AGAINST EVERYTHING

On Dishonest Times

Mark Greif

VERSO
London • New York

This paperback edition first published in the UK by Verso 2017
First published in the UK by Verso 2016
© Mark Greif 2016, 2017

1 3 5 7 9 10 8 6 4 2

Verso
UK: 6 Meard Street, London W1F 0EG
US: 20 Jay Street, Suite 1010, Brooklyn, NY 11201
versobooks.com

Verso is the imprint of New Left Books

ISBN-13: 978-1-78478-593-2
ISBN-13: 978-1-78478-594-9 (EBK)

British Library Cataloguing in Publication Data
A catalogue record for this book is available from the British Library

Printed and bound by CPI Group (UK) Ltd, Croydon, CRO 4YY

"Greif's book proposes the impossible thing, a phenomenology of the present—at a moment in which the present is slipping by so fast that anything we dare call that is already signed, sealed and delivered to the past. Hip-hop, food shows, current events like war and the police, hipsters, exercises, the youth culture—this list omits the deliberate and attractive heterogeneity of Greif's notes on the everyday, his attempt to capture its random contents before they are incorporated into some official academic field or trivialized into familiar themes and slogans by an omnivorous public sphere. It isn't a novel, it isn't a journal either (which you could 'dip into'), it's probably not a blog, it is deliberately unfinished (in the sense of 'to be continued,' but maybe by all or each of us); but it is certainly wonderful reading which cuts into the present before the latter disappears."

Fredric Jameson

"I love Mark Greif. No living essayist effects the destruction of everything other people hold dear with a lighter or more elegant touch. An unmitigated delight."

Elif Batuman, author of *The Possessed*

"The ideas and images I discover in Mark Greif's essays stay with me for years, and become part of the way I experience and understand the world. I couldn't be happier that this book is being published so I can read them all over again."

Sheila Heti, author of *How Should a Person Be*

"In *Against Everything*, Mark Greif makes a case for so much: for curiosity and precision, for second glances, for reconsidering, for paying attention to the world and not being satisfied by what it's become, or ever been. Greif is interested in blame and desire and how we coax and wrench meaning from our lives. He's interested in how we might remain alive to what matters while staying attuned—also—to the truth of mattering itself as something fluid, its contours up for grabs. His unexpected turns of thought come with such persuasive acuity they sound like common sense. I found the crackle of rigor in these essays, but also so much tenderness and awe."

Leslie Jamison, author of *The Empathy Exams*

"I was impressed above all by the resourcefulness of his prose, the concentrated intelligence of the exercise ... Greif doesn't lack for nerve and, whatever the object of discussion, his procedure is to 'look steadily at it, and think.'"

Stefan Collini, *London Review of Books*

"Greif's essay on the Kafkaesque nature of the modern gym, 'Against Exercise,' is already a classic; and his new book, *Against Everything*, tells us it's not just the gym, it's also our music, our culture, our political life—everything about us."

Aravind Adiga, *Guardian* Best Books of the Year

"This is how academics and intellectuals ought to write for the (mythical) general reader."
Robert Eaglestone, *Times Higher Education*

"A year that began in anxiety comes to an end in suspicion, fear and contempt ... How did we get here? The most convincing explanations I could find were contained in Mark Greif's *Against Everything* ... If we pay closer attention to the symptoms of our present situation then we might formulate better responses to its causes."
Ben Eastham, *Frieze* Highlights of 2016

"A brilliant and provocative ethnography of the present—you will never again look at hipsters, your fully stocked refrigerator, or the gym's weights section in the same way."
Ceridwen Dovey, *Australian* Books of the Year 2016

"The best essays ... read as if the Roland Barthes of *Mythologies* or the LA-exiled Theodor Adorno of *Minima Moralia* were deposited amid post-millennial American culture."
Brian Dillon, *4Columns*

"These essays are an earnest attempt to examine the points of friction between capitalism and our daily lives, as well as an attempt to discover their resolution. Greif has always been a remarkably prescient and insightful essayist ... but his elegance has grown with time."
Alex Christofi, *New Humanist*

"*Against Everything* embodies a return to the pleasures of critical discourse at its most cerebral and personable ... I would read anything he writes, anywhere."
Daphne Merkin, *New York Times Book Review*

"A book on a single subject: contemporary life, more specifically, the kind of life that someone who would buy such a book, or read a column about such a book—in short, yourself—might right now be living. It's meant to be consumed from beginning to end. It makes you think."
Louis Menand, *New Yorker*

"Greif is an eminently reasonable radical. Resisting everything, in his equation, is the opposite of despair."
Christian Lorentzen, *Vulture* Ten Best Books of the Year

"The essays in *Against Everything* are an intellectual wonderland, superior pieces of cultural criticism ... Greif brings a clarifying eye to the whirling chaos of contemporary life."
Michael Lindgren, *Washington Post*

"Dark, wonderful essays on contemporary derangement."
Gideon Lewis-Kraus, *Bookforum*

For Gabrielle and Simone

CONTENTS

This book represents a decade of writing. These are essays I wrote for *n+1*, the journal I founded with friends to publish a kind of literature that didn't exist elsewhere. Writers dead or famous have innumerable publications to air their views. If we made one venue for the unknown, might they say one thing as yet unsaid? Here are my published attempts. The additions are essays unpublished previously in English, inquiries I didn't want to share without context in America. They all reflected an effort, in my twenties and my thirties, to try to figure a few things out. What I was living for, principally, and why so much around me seemed to be false, and contemptible, yet was accepted without a great collective cry of pain.

This is not a book of critique of things I don't do. It's a book of critique of things I do. Habits in which I am joined by a class of people, call them the middle classes, or people in the rich nations, or Americans and Europeans and their peers the world over. Call them us, or call them you. I want to talk about you.

A lot of books tell you how to do the things you are supposed to do, but better. This book asks about those things you are supposed to do. Do you really do those things? For the reasons that are supposed? What if our true reasons, yours and mine, are not the ones usually proclaimed?

If the right reasons to do things, to be good and true and righteous, in fact are wrong? If the usual wisdom is unwise?

I begin with the body. It's the closest thing to us. In exercise, health, sexual desire, eating, childbearing. Youth and age. My notion is that once progress made it easy to acquire the necessities of bodily life, other forces set about making those needs complicated and hard. Much of daily life is turned over to life maintenance at the very moment you'd think we'd be free to pursue higher goals.

Spectacles, sights and sounds, measures and sums, are made from former areas of privacy. This exposure to sight generates all sorts of new pleasures and new fears. But the ceaseless grooming and optimizing of ordinary life stands in the way of finding out how else we could spend our attention and our energy. Adventurers are always coming back to tell us the thrills of daring acts that re-create more of the same. "I stood on the precipice and leaped!" "Into what?" "Into the known!"

Our hesitancy to know ourselves extends to things both bad and good. Identity theft has become such a general phenomenon these days, no wonder it goes so often unreported. The problem is not that others are stealing ours but that we are sneaking theirs. By the book's end, I will have asked what we call "experience" today and what we name "reality." Where glimmers of hope come from, especially within the popular culture, and why you might be embarrassed to own them. And what sight and the body could have to do with a nation's armies, police, and democracy.

I can imagine someone asking: "Against *everything*?" I'll tell you what the impulse means to me. My mother used to take me to a pond, when I was small, because it was a place to swim and walk in the suburbs where I grew up. Its name, Walden, also named a scandalous book.

My mother had never read the book. I was too young to read it. We circled the pond, many afternoons, and speculated. In olden days there had been a man named Thoreau. He walked and thought here. He had written in his book that the things people considered superior were often inferior. The best things might be in nobody's possession. Trash was treasure. Work was overrated, insofar as most people worked at the wrong things for the wrong reasons. Walking without a goal was superior to running. Conversation was the true purpose of everything, even of solitude and reading and thinking.

Our knowledge of his words was very dim. It came from short quotations reproduced on coffee mugs, bumper stickers, and T-shirts: "Beware of all enterprises that require new clothes." Our ignorance, though, did not mislead us as to the sense of what the philosopher had meant. Absence of detail proved to be the best instruction conceivable. "I wonder what he would have thought of that?" said my mother as we passed every folly, driving to the pond or coming home: billboards, luxury cars, malls, political signage, mansions, families fighting in backseats, radio insipidity, entreaties to good behavior from the road signs, the infinite unlovely and inane.

It was my task to do the wondering. The pact between us was that "he" knew how to question and discredit anything we might think of—things we doubted, but also things we did. My portion was to figure out exactly what his critique and alternative could be. I had to show how every commonplace thing might be a compromise. The standards universally supposed might not be "universal." Or they simply might not suit a universe in which my mother and I could happily live. I chattered—childishly, I guess, but buoyed by a medium other than youth and age—while kicking my sloppy sneakers against the dash. I taught myself to overturn, undo, deflate, rearrange, unthink, and rethink. "But it isn't really possible," my mother would warn. "You can't go down to the root. Some things don't change." "I'll bet *he* would think it's possible."

The most important thinker for me, ever, was thus just a principle when he mattered most, and his period of greatest importance was when I had not read him. I knew a "philosopher" to be a mind that was unafraid to be against everything. Against everything, if it was corrupt, dubious, enervating, untrue to us, false to happiness. And to attempt this was to try to be our friend, my mother's and mine.

I finally read *Walden* when I was seventeen, about to leave home to start life on my own. The book was more implacable than I could ever have imagined, and more hopeful and loving. I had with it the experience I've had with only a handful of books, of knowing I didn't deserve to finish it until I would no longer have to cast down my eyes, abashed, in the presence of its words. That kind of growing up, I thought uneasily, could take a lifetime.

I identify with my mother, as she was then, an adult, who knows that many things don't change, and with myself, as I was then, a child, who knew that life was not worth entering if it couldn't become better than it is. And I speak as myself now, still learning to be different than I am. To wish to be against everything is to want the world to be bigger than all of it, disposed to dissolve rules and compromises in a gallon or a drop, while an ocean of possibility rolls around us. No matter what you are supposed to do, you can prove the supposition wrong, just by doing something else.

I

AGAINST EXERCISE

Were "In the Penal Colony" to be written today, Kafka could only be speaking of an exercise machine. Instead of the sentence to be tattooed on its victims, the machine would inscribe lines of numbers. So many calories, so many miles, so many watts, so many laps.

Modern exercise makes you acknowledge the machine operating inside yourself. Nothing can make you believe we harbor nostalgia for factory work but a modern gym. The lever of the die press no longer commands us at work. But with the gym we import vestiges of the leftover equipment of industry to our leisure. We leave the office, and put the conveyor belt under our feet, and run as if chased by devils. We willingly submit our legs to the mangle, and put our stiffening arms to the press.

It is crucial that the machines are simple. The inclined planes, pins, levers, pulleys, locks, winches, racks, and belts of the Nautilus and aerobic machines put earlier stages of technical progress at our disposal in miniature. The elements are visible and intelligible for our use but not dangerous to us. Displaced, neutralized, they are traces of a necessity that no longer need be met with forethought or ingenuity.

A farmer once used a pulley, cable, and bar to lift his roof beam; you now use the same means to work your lats. Today, when we assume our brains are computers, the image of a machine man, whether Descartes's or La Mettrie's, has an old and venerable quality, like a yellowed poster on the infirmary wall. Blood pressure is hydraulics, strength is mechanics, nutrition is combustion, limbs are levers, joints are ball-and-sockets.

The exercise world does not make any notable conceptual declaration that we are mechanical men and women. We already were that, at least as far as our science is concerned. Rather, it expresses a will, on the part of each and every individual, to discover and regulate the machinelike processes in his own body.

And we go to this hard labor with no immediate reward but our freedom to do it. Precisely this kind of freedom may be enough. Exercise machines offer you the superior mastery of subjecting your body to experimentation. We hide our reasons for undertaking this labor, and thoughtlessly substitute a new necessity. No one asks whether we want to drag our lives across a threshold into the kingdom of exercise.

Exercise is no choice. It comes to us as an emissary from the realm of biological processes. It falls under the jurisdiction of the obligations of life itself, which only the self-destructive neglect. Our controversial future is supposed to depend on engineered genes, brain scans, neuroscience, laser beams. About those things, we have loud, public, sterile debates—while the real historic changes are accomplished on a gym's vinyl mats, to the sound of a flywheel and a ratcheted inclined plane.

In the gym you witness people engaging in a basic biological process of self-regulation. All of its related activities reside in the private realm. A question, then, is why exercise doesn't stay private. It could have belonged at home with other processes it resembles: eating, sleeping, defecating, cleaning, grooming, and masturbating.

Exerciser, what do you see in the mirrored gym wall? You make the faces associated with pain, with tears, with orgasm, with the sort of exertion that would call others to your immediate aid. But you do not hide your face. You groan as if pressing on your bowels. You repeat grim labors, as if mopping the floor. You huff and you shout and strain. You appear in tight yet shapeless Lycra costumes. These garments reveal the shape of the genitals and the mashed and bandaged breasts to others' eyes, without acknowledging the lure of sex.

Though we get our word "gymnasium" from the Greeks, our modern gym is not in their spirit. Athletics in the ancient institution were public and agonistic. They consisted of the training of boys for public contests. The gymnasium was closest to what we know as a boxing gym, with the difference that it was also the place adult men gathered to admire the most beautiful boys and, in the Athenian fashion, sexually mentor them. It was the preeminent place to promote the systematic education of the young, and for adults to carry on casual debates among themselves, modeling the intellectual sociability, separated from overt politics, that is the origin of Western philosophy. Socrates spent most of his time in gymnasia. Aristotle began his philosophical school in the covered walkway of a gymnasium.

The Socratic and Peripatetic methods would find little support in a modern gym. What we moderns do there belonged to mute privacy. The Greeks put their genuinely private acts into a location, an *oikos,* the household. To the household belonged all the acts that sustained bare biological life. That included the labor of keeping up a habitation and a body, growing food and eating it, bearing children and feeding them. Hannah Arendt interpreted this strong Greek distinction of the household from the public world as a symbol of a general truth: that it is necessary to keep the acts which sustain naked life away from others' observation. A hidden sphere, free from scrutiny, makes the foundation for a public person—someone sure enough in his privacy to take the drastic risks of public life, to think, to speak against others' wills, to choose with utter independence. In privacy, alone with one's family, the dominating necessity and speechless appetites can be gratified in the nonthought and ache of staying alive.

Our gym is better named a "health club," except that it is no club for equal meetings of members. It is the atomized space in which one does formerly private things, before others' eyes, with the lonely solitude of a body acting as if it were still in private. One tries out these contortions to undo and remake a private self; and if the watching others aren't entitled to approve, some imagined aggregate "other" does. Modern gym exercise moves biology into the nonsocial company of strangers. You are supposed to coexist but not look closely, wipe down the metal of handlebars and the rubber of mats as if you had not left a trace. As in the elevator, you are expected to face forward.

It is like a punishment for our liberation. The most onerous forms of necessity, the struggle for food, against disease, always by means of hard labor, have been overcome. It might have been naive to think the new human freedom would push us toward a society of public pursuits, like Periclean Athens, or of simple delight in what exists, as in Eden. But the true payoff of a society that chooses to make private freedoms and private leisures its main substance has been much more unexpected. This payoff is a set of forms of bodily self-regulation that drag the last vestiges of biological life into the light as a social attraction.

The only truly essential pieces of equipment in modern exercise are numbers. Whether at the gym or on the running path, rudimentary calculation is the fundamental technology. As the weights that one lifts are counted, so are distances run, time exercised, heart rates elevated.

A simple negative test of whether an activity is modern exercise is to ask whether it could be done meaningfully without counting or measuring it. (In sports, numbers are used differently; there, scores are a way of recording competition in a social encounter.) Forms of exercise that do away with mechanical equipment, as running does, cannot do away with this.

In exercise one gets a sense of one's body as a collection of numbers representing capabilities. The other location where an individual's numbers attain such talismanic status is the doctor's office. There is a certain seamlessness between all the places where exercise is done and the sites where people are tested for illnesses, undergo repairs, and die. In the doctor's office, the blood lab, and the hospital, you are at the mercy of counting experts. A lab technician in a white coat takes a sample of blood. A nurse tightens a cuff on your arm, links you to an EKG, takes the basic measurements of your height and weight—never to your satisfaction. She rewards you with the obvious numbers for blood pressure, body-fat ratio, height and weight. The clipboard with your numbers is passed. At last the doctor takes his seat, a mechanic who wears the white robe of an angel and is as arrogant as a boss. In specialist language, exacerbating your dread and expectation, you may learn your numbers for cholesterol (two types), your white cells, your iron, immunities, urinalysis, and so forth. He hardly needs to remind you that these numbers correlate with your chances of survival.

How do we acquire the courage to exist as a set of numbers? Turning to the gym or the track, you gain the anxious freedom to count yourself. What a relief it can be. Here are numbers you can change. You make the exercises into trials you perform upon matter within reach, the exterior armor of your fat and muscle. You are assured these numbers, too, and not only the black marks in the doctor's files, will correspond to how long you have to live. With willpower and sufficient discipline, that is, the straitening of yourself to a rule, you will be changed.

The gym resembles a voluntary hospital. Its staff members are also its patients. Some machines put you in a traction you can escape. Others undo the imprisonment of a respirator, cuing you to pump your lungs yourself, and tracking your heart rate on a display. Aided even by a love that can develop for your pains, this self-testing becomes second nature. The curious compilation of numbers that you are becomes an aspect of your freedom, sometimes the most important, even more preoccupying than your thoughts or dreams. You discover what high numbers you can become, and how immortal. For you, high roller, will live forever. You are eternally maintained.

The justification for the total scope of the responsibility to exercise is health. A further extension of the counting habit of exercise gives a precise economic character to health. It determines the anticipated numbers for the days and hours of one's life.

Today we really can preserve ourselves for a much longer time. The means of preservation are reliable and cheap. The haste to live one's mortal life diminishes. The temptation toward perpetual preservation grows. We preserve the living corpse in an optimal state, not so we may do something with it, but for its own good feelings of eternal fitness, confidence, and safety. We hoard our capital to earn interest, and subsist each day on crusts of bread. But no one will inherit our good health after we've gone. The hours of life maintenance vanish with the person.

The person who does not exercise, in our current conception, is a slow suicide. He fails to take responsibility for his life. He doesn't labor strenuously to forestall his death. Therefore we begin to think he causes it. It may be a comfort to remember when one of your parents' acquaintances dies that he did not eat well or failed to take up running. The nonexerciser is lumped with other unfortunates whom we socially discount. Their lives are worth a percentage of our own, through their own neglect. Their value is compromised by the failure to ensure the fullest term of possible physical existence. The nonexerciser joins all the unfit: the slow, the elderly, the hopeless, and the poor. "Don't you want to 'live'?" we say. No answer of theirs could satisfy us.

Conceive of a society in which it was believed that the senses could be used up. Eyesight worsened the more vivid sights you saw. Hearing worsened the more intense sounds you heard. It would be inevitable that such a conception would bleed into people's whole pattern of life, changing the way they spent their days. Would they use up their powers on the most saturated colors, listening to the most intoxicating sounds? Or might that society's members refuse to move, eyes shut, ears covered, nursing the remaining reserves of sensation?

We, too, believe our daily lives are not being lived out or used up, but eaten up unfairly by age. And we spend our time desperately. Upon the desperate materialist gratifications of a hedonic society, commanding immediate comfort and happiness, we engraft the desperate economics of health, and chase a longer span of happinesses deferred, and comforts delayed, by disposing of the better portion of our lives in life preservation.

Exercise does make you, as a statistical person, part of different aggregate categories that die with less frequency at successive ages. It furnishes a gain in odds. This is the main public rationale for those billions of man- and woman-hours in the gym. The truth, however, is also that being healthy makes you *feel* radically different. For a segment of its most ardent practitioners, exercise in its contemporary form is largely a quest for certain states of feeling. A more familiar phenomenon than the young person who is unhappy physically from never exercising is the young exerciser who suffers from missing one or two days of exercise. Movement is a necessity. There is everything to be said just for moving, getting the lead out, shaking what your mama gave you, turning restlessness to motion and vitality; but exercise is not plain motion. It is more like oscillation. The most common phenomenon may be the individual who judges, in his own mind if not out loud, the total healthiness of his state at each moment, alternating satisfaction and disappointment, based on what he ate, what he drank, how much he exercised, when, with what feelings as he was doing it, and with what relation to the new recommendation or warning he just heard on the news hour's health report. One feels healthier even when the body doesn't feel discernibly different; one feels unhealthy even when the body is fine. Or the body does begin to feel different—lighter, stronger, more efficient, less toxic—in ways that exceed the possible consequences of the exercises performed; but the feelings cannot last, they require more work. This may be a more important psychic "medicalization of human life" than anything a doctor can do with his tests.

The less respectable but even more powerful justification for day-to-day exercise is thinness. It involves the disciplining of a depraved will, rather than the righteous responsibility to maintain the health of the body-machine and its fund of capital.

Women strip their bodies of layers of fat to reveal a shape without its normal excess of flesh. Despite the new emphasis on female athleticism, the task of the woman exerciser remains one of emaciation. Men thin themselves, too, but more importantly bloat particular muscles, swelling the major clusters in the biceps, chest, and thighs. They awaken an incipient musculature that no work or worldly activity could bring out like this. Theirs is a task of expansion and discovery.

Women's emaciation is a source for feminine eye-rolling and rueful nicknames: the "social X-ray," the actress as skin and bones. Men's proud expansion and discovery of six muscles of the lower abdomen, reminiscent of an insect's segmented exoskeleton, likewise becomes a byword and a joke: the "six-pack," bringing exercise together with the masculinity of beer.

Unlike the health model, which claims to make a continuous gain on mortality, thinness and muscle expansion operate in a cruel economy of accelerated loss. Mortality began when the first man and woman left the Garden. Everyone has to die, but no one has to shape a physique, and once this body altering begins, it is more implacable than death. Every exerciser knows that the body's propensity to put on weight is the physical expression of a moral fall. Every exerciser knows that the tendency of the body to become soft when it is comfortable or at rest, instead of staying perpetually hard, is a failure of discipline. This is the taste of our new Tree of Knowledge. In our era of abundance, we find that nutrition makes one fat rather than well fed, pleasures make one flabby rather than content, and only anorexics have the willpower to stop eating and die.

Exercise means something other than health to a young person who conceives sexual desirability as the truth about herself most worth defending. And youth is becoming permanent, in the demand that adults keep up an outward show of juvenescence. The body itself becomes the location of sexiness, rather than clothes or wit or charisma. Yet this is probably less true for society—which values personality still—than for the exerciser herself, who imagines an audience that doesn't exist. Saddest of all is the belief that an improved body will bestow bliss on the unloved.

The shock troops of modern exercise are women just past the college years. Only recently the beneficiary of a sexually mature body, and among our culture's few possessors by native right of the reduced body type we prefer—which we daily prefer more openly, more vehemently— the girl of twenty-two is a paradoxical figure as an exemplar of exercise. She is not yet among the discounted. But she knows her destiny. She starts immediately to get ahead in the race to preserve a form that must never exceed the barest minimum of flesh. A refreshing honesty can exist among exercisers who are not yet caught up in the doctrine of health. The rising incidence of smoking among young women, which worries public health advocates, is coincident with the rising incidence of gym exercise, which doesn't. While the cigarette suppresses appetite (rebelliously), the StairMaster attacks calories (obediently). Each can become intensely, erotically pleasurable, and neither is really meant for health or longevity.

The doctrine of thinness introduces a radical fantasy of exercise down to the bone. It admits the dream of a body unencumbered by any excess of corporeality. Thanatos enters through the door opened by Eros, and exercise flirts with a will to annihilate the unattractive body rather than to preserve its longevity. Without an accompanying ideology of health, thinness would in fact liquidate all restraints, generating a death's-head vision of exercise. Health curiously returns as the only brake on a practice that otherwise can become a kind of naked aggression against the body.

With health in place, the aggression is more likely to be carried on psychically. It pools, then starts an undercurrent of hatred for this corrupt human form that continually undoes the labor you invest in it. One hundred twenty pounds of one's own flesh starts to seem like the Sisyphean boulder. Yet the bitterness of watching your body undo your work is restrained by a curious compensation that Sisyphus did not know. If the hated body is the scene of a battle, a certain pleasure still emerges from the unending struggle, and in a hedonistic order divided against its own soft luxuries, at least this pleasure, if no other, can be made to go on forever.

An enigma of exercise is the proselytizing urge that comes with it. Exercisers are always eager for everyone else to share their experience. Why must others exercise, if one person does?

No one who plays baseball or hockey demands everyone else play the sport. Sports are social. Their victories become visible in the temporary public arrangements of a game. Perhaps accomplishments recognized by others in the act of their occurrence can be left alone. The gym-goer, on the other hand, is a solitary evangelist. He is continually knocking on your door, to get you to recognize the power that will not give him peace. You, too, must exercise. Even as he worries for your salvation, nevertheless, he has the gleam of someone who is ahead of you already, one chosen by God.

Running is most insidious because of its way of taking proselytizing out of the gym. It is a direct invasion of public space. It lays the counting, the pacing, the controlled frenzy, the familiar undergarment-outergarments and skeletal look, on top of the ordinary practice of an outdoor walk. One thing that can be said for a gym is that an implied contract links everyone who works out in its mirrored and pungent hangar. All consent to undertake separate exertions and hide any mutual regard, as in a well-ordered masturbatorium. The gym is in this sense more polite than the narrow riverside, street, or nature path, wherever runners take over shared places for themselves. With his speed and narcissistic intensity the runner corrupts the space of walking, thinking, talking, and everyday contact. He jostles the idler out of his reverie. He races between pedestrians in conversation. The runner can oppose sociability and solitude by publicly sweating on them.

No doubt the unsharability of exercise stimulates an unusual kind of loneliness. When exercise does become truly shared and mutually visible, as in the aerobics that come close to dance, or the hardcore bodybuilding that is always erotic and fraternal, it nears sport or art and starts to reverse itself. When exercise is done in a private home, or in untenanted landscapes, or without formal method, apparatus, or counting, it recovers certain eccentric freedoms of private techniques of the self. You could be dancing. However, the pure category of modern exercise is concerned not with the creative process of reproduction (as in activities in common) or the pure discoveries of solitude (as in private eccentricity). It pursues an idea of replication. Replication in exercise re-creates the shape and capabilities of others in the material of your own body, without new invention, and without exchange with others or crossing-over of material between selves.

It is a puzzling question, in fact, whether "you" and "your body" are the same in exercise. If on the one hand exercise seems strongly to identify exercisers with their bodies, by putting them to shared labor, on the other hand it seems to estrange them from the bodies they must care for and manage. Where does "fitness" actually reside? It seems to be deep inside you; yet that inside has risen to a changeable surface. And this surface is no longer one you can take off, as you did a costume in earlier methods of improving your allure. Fashion historians point out that women freed themselves from corsets worn externally, only to make an internal corset, as they toned the muscles of the abdomen and chest, and dieted and exercised to burn away permanently the well-fed body that whalebone stays temporarily restrained. Though the exerciser acts on his self, this self becomes ever more identified with the visible surface. Though he works on his body, replication makes it ever more, so to speak, anybody.

The exerciser conforms, in a most virulent practice of conformism. But exercise itself pushes the norms of medicine and sexual allure toward further extremes. The feedback does not stabilize the system but radicalizes it, year by year. Only in a gym culture does being overweight become the "second leading cause of death" (as the news reported this spring) rather than a correlation, a relative measure, which positively covaries with the heart attacks, the cancers, the organ failures, and final illnesses that were formerly our killers. Only in a gym culture do physical traits that were formerly considered repellent become marks of sexual superiority. (We are hot now for the annihilation by exercise and dieting of once voluptuous feminine flesh, watching it be starved away in natural form and selectively replaced with breast implants, collagen injections, buttock lifts. We've learned to be aroused by the ripped, vein-popping muscles that make Incredible Hulks of men who actually push papers.) Because health and sex are the places we demand our truth today, newly minted ideals must be promulgated as discoveries of medical science or revelations of permanent, "evolutionary" human desires. The technical capabilities of gym exercise drive the social ideals and demands.

Does this critique imply a hatred of the body? On the contrary.

The ethos of gym exercise annihilates the margin of safety that humans have when they relate to their own bodies. Men and women seem more ashamed of their own actual bodies in the present environment of biological exposure than in a pre-gym past. An era of exercise has brought more obsession and self-hatred rather than less.

A feminist worry becomes important. It is certainly possible to make people used to displaying to others' eyes the biological processes of transformation. And this has been, at times, the aim of feminists, who intended to attack a patriarchy that vilified the natural body or that made biological processes a source of shame and inferiority. But the forms of exposure that have recently arisen are not in line with feminist liberation of the unconditioned body.

Patriarchy made biology a negative spectacle, a filth that had to be hidden. The ethos of exercise makes it a positive spectacle, a competitive fascination that must be revealed. The rhetoric of "loving the body" can thus be misused. With the extension of the cliché that one should "not be ashamed" of the body, people are less able to defend themselves against the prospect that their actual bodies, and biological processes, may be manifest at every moment, in new states of disciplining neither public nor private. It becomes a retrogression, a moral failing in these people, to wish to defend against exposure, or to withdraw their health, bodies, arousal, and self-regulation from the social scene, as if privacy of this kind were mere prudery or repression.

Once subjected to this socialization of biological processes, the body suffers a new humiliation no longer rooted in the distinctions between the revealed and the hidden, the natural and the shameful, the sexual ideal and the physical actuality, but in the deeper crime of merely existing as the unregulated, the unshaped, the unsexy, the "unfit."

Our practices are turning us inside out. Our hidden flesh becomes our public front. The private medical truth of bodily health becomes our psychic self-regard. Action in public before strangers and acquaintances loses its center of gravity in the lived experience of the *citizen* and is replaced by the activity of exercise in public, as speech gives way to biological spectacle.

Your exercise confers superiority in two contests, one of longevity and the other of sex. Facing mortality, the gym-goer believes himself an agent of health—whereas he makes himself a more perfect patient. Facing the sexual struggle, the gym-goer labors to attain a positive advantage, which spurs an ever-receding horizon of further competition.

The consequences are not only the flooding of consciousness with a numbered and regulated body, or the distraction from living that comes with endless life-maintenance, but the liquidation of a sense of the public, and what can be made collectively in public, along with the last untouched spheres of privacy, such that biological life, good and bad, will be always seen, in all locations, and all we have.

"You are condemned. You are condemned. You are condemned." This is the chant the machines make with their grinding rhythm, inside the roar of the gym floor. Once upon a time, the authority of health, and the display of our bodies and biological processes, seemed benign, even liberating. We were going to overcome illness, we were going to exorcise the prudish Victorians. But our arrows were turned from their targets, and some of them punctured our privacy.

The thinness we strive for becomes spiritual. This is not the future we wanted. That prickling beneath the exerciser's skin, as he steps off the treadmill, is only his new self, his reduced existence, scratching the truth of who he is now, from the inside out.

[2004]

AFTERNOON OF THE SEX CHILDREN

Not long ago I took part in one of the conversations you're not sup-posed to have. It turned on whether Vladimir Nabokov, author of *Lolita,* really desired underage girls. The usual arguments came out: Nabokov was a master of personae, and Humbert Humbert a game to him. Kinbote, analogous narrator of *Pale Fire,* didn't make you think Nabokov loved boys. The late novels were Nabokov's allegories of the seductions of aestheticism, which transfigures the forbidden into the beautiful; or moral paintings of our acceptance of crime, when crime is presented alluringly. So love of the wrong object becomes a metaphor for art, ethics, personality, and so forth.

I was reluctant to say that I felt these explanations were inadequate and even in bad faith. The trouble with *Lolita* is plainly its ability to describe what a sexual twelve-year-old looks like. What her dress is like when it brushes her knees, what her toes are like with painted nails, how the color sits on the plump bow of her lips—the phrase for this is that it is "too real"; that's the scandal. It continues to be the scandal fifty years after publication, and it will be a scandal whenever any adult acknowledges the capacity to upend his vision and see a child, protected larval stage of the organism, as a sexual object. The girl is still a child, only now she is a sex child. Yet this makes me feel Nabokov was not a pedophile, but something he is not credited with being—a social critic.

You, too, see it, or should. The trend of these fifty years has been to make us see sexual youth where it doesn't exist, and ignore it as it does. Adults project the sex of children in lust, or examine children sexually with magnifying glasses to make sure they don't appeal to us. But these lenses became burning glasses. The hips of Betty Grable melted and disappeared. The breasts of Marilyn Monroe ran off and were replaced with silicone. The geography of fashion created new erogenous zones—pelvic midriff, rear cleavage—for dieters starving off their secondary sex characteristics, and for young teens, in the convergence of the exerciser and the pubescent child. The waif and the pixie became ideal. Mama and daughter look the same again before the bedroom mirror—not dressed up in Mama's pearls and heels, this time, but in children's wear. The dream belongs to sixteen, or to those who can starve themselves to sixteen.

The critic Philip Fisher has noted that *Lolita,* tightly plotted as it is, repeats one scene twice. Humbert spies a lit window far opposite. Because he longs to see a nymphet, he sees one. The wave of arousal returns, its tide dampening him up to his knees. As he nears the climax, the form is refocused as an adult woman or man. Disgusting! But this is a simple inversion of a characteristic experience of our time. A man will see a distant form, in low-cut top and low-slung jeans, and think he is on the trail of eroticism; draw near, and identify a child. Revolting! The defenses against it continue the problem. The more a whole nation inspects the sex characteristics of children to make sure it is not becoming aroused by childishness, and slyly hunts around to make sure its most untrustworthy members are not being so aroused, the more it risks creating a sexual fascination with the child. However you gaze, to accept the fantasy, or to assure yourself you see nothing, you join in an abomination.

We live in the afternoon of the sex children; Nabokov just saw the dawn.

Now children from junior high to high school to college live in the most perfect sex environment devised by contemporary society—or so adults believe. Now they are inmates in great sex colonies where they wheel in circles holding hands with their pants down. Henry Darger, emblematic artist of our time with his girl armies, made for our sensibilities what Gauguin's Tahitian beauties were to the French nineteenth-century bourgeoisie—repositories of true, voluptuous, savage, inner nature.

Yet in public we want to believe that children are not prepared for sex as we are, do not understand it, and have a special, fragile, glassy truth inside them that will be endangered by premature use—as if the pearls of highest value for us, our chase after sex, our truth of "sexuality," should not also be the treasure for them.

It took the whole history of postwar American culture to make the sex child. It required a merging of old prurient fantasies, dating from the Victorians and the Progressives, with the actual sexual liberation of children after mid-century. You needed the expansion of the commercial market for children—selling to kids with sex as everything is sold with sex. You needed the bad faith of Madison Avenue advertisers and Seventh Avenue fashion writers. You needed the sinister prudery of Orange County evangelicalism and the paraliterature of child sex that arises in antipedophilia crusades (*Treacherous Love; It Happened to Nancy*)— erotica purveyed to middle-school libraries. You needed the Internet.

Victorian child-loving is only loosely the background for our current preoccupation with the pedophile and the sexual child. With Lewis Carroll and Alice, John Ruskin and Rose La Touche, the fantastic young bride and her gauzy innocence, we know we are in the realm of adult prurience. It is *child sexual liberation* that transforms the current moment. We can no longer say it is only fantasy that exists about the sex lives of children. Or, rather—maybe this is the better way to say it— children have been insistently invited into our fantasy, too, and when they grow up they'll furnish the adult continuity of this same madness.

Is it necessary to say that the majority of the sex children we see and desire are not legally children? The representatives of the sex child in our entertainment culture are often eighteen to twenty-one—legal adults. The root of their significance is that their sexual value points backward, to the status of the child, and not forward to the adult. So there is Britney, famous at the age of eighteen for a grind video to "Oops! . . . I Did

It Again" (*"I'm not that innocent"*), and Paris, nineteen years old in her amateur porn DVD (*1 Night in Paris*); alumnae of the Mickey Mouse Club like Christina, licking her lips at twenty on the *Rolling Stone* cover, miniskirt pulled open, with the headline "Guess What Christina Wants"; and Lindsay, veteran of Disney children's films, whose breast size, extreme dieting, and accidental self-exposures on the red carpet are the stuff of *Entertainment Tonight*. It's important that these are not adult "stars" in the way of Nicole Kidman or Julia Roberts; not called beautiful, rarely featured in adult films. Instead they furnish the core of entertainment news to two distinct audiences: children nine to fourteen, who enjoy their music and films on these works' own terms, and adults who regard them—well, as what?

Oddly, those of us who face these questions now have been sex children ourselves; we come after the great divide. You would think we'd remember. Our sex was handed to us, liberated, when we appeared in the world. We managed to feel like rebels with all the other twelve-year-olds, deluded, but not to be blamed for that. A great tween gang of sexual ruffians, trolling the basement TV for scrambled porn, tangling on couches, coming up for air in clouds of musk, shirts on backward; what did we learn? Having lived in the phantasm evidently does not diminish the phantasm. One still looks at those kids enviously; that is one of the mysteries to be solved. It is as if crossing the divide to adulthood entailed a great self-blinding in the act of seeing what is not, precisely, there; and forgetting what one oneself experienced. If we turn to the sex children as avidly as anyone, it must be because they are *doing something for us, too,* as participants in this society and as individuals. And the supplement will not be found in their childhood at all, but in the overall system of adult life.

The lure of a permanent childhood in America partly comes from the overwhelming feeling that one hasn't yet achieved one's true youth, because true youth would be defined by freedom so total that no one can attain it. Presumably even the spring-break kids, rutting, tanning, boozing with abandon, know there is a more perfect spring break beyond the horizon. Without a powerful aspiration to become adult, without some separate value that downplays childhood for sharper freedoms in age and maturity, the feeling of dissatisfaction can proceed indefinitely, in the midst of marriage, child rearing, retirement, unto death.

The college years—of all times—stand out as the apex of sex childhood. Even if college is routinized and undemanding, it is still often residential, and therefore the place to perfect one's life as a sex child. You move away from home into a setting where you are with other children—strangers all. You must be patient for four years just to get a degree. So there can be little to do but fornicate. Certainly from the wider culture, of MTV and rumor, you know four years is all you will get. Academic semesters provide interruptions between institutionalized sex jubilees: spring break, or just the weekends. The frat-house party assumes a gothic significance, not only for prurient adults but for the collegians themselves who report, on Monday, their decadence.

As a college student today, you always know what things *could* be like. The *Girls Gone Wild* cameras show a world where at this very moment someone is spontaneously lifting her shirt for a logoed hat. You might think the whole thing was a put-on except that everyone seems so earnest. The most earnest write sex columns ("Sex and the Elm City") in which the elite and joyless of Yale aspire to be like the déclassé and uninhibited of Florida State. The new full-scale campus sex magazines (e.g., Boston University's *Boink* and Harvard's *H Bomb*) seek truth in naked self-photography and accounts of sex with strangers as if each incident were God's revelation on Sinai. The lesson each time is that sleeping with strangers or being photographed naked lets the authors know themselves better. Many of these institutions are driven by women. Perhaps they, even more than young men, feel an urgency to know themselves while they can—since America curses them with a premonition of disappointment: when flesh sags, freedom will wane.

From college to high school, high school to junior high, the age of sex childhood recedes and descends. "The Sexual Revolution Hits Junior High," says my newspaper, reporting as news what is not new. Twice a year *Newsweek* and *Time* vaunt the New Virginity. No one believes in the New Virginity. According to polls of those who stick with it, their abstinence is fortified with large measures of fellatio. Eighty percent of people have intercourse in their teens, says the Centers for Disease Control. (Why the Centers for Disease Control keeps records of sexual normalcy, unsmilingly pathologized as an "epidemic," is its own question.) My newspaper tells me that menstruation starts for girls today at eleven, or as early as nine. No one knows why.

Yet the early reality of sex childhood is its restrictive practical dimension. It exists only in the context of the large institutions that dominate children's lives, the schools. In these prisonlike closed worlds of finite numbers of children, with no visible status but the wealth they bring in from outside (worn as clothes) and the dominance they can achieve in the activities of schooldays (friend making, gossiping, academic and athletic success), sex has a different meaning than in adult licentiousness or collegiate glory. Sex appeal is demanded long before sex, and when sex arrives, it appears within ordinary romantic relationships. New sexual acts are only substitutes for any earlier generation's acts, as you'd expect. Where petting was, there shall fellatio be.

It will simply never be the case that children can treat sex with the free-floating fantasy and brutality that adults can, because we adults are atomized in our dealings with others as children in school are not. If I do something rotten on a blind date, I never need to see the only witness again. A child does something rotten, and his date is sitting next to him in homeroom. The adult world sends down its sexual norms, which cannot blossom in a closed institution (though alarmists say they *originate* there), but which the children tuck away to fulfill just as soon as they can. Children are the beneficiaries of a culture that declares in all its television, jokes, talk, and advertising that if sex isn't the most significant thing in existence, it is the one element never missing from any activity that is fun. They are watchers, silent, with open eyes, and they grow in the blue light.

So much for the decadent reality of childhood.

But adults then look back from exile and see wrongly, thinking the children are free because we've hemmed them in with images of a transitory future freedom. Never mind that we ourselves led carnal lives that would make old men weep. Those lives hardly counted: inevitably we were caught in actual human relationships with particular people, in a matrix of leaden rules and personal ties. Envy of one's sexual successors is now a recurrent feature of our portion of modernity. Philip Larkin:

> When I see a couple of kids
> And guess he's fucking her and she's
> Taking pills or wearing a diaphragm,
> I know this is paradise
>
> Everyone old has dreamed of all their lives—
> . . . .
> . . . everyone young going down the long slide
>
> To happiness, endlessly. I wonder if
> Anyone looked at me, forty years back,
> And thought, *That'll be the life;*
>
> . . . .
> . . . *He*
> *And his lot will all go down the long slide*
> *Like free bloody birds . . .*

("High Windows")

Larkin's solace in the poem was high windows and the icy blue; in real life, an enormous collection of pornography.

The dirty magazines and their supposedly legitimate counterparts in fact play a significant role in the system of sex childhood. In Larkin's life, the poetry of longing went hand in hand with the fulfillments of porn, and all of us share in this interchange at a more banal level. The colloquialisms "men's magazines" and "women's magazines" generally seem to name two very different sets of publications. "Women's magazines" are instructional—how to display oneself, how to serve men, and nowadays (maybe always) how to steal sexual and emotional pleasure from men, outwitting them, while getting erotic and affective satisfactions, too, in the preparations for your self-display. "Men's magazines," for their part, are pornographic—how to look at women, how to fantasize about women, how to enjoy and dominate, and what one becomes while fantasizing this domination. The two genres are distinct, but continuous.

The women's advice and fashion magazines, *Cosmopolitan, Glamour, Elle, Vogue,* hold a permanent mandate for an erotic youthfulness, though not literal sexual youth. They provide shortcuts to staying young for old and young alike: how to keep your skin young, how to keep your muscles young, how to keep your ideas young, how to feel perpetually young, how to siphon vitality from elsewhere to be "young" even if you're not, literally, young, and how to use your youth if you are. You learn early what you'll lose late, and get accustomed to denying the aging that you might never have minded as much without this help.

Men's magazines fix readers' desires in the range of women's shapes and bodies and modes of seduction and subordination—fragmenting the market by body part and sex act and level of explicitness, but also by age. Pornography has a special investment in youth. The college girl is a central feature of *Playboy* in its "Girls of the Big Ten" pictorials; *Hustler* has a relentless *Barely Legal* franchise in magazines and videos, aped by *Just 18* and *Finally Legal* and all the bargain titles behind the convenience-store counter. In the demimonde of the Internet, an even more central category of all online pornography is "teen." Of course it is profoundly illegal in the United States to photograph anyone under eighteen sexually; in what is called 2257 compliance, producers of pornography must keep public legal records proving that every model is eighteen or older. Technically, therefore, there are only two ages, eighteen and nineteen, at which "teen" models can be actual teens. Nor do the models ever seem to be sexually immature; child pornography doesn't seem to be what the sites are for. Rather, putative teen models are made *situationally* immature—portrayed with symbols of the student life, the classroom, the cheerleading squad, the college dorm, the family home, the babysitting, the first job; not the husband, not the child, not the real-estate brokerage or boardroom or bank office, never adult life.*

Thus a society that finds it illegal to exploit anyone beneath the age of legal majority is at the same time interested in the simulation of youth—often by people who are sexually mature but still only on the cusp of adulthood. And in its legitimate publications, as in its vice, it encourages a more general, socially compulsory female urgency to provision youth across the life span, and a male rush to take it.

Though the young person has never been old, the old person once was young. When you look up the age ladder, you look at strangers; when you look down the age ladder, you are always looking at versions of yourself. As an adult, it depends entirely on your conception of yourself whether those fantastic younger incarnations will seem long left behind or all-too-continuous with who you are now. And this conception of yourself depends, in turn, on the culture's attitudes to adulthood and childhood, age and youth. This is where the trouble arises. For in a culture to which sex furnishes the first true experiences, it makes a kind of sense to return to the ages at which sex was first used to pursue experience and one was supposedly in a privileged position to find it. Now we begin to talk, not about our sex per se, but about a fundamental change in our notion of freedom, and what our lives are a competition for.†

---

* Feminist critiques of pornography rooted in an idea of male violence and revenge against the threat of women's liberation might have predicted a different outcome in our age of equality: representations of the literal humiliation or subordination of adult women in power—bosses, senators, spokespeople. What they did not anticipate was a turn to sexualized youth. Though the two lines of critique are not at all incompatible (i.e., youth still may be a way of denying adult equality), one sees now that feminist critiques of youth and aging are proving to be more significant historically than porn critiques.

† I want to acknowledge two lines of thought that insist on the attraction to sexually mature children as natural, not social, contravening my account. One is the commonsense historical argument that until recently sexually mature children of the middle teen years *were* adults, because human beings used to marry in their teens. Natasha, the dream of Russian womanhood in *War and Peace,* one of the greatest novels of the nineteenth century, set in that century's early years, is fourteen when she becomes the object of her first suitors' attention—and admirable suitors too: hussars in the tsar's army, and a count. Her girlishness is treated matter-of-factly by those who are drawn to it as an

We must begin to talk directly about the change that was well begun in Nabokov's day and is well advanced in ours, the transformation that created the world in which we are both freed and enslaved. That was sexual liberation.

---

appealing aspect of her personality, and it is considered realistically by her parents, who are concerned she may be too immature yet to leave home and run a household. In the United States, as the historian Philip Jenkins has summarized, the standard age of sexual consent was ten years old until the 1890s, when it was raised to sixteen or eighteen depending on the state.

The other argument is one occasionally offered explicitly, but much more often implicitly, in the field of evolutionary psychology. Evolutionary psychology explains behavioral dispositions in modern human beings by the optimal strategies for passing on genes, through patterns hardwired into our brains by our evolutionary past and the continuing reproductive demands of the present. "Youth is a critical cue," writes evolutionary psychologist David M. Buss in the standard book on the subject of sex, "since women's reproductive value declines steadily with increasing age after twenty. By the age of forty, a woman's reproductive capacity is low, and by fifty it is close to zero" (*The Evolution of Desire*). The desire for children from the moment of visible pubescence (say, twelve today) to the maximum age before reproductive decline (age twenty) may therefore be the best means for passing on genes. This inclination would be set beneath the level of consciousness, as men's desire is targeted to females who are fertile, healthy, and poised for the longest period of childbearing possible before the decline sets in. On evolutionary-biological presuppositions, it ought to be the case that human males today and yesterday, and in every society, should be maximally attracted to newly post-pubescent girls unless it be determined statistically that there is some ramping-up of reproductive success in the years after menarche—in which case, certainly, no later than fourteen or fifteen.

Neither the historical nor the biological argument seems to meet the problem of the sex child as we now know it, because, I think, neither captures our current experience of desire, in which the sex children come in only secondarily, through some kind of mediation of fancy; in our real lives adults feel the sexual appeal of other adults. Unless sexual desire is wholly unconscious, and the social level entirely a screen or delusion—a very complex delusion to cover biological determinism—then with the sex children it's my sense that we are dealing primarily with the sexual appeal of *youth* rather than the actual determinative sexual attractiveness of *youths,* even if the latter also exists (even with biological bases). The social appeal would be something like a desire for the sex child's incipience, the child's taste of first majority before the rules clamp down: youth as eternal becoming, in eternal novelty of experience. Apart from such fancies, the appeal of sexually mature children seems to me relatively weak in culture, not strong. But I understand that introspection is not science, and I am aware this may not satisfy partisans of determinist "natural" views.

. . .

Liberation implies freedom to do what you have already been doing or have meant to do. It unbars what is native to you, free in cost and freely your possession, and removes the iron weight of social interdiction. Even in the great phase of full human liberation that extended from the 1960s to the present day, however, what has passed as liberation has often been *liberalization*. (Marcuse used this distinction.) Liberalization makes for a free traffic in goods formerly regulated and interdicted, creating markets in what you already possess for free. It has a way of making your possessions no longer native to you at the very moment that they're freed for your enjoyment. Ultimately you no longer know *how* to possess them, correctly, unless you are following new rules that emerge to dominate the traffic in these goods.

In sexual liberation, major achievements included the end of shame and illegality in sex outside of marriage (throughout the twentieth century); the disentangling of sex from reproduction (completed with the introduction of the oral contraceptive pill in 1960); the feminist reorganization of intercourse around the female orgasm and female pleasure (closer to 1970); and the beginning of a destigmatization of same-sex sexuality (1970 to the present). The underlying notion in all these reforms was to remove social penalties from what people were doing anyway.

But a test of liberation, as distinct from liberalization, must be whether you have also been freed to be free *from* sex, too—to ignore it, or to be asexual, without consequent social opprobrium or imputation of deficiency. If truly liberated, you should engage in sex or not as you please, and have it be a matter of indifference to you; you should recognize your own sex, or not, whenever and however you please. We ought to see social categories of asexuals who are free to have no sex just as others are free to have endless spectacular sex, and not feel for them either suspicion or pity. One of the cruel betrayals of sexual liberation, in liberalization, was the illusion that a person can be free only if he holds sex as all-important and exposes it endlessly to others—providing it, proving it, enjoying it.

This was a new kind of unfreedom. In hindsight, the betrayal of sexual liberation was a mistake the liberators seemed fated to make. Because moralists had said for so many centuries, "Sex must be *controlled* because it is so powerful and important," sexual liberators were seduced into saying, in opposition, "Sex must be *liberated* because it is so powerful and important." But in fact a better liberation would have occurred if reformers had freed sex not by its centrality to life, but by its triviality. They could have said: "Sex is a biological function—and for that reason no grounds to persecute anyone. It is *truthless*—you must not bring force to bear on people for the basic, biological, and private; you may not persecute them on grounds so accidental. You must leave them alone, neither forcing them to deny their sex nor to bring it into the light."

This misformulation of liberation became as damaging as it did only because another force turned out to have great use for the idea that sex is the bearer of the richest experiences: commerce. The field of sex was initially very difficult to liberate against a set of rival norms that had structured it for centuries: priority of the family, religious prohibitions, restraint of biology. Once liberation reached a point of adequate success, however, sex was unconscionably easy to "liberate" further, as commerce discovered it had a new means of entry into private life and threw its weight behind the new values. What in fact was occurring was liberalization by forces of commercial transaction, as they entered to expand and coordinate the new field of exchange. Left-wing ideas of free love, the nonsinfulness of the body, women's equality of dignity, intelligence, and capability, had been hard-pressed to find adequate standing before—and they are still in trouble, constantly worn away. Whereas incitement to sex, ubiquitous sexual display, sinfulness redefined as the unconditioned, unexercised, and unaroused body, and a new shamefulness for anyone who manifests a *non*sexuality or, worst of all, willful sexlessness—that was easy.

Opposition to this is supposed to be not only old-fashioned but also joyless and puritanical—in fact, ugly. Sex talk is so much a part of daily glamour and the assurance of being a progressive person that one hates to renounce it; but one has to see that in general it is commercial sex talk that's reactionary, and opposition that's progressive. Liberalization has succeeded in hanging an aesthetic ugliness upon all discussions of liberation, except the purely ornamental celebrations of "the Woodstock generation" one sees on TV. Original liberators are ogres in the aesthetic symbolism of liberalization. They don't shave their legs! They're content to be fat! They have no fun. To say that a bodily impulse is something all of us have, and no regimentation or expertise or purchases can make one have it any more, is to become filthy and disgusting. It is to be nonproductive waste in an economy of markets, something nonsalable. It is not the repression of sex that opposes liberation (just as Foucault alerted us), but "inciting" sex as we know it—whatever puts sex into motion, draws it into *publicity,* apart from the legitimate relations between the private (the place of bodily safety) and the public (the sphere of equality).

The question remains why liberalization turned back to gorge itself on youth.

How should a system convince people that they do not possess their sex properly? Teach them that in their possession it is shapeless and unconditioned. Only once it has been modified, layered with experts, honeycombed with norms, overlaid with pictorial representations and sold back to them, can it fulfill itself as what its possessors "always wanted." Breasts starved away by dieting will be reacquired in breast-implant surgery—to attain the original free good, once destroyed, now re-created unnaturally.

How to convince them that what appears plentiful and free—even those goods that in fact are universally distributed—is scarce? Extend the reach of these new norms that cannot be met without outside intervention. Youth becomes a primary norm in the competition for sex. The surprise in this is not that youth would be desirable—it has always had its charm—but that you would think youth ought to be competitively *ineffective,* since it is universally distributed at the start of life. Yet youth is naturally evanescent, in fact vanishing every single day that one lives. It can be made the fundamental experience of a vanishing commodity, the ur-experience of obsolescence. Plus, it was everyone's universal possession at one time; and so artful means to keep it seem justified by a "natural" outcome, what you already were; and youth can be requalified physically as an aspect of memory, for every single consumer, in minutiae of appearance that you alone know (looking at yourself every day in a mirror, you alone know the history of your face and body) even while other people don't. We still pretend we are most interested in beauty, and it covers our interest in youth. Beauty is too much someone else's good luck; we accept that it is unequally distributed. Youth is more effective precisely because it is something all of us are always losing.

From the desire to repossess what has been lost (or was never truly taken advantage of) comes, in the end, the ceaseless extension of competition. It is easily encouraged. It doesn't require anything nefarious or self-conscious, certainly not top-down control, though it's sometimes convenient to speak of the process metaphorically as a field of control. All it requires is a culture in which instruments of commentary and talk (news, talk shows, advice magazines) are accompanied and paid for by advertisers of aesthetic and aestheticizable products—everything from skin cream to Viagra to cars. This is supremely prosaic; but this is it. Once people can be convinced that they need to remain young for others to desire them, and that there are so many instrumentalities with which they can remain young; once they can be encouraged to suspect that youth is a particularly real and justifiable criterion for desire, then the competition will accelerate by the interchange of all these talkers: the professional commentators and product vendors and the needy audiences and ordinary people. Norms will not be set in advance, but are created constantly between the doubting individual and the knowing culture, or between the suddenly inventive individual and the "adaptive" and trend-spotting culture; a dialectic ultimately reproduced inside individuals who doubt ("I'm growing old") but seek know-how ("I'll be young")—in the channeling of desire in the bedroom, in conversation, in the marketplace.

For our object lessons and examples, it becomes advantageous for those searching for sexually desirable youthfulness to follow the trail to those who actually have youth. Thus young people in all forms of representation—advertising, celebrity following, advice literature, day-to-day talk and myth—augment the competitive system of youth whether or not they are the "target market" of any particular campaign.

And yet the young are off-limits sexually, by law and morality and, more visibly, because of institutions that instruct and protect them. An adult simply will not get his or her hands on a college student—in large part because that student is in a closed institution. Professors have increasingly learned to stay away from students by threat of firing and public shaming. An adult should never wind up in sexual contact with a high-school student unless conscience is gone and jail holds no fear; but neither will he run into many of them. The real-world disastrous exceptions of abuse, as we well know, come from those inside the institutions that instruct and protect the child: teachers, priests, babysitters, and, far and away most frequently, parents and family members. This criminal subset has an ambiguous relation to the wider fascination. For society as a whole, gazing at those youths who are sexually mature but restricted from the market institutionally or legally, sex children become that most perfect of grounds for competition, a fantastic commodity unattainable in its pure form.

Hence the final double bind of social preoccupation with the sex children in a commercial society regimented by a vain pursuit of absolute freedom. On one side, the young become fascinating because they have in its most complete form the youth that we demand for ourselves, for our own competitive advantage. They are the biologically superrich whose assets we wish to burgle because we feel they don't know the treasures they keep; they stand accidentally at the peak of the competitive pyramid. *Desire for sex childhood is thus a completion of the competitive system.* On the other side, the sex child as an individual is the only figure in this order who is thought to be *free* from competition; who holds sex as still a natural good, undiminished, a capability, purely potential—not something ever scarcer and jeopardized by our unattractiveness and our aging. For sex children, sex remains a new experience of freedom and truth that retains its promise to shape a better self. The kids are not innocent of carnality but they are innocent of competition. *Desire for sex childhood thus becomes a wish for freedom from the system.* The sex child can be a utopia personified, even as she props up the brutal dystopia to which her youth furnishes the competitive principle.

As I attempted the first draft of this essay, the news was filled with reports about a twenty-two-year-old North Dakota college student, Dru Sjodin, who was abducted and murdered as she left her retail job at Victoria's Secret. Police arrested a fifty-year-old level 3 sex offender who had been identified in the mall parking lot though he lived thirty miles away in Minnesota. The man had Sjodin's blood in his car; police couldn't find the girl. But the news kept showing a college glamour picture, comparing her to other abducted youths, and dwelling on her workplace with its lingerie.

At the time, I thought: We can expect this to keep happening as long as sex with the sex children is our society's most treasured, fanta-sized consumer good. There was something inevitable about a murderer going to the mall to abduct a sex child—though under the circum-stances it seemed terrible to say so. The whole tragedy was too depress-ing. So I stopped writing.

During the second attempt, I reached the clinical literature on child molestation. Some of it is tolerable. This includes the accounts of abused children who enter therapy and meet child psychologists who then record their cures in a whole hopeful literature on the side of healing. What is mostly intolerable, on the other hand, is the literature about child molesters. There are valuable contributions to criminol-ogy and psychology on the library shelves, which outline the problems of pedophilia and sexual abuse and molestation, often with in-depth interviews. I couldn't read very much of them. Sorry as I felt for these men, it seemed clear to me they should be destroyed. But this was really insane, and went against my other beliefs. So I began to consider: What is the meaning of abomination today, in a nonreligious age? It must be that there are points of cultural juncture at which phenomena are pro-duced that, though explicable, are *indefensible* in the terms of any of the structures that produce or analyze them. You don't want to appeal to trauma, rehabilitation, socialization, or biological inclination. You can't just run away from the phenomena, and yet they can't be brought into the other terms of social analysis without an unacceptable derangement of values. This explains the impasse in which the annihilative impulse takes hold. So I stopped a second time.

In an increasingly dark mood, I came to the darkest way to frame the enigma of the sex children. A fraction of young people are extraordinarily highly valued, emulated, desired, examined, broadcast, lusted after, attended to in our society. These legal ex-children are attended to specifically as repositories of fresh sexuality, not, say, of intellect or even beauty. As their age goes up to seventeen, eighteen, and nineteen, the culture very quickly awards them its summit of sexual value. Yet as their age goes down from some indefinite point, to sixteen, fifteen, fourteen, and so on, the sexual appeal of childhood quickly reaches our culture's zone of absolute evil. Worse than the murderer, worse than the adult rapist of adults, and even worse than the person who physically and emotionally abuses children, is the person who sexually tampers with a child in any degree—who can then never be reintegrated into society except as a sex offender—or is simply the author of monstrous thoughts, a cyberstalker netted in police stings in chat rooms, or found downloading underage images to his hard drive. This is the "pedophile" whether or not he acts. Since the two zones—maximum *value* of sex and maximum *evil* for sex—are right next to each other, shouldn't we wonder if there's some structural relation in society between our supergood and absolute evil?

The most direct explanation is that we may be witnessing two disparate systems as they come into conflict at just one point. System A would be the sexual valuation of youth, spurred by the liberalization of sex and its attachment to youth in a competitive economy. System B would be adult morality, the moral impulse to shield beings who need protection from sexual tampering and attention—because of the cruel nonreciprocity inflicted on a young child who doesn't yet have sexual desire (in true pedophilia, molestation of those beneath pubescence); the equally cruel coercion of those old enough to desire but not to have an adult's power to consent or to see how their actions will look to a future self (molestation of adolescents); and the deep betrayal, in all acts of sexual abuse, of the order of society and of its future, in something like a society-level version of the taboo on incest. Now, system A (sexual value, commerce) possesses a major flaw in its tendency to drive sexual attention down the age scale relentlessly—even to those legal children who possess sex in its newest and most inaccessible form. System B would fight this tendency, trying to provide necessary restraints; but perhaps it becomes most destructively punitive just where it refuses to disavow system A entirely. By otherwise accepting the sexual value of youthfulness, in other words—with such threatening possible side effects—morality would have to narrow itself vengefully upon the single point of visible contradiction, and overpunish whoever pursues too much youth, or does so too literally.

What's really striking to anyone who watches the news is of course the *intensity* of punitive violence where the two systems clash. From the point of view of morality, the overpunishment of the pedophile and the sex offender (barred from living anonymously, unrehabilitatable, hounded from town to town and unable to return to society) makes perfect sense, because of the extreme moral reprehensibility of abusing a child—combined with a dubious contemporary doctrine that *desires* can never be rehabilitated. It would also make sense, however, to worry that the ruthlessness of this interdiction of pedophilia helped rationalize or reinforce the interests which confer extreme sexual value on youth just a bit up the ladder. *One fears our cultural preoccupation with pedophilia is not really about valuing childhood but about overvaluing child sex.* It would be as if the culture understood it must be so ruthless to stop actual tampering with real children *just because* it is working so hard to keep afloat the extreme commercial valuation of youth and its concrete manifestations in the slightly older sex child. Does the culture react so vehemently at just this point because were the screen of morality to collapse, the real situation would have to be confessed—the child's extreme uninterest in adults; the child's sexual "liberation" as a sub-effect of our own false liberation; the brutalization of life at all levels by sexual incitement?

One further step into the darkness is necessary to complete the critique. The most pitiful and recondite form of pedophilia is sexual attachment to children below the age of sexual maturity—true pedophilia, which seems so utterly unmotivated, a matter of strict pathology. But a certain amount of the permanent persistence of child molesting as a phenomenon must come not from a fixed psychic category but from the misdirecting of sexual impulse to young people who temporarily fill a place of temptation or fascination—especially in desire for teens who are sexually mature, but whom an adult may still do a profound wrong by addressing sexually. It seems likely that an incessant overvaluing of the sex of the young will *train* some people toward wrong objects. This should swell the numbers of the class of incipient or intermittent wrongdoers who might no longer see a bright line between right and wrong—because social discourse has made that beam wobble, then scintillate, attract, and confuse.

If this is so, such immoral attention is not just a matter of a "loosening" of morality, but the combination of liberalization (*not* liberation) with a blinkered form of cultural interdiction. The pedophilic sensibility of the culture is strengthened. Thus we may produce the obsession we claim to resent; the new pedophile would become a product of our system of values.

One rehabilitative solution would be to try to extinguish the worship of youth. Childhood is precisely the period when you can't do what you like. You are unformed and dumb. It is the time of first experiences; but first experiences can be read either as engravings from which all further iterations are struck and decline in clarity, or as defective and insufficient premonitions of a reality that will develop only in adulthood. We know the beauty of the young, which it is traditional to admire—their unlined features, their unworn flesh—but we also can know that the beauty of children is the beauty of another, merely incipient form of life, and nothing to emulate. One view of the young body is as an ideal. The other is as an unpressed blank.

A second solution would be the trivialization of sex. This is much harder, because every aspect of the culture is so much against it, counterliberators and prudes included. Aldous Huxley warned of a world in which we'd arrange sexual intercourse as we make dates for coffee, with the same politeness and obligation. That now seems like an impossibly beautiful idyll. At least coffee dates share out assets pacifically. You meet for coffee with people you don't really want to see, and people who don't want to see you agree to meet you, and yet everyone manages to get something out of it. If only sex could be like coffee! But sex has not proved adaptable to this and probably never will, despite the recent overcoming of a heretofore limiting condition—the inability to summon physical arousal at will. The new pharmacopoeia of tumescence drugs will soon give way, according to reports of current clinical trials, to libido drugs that act directly on the brain rather than the vascular system—and for both men and women. I'm not optimistic they will produce a revolution in etiquette.

The reason it seems a sex of pure politeness and equal access does not work is that the constant preparation to imagine any and every other person as a sexual object (something our culture already encourages) proves to be ruthlessly egocentric and antisocial, making every other living body a tool for self-pleasure or gain. At times I wonder if we are witnessing a sexualization of the life process itself, in which all pleasure is canalized into the sexual, and the function of warm, living flesh in any form is to allow us access to autoerotism through the circuit of an other. This is echoed at the intellectual level in the discourse of "self-discovery." The real underlying question of sexual encounter today may not be "What is he like in bed?" (heard often enough, and said without shame) but "What am I like in bed?" (never spoken). That is to say, at the deepest level, one says: "Whom do I discover myself to be in sex?"—so that sex becomes the special province of self-discovery.

Meanwhile, the more traditional way of de-emphasizing sex, by subordinating it to overwhelming romantic love, has diminished as an option as the focus on self-discovery has increasingly devitalized romantic love. Self-discovery puts a reflecting wall between the self and attention to the other, so that all energy supposedly exerted in fascination, attraction, and love just bounces back, even when it appears to go out as love for the other. When self-discovery is combined with the notion of a continually new or renewed self, and this newness is associated with literal or metaphorical youth—well, then you simply have a segment of the affluent first world at the present moment.

This means the de-emphasis of sex and the denigration of youth will have to start with an act of willful revaluation. It will require preferring the values of adulthood: intellect over enthusiasm, autonomy over adventure, elegance over vitality, sophistication over innocence—and, perhaps, a pursuit of the confirmation or repetition of experience rather than experiences of novelty.

The de-emphasis of sex and the denigration of childhood can still be put on the agenda of a humane civilization. However, I think it's basically too late for us. Perhaps I simply mean that I know it is too late for me. If you kick at these things, you are kicking at the heart of certain systems; if you deny yourself the lure of sex, for example, or the superiority of youth, you feel you will perish from starvation. But if I can't save myself or my children, probably, I still might help my grandchildren. The only hope would be, wherever possible, to deny ourselves in our fatuousness and build a barricade, penning us inside, quarantining this epoch that we must learn to name and disparage.

Let the future, at least, know that we were fools. Make our era distinct and closed so that the future can see something to move beyond. Record our testament, that this was a juvenile phase in liberation which must give way to a spiritual adulthood! Turn back to adults; see in the wrinkles at the side of the eye that catch the cobalt, the lines of laughter in the face, the prolific flesh, those subtle clothes of adulthood, the desire-inspiring repositories of *wisdom* and *experience*. Know that what we wish to be nourished upon is age and accomplishment, not emptiness and newness. Then, in sophisticated and depraved sexuality, rather than youth's innocence and the fake blush of truth, let our remaining impulses run in the sex of the old for the old—until they run out. Make a model for a better era. Once more, my moderns—in a superior decadence, in adult darkness rather than juvenile light—rise to the occasion! One effort more if you wish to be liberators.

[2006]

ON FOOD

Food riots have broken out this year in Haiti, Egypt, Mozambique, and Bangladesh. In New York, eight million people look into the refrigerator wondering what to eat.

Rice prices soar on the international market as shortages trigger unrest among people for whom rice is a dietary staple. The packaging of the rice on my pantry shelf tells a story about pristine fields and rare cultivation. "To keep our rice select, we inspect each grain . . . This may seem like a lot of extra work to you, but we care."

"Care" is one of the fluctuating words of our time. As CARE, it is an international rescue organization; as demotic speech, a matter of whim and interest; in official talk (as of health care), it essentially means nursing or medicine. In one sense, I could care less if I have rice. In another, I care (and care for myself) a great deal: I put all kinds of worry and concentration into whether I will have white rice, brown rice, basmati, arborio. . . . Does brown rice leave more of the fibrous husk (for health)? Is polished rice more suitable to the Cambodian cuisine I'll cook tonight (for experience)? And should I have salmon, which, with its omega-3s, is said to be good for my brain, heart, and mood? Or tofu, with its cholesterol-lowering soy protein, its isoflavones and selenium? Thus from taste or "choice" we stray outward to a vantage from which the wrong choice at dinner looks like death, where "care" becomes ambassador for compulsion.

Two generations ago, progress in the realm of food split along dual tracks. For those who don't yet have enough, the goal remains to gain plenty, by any technical means available. For those whose food is assured, the task becomes to re-restrict it. This second movement has been underacknowledged.

Having had our food supply made simple, we devote ourselves to looking for ways to make it difficult. The more we are estranged from the tasks of growing and getting food, the more food thought pervades our lives. It is a form of attention that restores labor, rarity, experience, and danger to food's appearance (its manifestations in the market and at the table) and its refusal (our rejection of unfit foods, our dieting). This parallels the new complication of other phenomena of bodily attention—specifically, modern exercise and sex. It will be objected that the care for food is a fascination only of the rich; this is false. Stretching from high to low, the commands to lose weight, to undertake every sort of diet for the purposes of health, to enjoy food as entertainment, to privatize food care as a category of inner, personal life (beyond the shared decisions of cooking and the family dinner), have communicated new thought and work concerning food to the vast middle and working classes of the rich Western countries, too.

I think there is something wrong with all this. Underlying my opposition is a presumption that our destiny could be something other than grooming—something other than monitoring and stroking our biological lives. Many readers will disagree. I respect their disagreement if they are prepared to stand up for the fundamental principle that seems to underlie their behavior: that what our freedom and leisure were made for, in our highest state, *really is* bodily perfection and the extension of life. One of the main features of our moment in history, in anything that affects the state of the body (though, importantly, not the life of the mind), is that we prefer optimization to simplicity. We are afraid of dying, and reluctant to miss any physical improvement. I don't want to die, either. But I am caught between that negative desire and the wish for freedom from control. I think we barely notice how much these tricks of care take up our thinking, and what domination they exert.

The reason to eat food is no longer mainly hunger. There is now no point in your day when if you were to go without a meal you would fall into physical jeopardy. You "get hungry," to be sure, but probably from birth to death never *go* hungry, though enough people in the world still do.* This is a change in life.

Confusion arises around any need that never gets fully activated. We know we have to eat because otherwise we will die. We direct our thoughts to the activation point, the terminal condition, even though we'll never approach it. We act as if we are under compulsion for decisions none of which are determined by this need—as if our "provisional necessity" were a "fatal necessity." "We have to eat"; but we don't have to eat anything in particular, so extensive are our food choices, any of which is sufficient for life. (Traditional societies always existed subject to conditions of scarcity; choice was circumscribed when one's food was given by whatever would grow.) "We have to eat"; but we don't have to eat at any given moment, so regularly do we eat, so lavish are our meals. (Though of course you get hungry just hours after eating—from sitting, or waiting, or being. Hunger is recalibrated in half-inches where once it was measured in yards.)

It's now considered possible for some of us to get ourselves to states in which eating once again feels medically necessary, even with respect to the timing of daily meals. "My blood sugar must be down." "Remember to stay hydrated." You become "hypoglycemic": that is, lacking in

---

* In 2005 USDA statistics, about 4 percent of American households, at some point during the year, found their normal eating habits disrupted because of lack of money to buy food. About one-third of those households faced disruption in one or two brief episodes; another third experienced disruption frequently. In the developing world, the problem is different—there, portions of the population may face starvation or disease from the inability to buy food. The World Food Programme puts the proportion of the developing world that experiences undernourishment at 16 percent of the total population.

sugars. You become "dehydrated": that is to say, thirsty. You reach a point where you get lightheaded, sick, unhappy without your food. Truer states of privation can be achieved through exercise. (A kind of confusion is deliberately maintained between thirst, which activates in shorter time spans, and hunger, which is slow-building and diverse in its fulfillment—so that a glass of orange juice becomes a palliative to thirst that also contains, in the solids and sugars and vitamins and tangible substance, a kind of food.) But you don't even have to wear yourself out to feel changes inside you. Enough of us monitor ourselves this closely in daily life. We become patients in a hypothesized emergency room, in which we move as specters.

These reduced states, and the ability to identify the feelings of them, go with a degree of discernment and class distinction. Lower-class people get hungry, and "we" get hypoglycemic. The redevelopment of biologically necessary hunger is considered morally superior to its wide-spread alternative, the lazy hunger of an addiction to abundance.

The poor say they want lunch. Don't believe them. Put aside the hunger of these people who endlessly crave "junk foods" and "drug foods," fats and sugars—the obese overeaters, one of the last classes of people it's socially acceptable to despise. The exalted need of the momentarily dizzy armchair athlete is counterpoised to the cravings of the obese underclass.

Historically, the *modern* project of food has always been associated with an end to scarcity. Before modernity, the multiplication of food meant that the supernatural had entered the mundane: as with the miracle of the loaves and fishes, Jesus's carbs and proteins. Not until the eighteenth and nineteenth centuries did plenty come into view as a practical possibility. Its realization crept up on theorists by gradual developments. Malthus declared it impossible that agricultural production's carrying capacity (arithmetically increasing) could ever catch up with the level of population (geometrically increasing) less than two decades before capacity proved him wrong. Malthus wrote in 1798. The last major "subsistence crisis" to strike the Western nations en masse, according to the agricultural historian John D. Post, occurred in 1816–17. (The starvation conditions in 1845–47 in Ireland and parts of Central Europe because of potato blight he disqualifies as an isolated last catastrophe.) Periodic famine would no longer be a recurring feature of Western life, though it had been a basic condition for all human societies since the early Holocene.

The early years of the twentieth century ushered in a second transformation. The embrace of agricultural mechanization spurred a transition from the mere end of famine to the permanence of plenty, even overplenty. The United States led the worldwide change, which took place from about 1915 to 1970. The application of machine power, specifically the arrival of tractors, made labor hours drop despite ever larger harvests. Crop yields increased per amount of acreage cultivated, massively so with the introduction of hybrid strains of corn. Bruce L. Gardner, reanalyzing most recently the agricultural and economic data for the period, notes that US farms produce seven times the amount of food they did in 1900, while having shed two-thirds of their laborers. "As late as 1950, food consumed at home accounted for 22 percent of the average US household's disposable income. By 1998 that percentage had been reduced to 7," while we manage to eat more.

We live far enough after the period of the modernization of food to condescend to its achievements. The technical achievement of superabundance led to a predictable but short-lived celebration of technicized food itself: a commercial fetishism of the techniques of freezing and refrigerated transport, Swanson dinners and Birds Eye vegetables, and a lust for the re-engineering, preservation, and shelf stability that made Cheez Whiz and Pringles out of smooth Wisconsin milk and bursting Idaho potatoes. Corresponding to modernization was an *early modernism* of food, a recognizable trajectory through attitudes well known to us from painting or design or writing. Postwar modernization theory held that modernizing was exclusively an economic-technical achievement, one that stood apart from the sorts of aesthetic regimes that succeeded one another in progress in the arts, but it was not so. "Food science" represented a moment of human progress, recognized and regnant, transformed into culture. When mid-century food technics are satirized today by right-thinking people as kitsch—Tang, fish sticks, and Wonder Bread—a moment of utopian progress is reduced to folly, as can happen with so much of the naive ecstasy and radiance of all products of the machine triumphant.

Today we participate in a *late modernism* and even a *postmodernism* of food. We witnessed, after the triumph of a previously unquestioned project, a characteristic latecoming struggle around the nature and direction of progress. First, in the late 1960s, came reactions against the inhuman technical character of food science and "agribusiness." Critics in this phase pitted themselves against consumer capitalism. This initial reaction was romantic and primitivist, associated with the late-1960s counterculture and the movement "back to the land," just a few decades after productivity gains had led an agrarian population to leave it. It brought a call to the East for mystic authenticity in the culture of "health foods"—tofu, brown rice, yogurt, seaweed, wheat germ, made from the live spirits and microbes excluded in industrial processing. (These were the parts that were said to live and germinate, against an antiseptic modernist technics of death: the Bomb and pasteurization were made by the same culture. I rely on the historian Warren Belasco, who has extensively documented both the actions and the imagination of the early food counterculture.) This counterculture, too, introduced its own countertechnics of food-medicine, in remedies either Western but crankish and eccentric (like the chemist Linus Pauling's early championing of Vitamin C, a scandal in its time) or Eastern against the West (macrobiotics, acupuncture).

Soon a more flexible capitalism proffered a new set of options that allowed the dissolution, or simply the side-by-side juxtaposition, of opposites, and a new field of cooperation. The standard of "health" perhaps foreordained that the dropouts would deliver themselves back into the hands of experts. Proselytizing pioneers of the counterculture became the arbiters, physicians, and best friends of an expanded version of the Western capitalist culture they believed they had critiqued: figures like Andrew Weil, MD, the "healer," and the organic "growers" of Cascadian Farm. The conceit of magic pre-existing "natural" remedies and supplements and minerals (red wine, chocolate, "fiber," "antioxidants," et cetera) was brought under the mantle of medical testing and food enhancement. Food scientists and processors ceased to fight their former opponents, as they were licensed by the counterculture to process and formulate new concoctions and mine new markets evaluated, not by *opposition* or refusal, but along the common metric of health. The postmodern moment can be identified whenever the tug of war between "scientific" food progress and "humane" food reaction produces more business for both sides. In our moment, the options exist in plural, and the most self-satisfied individuals graze from two troughs, the scientifically fashioned and the organically-romantically grown, with the same rationale of "health" for both.

(Food science, to make this clear, was not intrinsically evil or flawed, and the food counterculture was not just about optimizing toothsomeness and health. Both possessed utopian desires. Whenever utopians present the substance of their wishes and fight to make them actual, a fair number of their dreams will come true, often because the triumphant ideas have won less philanthropic allies. The best hopes for humanity will be used to pick the pockets of mankind.)

The contemporary transformations of food are associated with a new impersonality imparted to the field—making of eating a "hobby," one pastime among others.

I was watching a beauty pageant on television when it introduced video of the young women contestants addressing the camera about their favorite reliefs from schoolwork and pageantry. What were their hobbies? Many listed "eating." I suppose you could hear "eating," not "cooking," as a victory for feminist equality. It's not housework. Since, though, presumably, these women must constantly *not* eat for the sake of their figures and their competitiveness, the hobby pleasure of eating becomes slightly sinister. It seems like the frenzied entertaining that rides atop an alternative housework, when the body is the single-occupancy house.

New food entertainments have changed the character of the tradition devoted to cooking and dining. It has given interest in food an increasingly abstract character, as a "spectacular" function of food can be divided off from its practical, gustatory function. We learn to take our foods at a remove. First, the contemplation and nutritional analyses of our foodstuffs becomes a semi-autonomous "scientific" sphere independent of any particular meal or mouthful. Second, our entertainments create a standpoint of satiety or disinterest from which you can contemplate food without hunger and find pleasure in that contemplation.

We've had an explosion of "food writing," as the bookstore category is renamed from "cooking" to "food." We have memoirs in food, novels with recipes, high literature that expands to absorb a "canon" of twentieth-century food writers from A. J. Liebling to M.F.K. Fisher to Ruth Reichl. Chronicles appear of a single comestible through history, cod or salt. The newsstand purveys magazines that range from the scientific purism of *Cook's Illustrated,* to the aspirational luxury of *Gourmet,* to the academicism of *Gastronomica.* The Food Network delivers twenty-four-hour TV programming devoted to cooking and eating: interminable specials on barbecue, semi-celebrities peddling the delights of chipotle. (In *Harper's* a few years ago, a well-meaning critic devoted himself to exposing that channel's programming as "gastro-pornography," trapped by the same leveling action between food and sex that makes all of our basic bodily desires into just one thing.) And late at night on TV, between the other paeans to desperation ("Been in an accident?"; "Foreclosure problems?"), are the pitches for miracle metabolism supplements, fat-burning capsules, and colon cleansers.

It may seem odd to think of food warnings and diet plans as entertainment, too. Certainly they've taken on the same spectacular character, though, and offer a linked way to spend our time. Should we eat wild or farmed fish? Is chocolate healthy? And is red wine? Last month, the magazine *Health* featured an advertisement for its Web site: "Trying to figure out what fish or vegetable is safe to eat this week?" It wasn't a joke. Nor was it just about contamination—it concerned a *weekly* shift in knowledge. The whole idea of food "news" announces the end of thousands of years in which there couldn't be such a thing as "news" in food. On one channel, we have competitive eating, broadcast as sport; on another, a weight-loss game show, *The Biggest Loser.* On one, how an automated factory makes Ho Hos; on another, the nutrition report. The point is not that we're "schizophrenic" about food, as some say—celebrating gluttony and advocating dieting. The point is that although we're collectively amused along two separate tracks, both may have a common meaning and, perhaps, purpose.* Their meaning lies in making food "discursive" along every axis. Their purpose? They may constitute a more fully integrated system at the level of social regulation, underlying what look like contradictory temperaments and local interests.

And this allows the step backward from immediacy that perhaps lets us think of our mortality, our bodily incarnation in its journey toward death, as likewise groomable, accessible to recipe—and preparation, and taste—if not yet subject to an absolute choice of when we die.

The most modern and elite of our eaters find that careful discriminations, taboos, and rigorous exclusions still lead down both paths without contradiction: toward the totally engineered and compressed vitamin pill; and toward the organic, sourced, inherited, unmodified "whole" food—not "made" but harvested, not altered (in this imagination) except by joyful labor. You can eat your PowerBar, product of

---

* This raises the matter of commensurability. Right now, your actions every day become foods, or the wiping away of foods, their eradication. If you do a certain number of minutes on the treadmill, measured in calories, that wipes out a bagel. But so does having sex wipe out calories. We're frequently told this, too, by the health magazines. With the three central bodily activities of our time (exercise, food, and sex), whatever draws the links to make them all expressible in a common measure contributes to the underlying attitude. Which leads to a troubling question: Why *would* it be necessary or useful to express all the forms of bodily life in common metrics? The instinctive suspicion is that when incommensurable goods and activities are modified to be expressible through some common medium, it is because the transformed goods are easier to "monetize," or to render accessible to either commercial or social-functional intervention. Because it is a way of reducing all things to a common coin, outside our control, when all the processes of the body are evaluated in the same metric, which we have no access to on our own, it helps the effort of convincing someone that he needs tangible equipment, or intangible expert knowledge, to accomplish what he did previously without it—for example, eat. Whenever formerly private and habitual practices are penetrated by a need for outside equipment and specialized knowledge, the individual hands himself over to experts, and integrates both his time and his spending power into the wider system.

an engineering as peculiar as most the world has known, and wash it down with unpasteurized unfiltered cider pressed by Mennonites, and on both fronts, you find it good.

A friend of mine sighs and says he wishes he didn't have to eat. He wishes he could take a pill that would cover all of his physical hunger for two weeks, say, or a month. Then he would have meals only when he wanted to, purely for pleasure: he would be completely free. Another friend wishes for a magic food that could be eaten all the time, in satiating quantities, in different flavors, that would require exactly as many calories to chew and digest as it contained. Truly magic food would be calorically null. Then she wouldn't have to monitor what she ate; she could eat the largest quantities of food she wanted, to gratify any hint of hunger, without it being incorporated into her body as weight. When a third friend is about to eat a food that has fat, especially meat fats or hydrogenated oils, he imagines the interior arteries of his heart becoming clogged with a yellow-white substance, like margarine or petroleum jelly. When he eats calories or fats, he imagines individual particles entering shrunken fat cells in his belly and seeing them stretch and become oblong. When he eats meat, he imagines it passing through his colon with a rough texture that scrapes the walls, roughening them, to make them susceptible to cancer. He conceives an evil superfat, beyond palm oil, soybean oil, and trans-fatty-acidic frying oil, one that can spread from food into every cell, hardening the arteries, clotting as plaque, making him obese. No true account of our food predicament can leave out our weird food imagination.

Taste is conditioned by ideas. The most confusing foods to taste now are those that are bad for you but delightful and delicious, and those that are "natural" or rare but flavorless. You learn to taste artificial grape flavor as "cheap" or chemical. With "refined sugar" or fried food, you say, "I enjoy having a Coke and onion rings, but I get a headache afterward"—and then you get the headache. Meanwhile, a "healthy" taste will be the aggregate of all the carrots, apples, breakfast bars, protein shakes, fruit smoothies, chewable vitamin C tablets, tempeh, green tea, and zinc lozenges that have crossed your lips. When you eat the supermarket tomato that tastes terrible, it is "terrible"; when you bite into the heirloom tomato that happens to be tasteless and watery, you adjust it to taste "real."

Then we're asked to picture our insides and *feel* toward them. "Beautify your insides"—an advertisement to young women for Metamucil, illustrated by a presumably gut-emptied fashion model complacently reclining against a drape. "Fall in love with your numbers"—the campaign for a blood-sugar-managing diabetes medication. We have developed the imagination to read advertisers' incongruities without halting: "A jolt of health." "All of the good fats you need, without any of the bad fats you should avoid." "Imagine getting the benefit of a whole growing season in one tablet." "Discover how good your body was designed to feel." "Stress less with the best-selling, multi-award-winning anti-stress drink." "The twenty most powerful superfoods of the moment." "Our products are sweet. Knowing where they come from makes them sweeter." Each sentence is worthy of contemplation.

Beside the familiar "design" perversion of the theory of evolution, the strangest and deepest implicit principle on view may be the dogma of total effect. "Everything that goes into food goes into you," runs the frightening apothegm of one last health-food advertisement. There is nothing that goes through your body, on this principle, that doesn't permanently change its makeup. Nothing fails to be incorporated. It is like the idea of a perfect ledger of what you consumed over a life, as if your body grew or aged differently based on every single item to pass your lips, or could be audited for the sums in different columns. Not for us, the quite reasonable supposition that the majority of what we eat doesn't change us, that human beings have been digesting so much for so long that they eat disparate foods with identical outcomes.

As ideal types, the gourmet and the foodie may best represent the imagination of food as it has subtly modulated for its most elite connoisseurs. The gourmet of past decades wed himself to a single place: Western Europe, and more particularly France. He learned to cook a single alien cuisine, French, and his time and attention went toward two basic activities, cooking and importing. He cooked a limited palette of dishes and learned a set sequence of techniques. The gourmet knew foods that lent themselves to travel: wine, cheese, sausages (or charcuterie), pâtés, later coffees and chocolates. He would have a shop in his wealthy town that sold these items (the "gourmet shop," the "wine and cheese shop"), and as an "expert" he could match wits with the experts who worked and shopped there. Julia Child exemplified the old gourmet.

The foodie differs in having the whole world at his fingertips. There is no single preferred region. There is the globe. If his cookbooks are European, they gravitate first to Europe's warm and "savage," uncivilized places (Provence, southern Italy), then quickly slide to brightly illustrated new books carrying him to Turkey, Morocco, Vietnam, India. No single tradition exists for him to learn, no singular importers to patronize, but rather an ocean of ingredients that wash up on his shores—in the high-end supermarkets, which pretend to adventure among wild foods (the one nearest the *n+1* office is called Foragers; Trader Joe's represents the supermarket as a colonial trading station), in the old gourmet shops that survive on sufferance, and in the ethnic groceries, where the "ethnic" food may even include the foodie's native, childhood cuisine.

The foodie wades out and swims in possibility. And then, surprisingly, many a foodie will deliberately restrict his range. He begins to set rules or laws for himself that make the quest for food harder and the thinking more complex. Undiscovered foods only; "authentic" restaurants only, or kitsch diners, or barbecue joints; organic food only; local or farmers' market food; historically reconstructed food; raw food or slow food only.

A foodieism even exists of carnivorousness, or disgust: eating body parts that have become disreputable or rejected. Anthony Bourdain, traveling five thousand miles in business class to eat a sheep's eyeball, is one type of foodie hero, the authenticity-, nature-, and experience-devouring buccaneer who acknowledges disgust only by appalling, cautious, philistine eaters. The rules or laws of his restrictions may be contradictory, operating in different food spheres; yet the true foodie can keep several going simultaneously, or slip from one regime to another. Not everyone undertakes the path of restriction, or follows it rigorously, but enough do, and the trait is essential.

The gourmet was always close to the snob. He wanted to be an aristocrat and identified with tradition. The foodie comes after the eradication of tradition's limits. He is not like an aristocrat, but like someone who has stumbled into obscene wealth by happenstance—as, judging globally, any of us in the rich countries has stumbled into wealth by the luck of where we live, and into food wealth by our system of cheap overabundance, and our access to all the migrant cuisines that shelter in America and Europe. There is no food we can't access. There is no traditional food, moreover, that can't be further enchanted by our concentration, restriction, choice, and discrimination between better and worse specimens. Would you like some chipotle with your lemongrass? We add the value of our intellectual labor, our "finishing" of the world's raw materials. Foodieism is a natural hobby for first-world professionals, ostensibly taking up the world, but referring back to domination and the perfection of the enriched, physical self.

It would be foolish to suggest that we have not had strong critiques of the new food order. They come in two forms, and can represent a kind of fraternal warfare. First, we have exposés of our "fast-food nation" and brilliant critiques of the national addiction to corn syrup. These come from the partisans of "nature," who fight industrial or mass food. Second, standing against them, the chef-, kitsch-, or ethnic-food-worshipping gourmands occasionally strike back. They accuse the nature lovers of tampering with pleasure, acting like killjoys, or speaking condescendingly from a position of purism (from which the gourmands also often speak, differently, but never mind).

Occasionally the two sides coalesce in a single figure. The most prominent recent voice ostensibly of the nature-oriented critique of food is the journalist Michael Pollan. His *Omnivore's Dilemma* (2006) has been presented as the *Silent Spring* of this decade. It takes its great moral gravity from the orientation with which Pollan starts: that of the public good, the good of the environment, even the interests of animals. Yet it, too, flops over into a gourmandizing vision of a rich person's rare satisfactions, and sutures the seeming incompatibilities through a double appeal to health and the environment.

Part of the book is superb, among the best expositions of its kind. Pollan does investigative journalism to dramatize the contemporary critique of corn overproduction caused by the United States' celebrated twentieth-century mechanization of agriculture and planting of hybrids. Others have put together the analytical pieces of this puzzle of unintended consequences, but Pollan makes it live. The consequence of reliance on a single crop and the necessary introduction of artificial fertilizers has been land damage. Tractorized corn farming causes overexpenditure of fossil fuels in an artificial economy sponsored by the state (leading to carbon pollution and resource depletion). It cheapens the feed for food animals, particularly beef cows and broiler chickens, whose expanded ranks likewise add wastes to the environment, while the removal of animals from dependence on grassland allows humans to abuse them in ever more confining pens. The consequent lowering of the price of meat leads humans to eat too much of it, because they can afford it, and thus to suffer new health problems. Meanwhile, the processing of large quantities of corn into too cheap a form of "unhealthful" nutrition, in the use of corn syrup to sweeten and calorify just about every processed food, creates obesity and ill health by a second route. And corn is further processed into all sorts of tertiary food products (fillers, binders, emulsifiers) not easily found on their own in nature, with ambiguous effects on human mortality.

The degradation of Pollan's argument occurs as he switches track from large-scale phenomena of environmental effects and collective public health to the small-scale phenomena of human body composition and optimization. Seemingly the most memorable moment in the early part of the book occurs when Pollan gets chemical tests to prove how much of the average American body has been built from molecules originating in corn. More than one person I know who read it has recalled to me how he developed a visceral disgust for all corn not recognizably in the form of yellow kernels. But this implies a dream of internal differentiation and superior makeup that works against humanity. The expanded use of staple crops was one of the great dreams of the progress of food: a single source of nutrition, widely growable, that could feed everyone, or be broken down and re-created in any form—a dream of man since the fantasy of manna. For dwellers on each home continent, your body *should* show molecules traceable to one particular staple: rice, wheat, millet, sorghum, or cassava, for example. It's not surprising for North and South Americans to be people of maize. Instead, the sophistication of a thousand different foodstuffs making up your elegant body is a rival fantasy that, chemically analyzed, points to excessive wealth.

Pollan's critique becomes increasingly privatistic as the book advances (in worries about individual weight gain and disease from meat and corn syrup), and it shades into a hostility to the widespread, easy provision of food itself. He attacks the large-scale success of organic farming, which he believes has caused the organic movement to lose its soul. I'm all in favor of countercultural soul. But the lone "grass farm" that Pollan prefers as an alternative, where livestock farming depends on the successful management of grass, casts agriculture as an artisan enterprise requiring a high degree of charismatic genius just to run from day to day. Its master farmer may be doing something for his soul, but I think Pollan is not. His championing of it entrenches a form of localism that stays dependent on the patronage of a few buyers at the very top of the income distribution, where Pollan seems to sit.

After this, *The Omnivore's Dilemma* becomes openly self-directed. Can Pollan forage food? He learns to pick extremely expensive mushrooms. Can he kill his meat? He hunts a wild boar. (What difference does it make to have killed this one rare creature, among the thousands that will die to feed him before and after?) How will Pollan enjoy his book-ending meal, a dinner so maddeningly elite (the fava beans don't help) as to make one momentarily sympathetic to Pollan's most petty critics—those who say he defends "nature" at all only to justify the sort of egotistic luxury trade that pays the rent on a thousand Whole Foods Markets?

Whether or not one admires Pollan's conclusions, in his reasoning from first principles he is undeniably antiprogressive. He defends nature but moves quickly from outer nature (trees, earth) to an inner nature (or "human nature") that he believes is fixed in crucial respects. The invariant parts of human nature, for Pollan, are rooted in our evolutionarily acquired attitudes to just such things as food. As is true for much other conservative thought about human nature (conservative with a little *c*), Pollan has a fundamental belief that past practices are likely to be superior simply because they were the past, "our" past. They must suit us in some deep way. He holds an underlying preference for the nature to be found beneath the vanity of reason. This line of thought intensifies in his short follow-up, *In Defense of Food* (2008). Pollan cuts through contemporary, ever-changing studies of nutritional science by appealing to his evolutionary model, in which human beings are adapted to eat many very different traditional diets, so long as that diet is not the new "Western diet" of twentieth-century invention. He seems to believe, against present food culture, that adopting any traditional diet of his grandparents' generation or earlier would lead us now, when combined with modern medicine, to live longer than we will on our own current diet (post–World War II Western foods). He has much to say in this book that is more honest than what other mainstream figures will allow themselves to say—not least, that food anxiety is beneficial to "the food industry, nutrition science, and—ahem—journalism." (Pollan's brand of journalism is almost uniquely beneficial to one particular food industry, the luxury food trade, and to one particular nutrition science, the luxury "alternative" one, though I fear this isn't what he thinks he's saying.) But Pollan's philosophical commitment to tradition as his truest guide, and his Burkean-Hayekian imputation that reason is always inadequate to decide anything "complex," like human dietary or social practices, distorts his thought in a particular direction.

The most progressive food philosophy of the present day, in the strict sense of progress as opposed to conservation, is vegetarianism. On the basis of reason and morality, it calls for a wholesale change in the way that human beings have always eaten, and a renunciation of a central part of the human dietary past and all its folkways. Vegetarianism has not given up on utopia. The point in *The Omnivore's Dilemma* at which Pollan must lose the goodwill of many of his readers, I think, is in his discussion of vegetarianism. I speak as a nonvegetarian. (Nonvegetarian because I am immoral, not because I think there are superior arguments for carnivorousness. It is not true, as some philosophers say, that genuinely to hold a belief is necessarily to act on it. I hope to behave better, by and by.) Everything in Pollan's book concerning meat animals and their damage to the environment really points to the conclusion that we should stop eating meat in any serious way. It is at this point that Pollan's traditionalism splits with his hope for social change, and one sees which matters more. "What troubles me most about . . . vegetarianism is the subtle way it alienates me from . . . a whole dimension of human experience . . . For although humans no longer need meat in order to survive . . . we have been meat eaters for most of our time on earth." That's a peculiar "we"—Pollan doesn't seem to mind being alienated from his living countrymen who eat burgers and chicken nuggets and tacos and dumplings, as much as he does from his imaginary past with evolving *Homo sapiens.*

Vegetarians are often the eaters who seem to have the greatest stake in *progressive* food industry and food chemistry while still paying attention to the socially harmful forms of overproduction that critics like Pollan identify. For them, Quorn (protein made of fungus) or Boca Burgers (protein made of soy) and multivitamin pills all have their place in a rational and future-oriented diet, just as heirloom lentils do, or quinoa, or Thoreau's beloved beans.

The health impulse may be expanded to include what our medicalized culture calls "quality of life"—satisfaction of the palate, crumbs of happiness, dinner-table sociability, and Pollan's sort of conservative natural piety—but it never ceases to be medical health. Its fulfillment may accidentally require progress in science and progress in medicine. But it is always, fundamentally, antiprogressive progress in an antisocial mode. Though health claims to purify and strengthen the body politic, health has nothing to contribute to (horizontal) solidarity and democracy. It leads individuals back into themselves, as those selves try to meet the (vertical) demands of experts. Too much focus on purity and optimization has a way of contravening the attitude of democracy. Democratic imagination desires that which is unlikely, unfitted to itself, unfit. It incorporates the sick and unknown not just for the sake of justice, but for a reckless joy.

Could there be anything I know that the usual food critics, like Pollan, don't? I know that each of them can escape the system of flawed nutritional science only by looking for more and different science. And yet if one were really to get out of this system, one would have to embrace a will to discover a different origin for value. The rules of food, of sex, of exercise, of health, give us ways to avoid facing up to a freedom from care that we may already have within reach. This would be an accomplished freedom from biology, lacking nothing, which we simply don't know what to do with. What if life were *not* really a possessive commodity that came in quantities that you gained or lost by your efforts? What if there were no further overcoming of some obstacle (disease, mortality) still to be attained, and we are now *in* the era of life assured and made free?

"Know thyself," said the ancient injunction. "The unexamined life is not worth living," added Socrates. Modern prophets reformulated this for our changed times, once we had become complacent about scientific examination, but stayed mystified by how to be: *Become what you are.*

"Know thy food," says the health ideology. Unexamined food is not worth eating. Commonsense wisdom used to say, "You are what you eat," which meant, "Put that donut down and pick up an apple. Choose God's first fruit over fried fluff." The health ideology says something that sounds similar, but is really very different, for it has become existential and grave, crowding out both common sense and the contemplation of true goals: *Become what you eat.*

What is health? It is stored care. It is good foods intaken, converted into a kind of currency, with your body as piggy bank. It is vile, careless pleasures kept from the mouth, rejected. It is a set of predictions about the future of your body based on correlations from others' lives. It is a set of attitudes and feelings about your body as it is now, based on introspection, feeling, combined with chancy outside expert information. It is putting in the hours of exercise to keep your heart pumping far into your old age. It is not bad, nor good. It is not assailable, nor is it the only truth.

I find it hard not to want to live longer. I also want to live without pain. This means I want "health." But when I place myself at a point within the vast constellation of health knowledge and health behaviors, I can't help feeling that these systems don't match up with my simple projects of longevity and freedom from pain. There is something too much, or too many, or too arbitrary, or too directed—too doom-laden, too managerial, too controlling.

The ultimate quarry and ultimate obstacle in any different way of thinking about food is this concept of health. How would one truly get outside of the rules of the game? By rejecting health as a goal, and choosing some other reason for living?

We have no language but health. Those who criticize dieting as unhealthy operate in the same field as those who criticize overweight as unhealthy. Even those who think we overfixate on the health of our food call it an unhealthy fixation. But choosing another reason for living, as things now stand, seems to be choosing death. Is the trouble that there seems to be no other reason for living that isn't a joke, or that isn't dangerous for everyone—like the zealot's will to die for God or the nation? Or is the problem that any other system than this one involves a death-seeking nihilism about knowledge and modernity, a refusal to admit what scientists, or researchers, or nutritionists, or the newest diet faddists, have turned up? As their researches narrow the boundaries of life.

Health is our model of all things invisible and unfelt. If, in this day and age, we rejected the need to live longer, what would rich Westerners live for instead?

[2008]

OCTOMOM AND THE MARKET IN BABIES

The news crews that arrived at Nadya Suleman's parents' house, where the young mother lived, in January 2009, thought they were reporting on a different kind of story than the one they got. They came to celebrate the minor miracle of only the second set of octuplets to have been born alive in the United States. But a few days later, Nadya, now "Octomom," had been made the most hated woman in America, through this same media's ministry.

I suppose it will be the octuplets who go into the history books, if any of it does. On the 26th of January, eight babies were born by cesarean section. They ranged in size from one pound, twelve ounces, to two pounds, nine ounces. Only seven had been noted on ultrasound. The eighth, emerging as a minuscule hand clinging to the ob-gyn's latex glove, amazed the delivery room.

I think Octomom deserves another glance, in the midst of our compulsive forgetfulness, as the central actor in perhaps the only non–Bernard Madoff, ostensibly nonfinancial story to stir the boiling pitch of the nation's passions in those historic months of September 2008 to March 2009, when American news outlets were trying to cope with the greatest financial collapse since the Great Depression. (Also enacting their own greatest moral collapse since their collusion in the 2003 Iraq War, at a rare moment when different messengers might really have led

American society on a different path into history.) In those months, not only the red-faced steam kettles of Fox or MSNBC, and the sawdust-shedding Pinocchios of network news and *Time,* but the puff purveyors at *People* and *Us Weekly,* felt an obligation, before saying much else, to acknowledge the meltdown of the American economy—if only because they were addressing audiences who were newly unemployed, foreclosed on, picked clean of retirement funds, and blamed for *their* poor judgment, despite twenty years of sky's-the-limit blandishments in "money news" and vast structural mischief by finance architects. The babies were supposed to be an oasis in the midst of the day's gloomy news of AIG perfidy, mortgage defaults, bank closures, toxic assets, and spiking unemployment. Instead, the camera teams camped on the lawn of the nice one-story house in Whittier, California, in the glitter of an LA winter, stumbled on an in vivo accompaniment to the crisis.

Who was Nadya Suleman? Not so unreasonable a person: dark-haired, thirty-three years old, Caucasianesque, with that slightly ethnic Coppertone cast that's the norm for new celebrities originating in Southern California; well-spoken enough, and not obviously unattractive—a figure, that is, that television could take seriously. She had a college degree, a former life as a medical technician, and credits from graduate work in counseling. She was churchgoing, shampooed—a slightly droopy flower raised in the warm air of Orange County, who had always known her "passion in life" was to be "a mom."

Who was the dad? Here was trouble. A single mother nowadays is a media Madonna: righteous in the face of the absentee father, and promised our support. She becomes a harpy if we learn she pushed the father away. It was tougher for the reporters to explain that in this case, as they quickly learned, there never had been a father, or any thought of one. The babies had been created in vitro and implanted as embryos. The search turned quickly to a male donor. The sperm had originated somewhere. Perhaps the octuplets' begetter could be found? (On cable news, odd debates took place on whether an unwitting donor could be made responsible for the children's upkeep.) The Suleman family said the donor was "David Solomon," nicely linking Nadya's brood to a Charles Murray–ish *Bell Curve* fantasy of the intellectual superiority of Ashkenazi Jews (had she given life to a race of supergeniuses?), until everybody noticed that this patrimony was just a transformation of Nadya's own last name. No such father could be located among all the David Solomons of Los Angeles. Instead of a father, the octuplets had a doctor, Michael Kamrava—a Beverly Hills fertility-clinic director with a controversial IVF practice near Rodeo Drive. Thus the shadow of Hollywood vanity crept over Nadya Suleman's story. At her request, she said, Dr. Kamrava had implanted six embryos in her womb, a number wildly above all professional recommendations. Suleman claimed two had split, adding pairs of twins.

It emerged that the house Nadya lived in was being foreclosed on. This made it like everyone else's house, it seemed, in certain towns, from Stockton to Bakersfield, all over California, where the state couldn't fund its budget anymore and would soon be issuing IOUs even to the people who filled its soda machines. Could Octomom also be a victim of the financial crisis? Well, she'd had no job to have lost. She hadn't for a while. The *Los Angeles Times* reported $2,379 a month in federal public assistance and $490 in food stamps, information available in public records. Suleman played down the food stamps. As for the public assistance, it was for her disabled children, three of her first six—her children *before* the octuplets. It seemed that Dr. Kamrava had performed other multiple-implantation procedures for Nadya in recent years. That half her previous babies arrived with birth defects, physical or mental, was not an entirely unlikely outcome when more than one or two were gestated at a time. A womb provides only limited real estate for the development of bodies and brains. And Nadya was opposed on principle to "selective reduction"—that is, the abortion of some among multiple developing embryos or fetuses, even embryos or fetuses that are identified in utero as less likely to survive, and more likely to be underdeveloped or disabled at birth—even though to do so would give the others a better chance. This detail was passed over lightly in the press, in recognition of sensitivities about "the unborn."

Too few commentators, I think, explained why Nadya said she had undertaken the pregnancy leading to octuplets in the first place. It was a consequence of the conjunction of Suleman's pro-life views and her doctor's unusual implantation methods. Dr. Kamrava supposedly informed her that multiple extra embryos created for her earlier IVF treatments were going to be thawed and disposed of. As Suleman explained to television viewers later: "Because they're frozen doesn't mean they're not alive. And they're still—they are alive. They're human lives!" Which meant she ought to help them to a better place. While the Catholic Church opposes IVF because it creates embryos outside of the mother's womb, most Protestant antiabortion groups don't, and may even propose it as a resort for couples who want to attain the ultimate goods of Protestant antiabortion ideology: babies, and the part Suleman skipped—traditional biparental family. Her church, she said, was the Evangelical megachurch of Calvary Chapel Golden Springs, average attendance thirteen thousand, but no staff member could confirm her as a congregant in that crowd. The pastors went so far as to deny her in multiple press releases. She had apparently come away anyway with her own syncretistic consumer theology.

The human-uplift story unwound as rapidly as the markets had done six months earlier. Fury emerged even before journalists established that the seed capital for Suleman's mother career had come from more than $160,000 in disability payments—which she had received for a back injury, it turned out, that she had endured as a *psychiatric* medical technician, when a state hospital inmate overturned a wooden desk on Nadya in a riot. (Anyone could see she was strong enough to carry a bellyful of kids, and then swan for Ann Curry on NBC.) The talk-show hosts went mental once "public assistance" was the red cape flourished before their horns. They could debate the merits of $700 billion in welfare to Russian-roulette-playing insurers and mismanaged banks, but they drew the line at supporting a houseful of kids. How on earth did an unemployed woman living with her parents pay for Hollywood IVF, with all those multiple trials and implantations? The talking heads, you could tell from their demeanor, knew what IVF cost—natural enough, since some of the female anchors, and the male anchors' wives, likely had used it, or their friends or producers had. Who was going to pay in the future for fourteen diaper-soiling, unsupervised, potentially handicapped babies as they grew? This during the weeks when the famous octuplets still had not been released from care at the Kaiser Permanente hospital in Bellflower, California, which was looking to Medi-Cal, the state's version of Medicaid for more than $100,000 in reimbursement for the Suleman kids' stay.

Nadya's volunteer PR person, Joann Killeen, on the job for the blink of an eye before abandoning the task, claimed to have recorded eighty-eight thousand e-mails in a week, including death threats (this from an "exclusive interview" with the *Whittier Daily News*):

> Emails and voicemail messages. People would call our office and just scream profanities into the phone. "F-you! F-you!" Or they would just say, "I'll get on a plane and come to California and I hope you die!" . . .
>
> Generally, [the e-mails] say the same thing. People are really angry. They are mad about the economy. They are mad their homes aren't worth what their mortgages are. They're mad they lost their 401(k).
>
> They're really disappointed in government because they pay their taxes and they've been a good citizen.
>
> They've controlled the number of children they can afford to have and they feel that, based on their perceptions of reading everything, they've jumped to shame and blame and judgment kind of comments about Nadya and that she has, according to them, milked the system—figured out a way to leverage the system so she can stay home and overpopulate the world.

To summarize in the language we were all then coming to learn: Nadya had leveraged her disability payments into six babies, collateralized them (as a state liability likely to pay revenues for years to come), and then quite brilliantly leveraged those six babies into eight more.

When Wall Street had done this—tried to wring profit out of bad risk by climbing deeper into the hole—the taxpayer money doled out to rescue their misbegotten investments was called a much-needed *"bail-*

out." On Fox News and MSNBC, Nadya Suleman was called assorted names.

By analogy, Nadya was made equivalent to the risk engineers who had sapped the economic system and run away with outsize rewards. Judge Judy, not normally notable as an economics commentator, spoke on CNN: "She's really no different from AIG—only in a little microcosm. Her actions were reckless, irresponsible, and she's using taxpayer money." "Octomom" was a tentacular comic-book monster, slithering her baby-oiled limbs into the American money pot, for those who wanted to blame the little people for what big people had done. Doughy as she was still from pregnancy, soft-spoken, rabbit-eyed, naively mendacious, she was so easy to hate. The true lesson, as the official news sources made it out, was that here, before our eyes, in Nadya Suleman, we had the essence of the faceless ones who caused the crisis: the buyer of the five-thousand-square-foot home his family couldn't afford, the taker of the $500,000 mortgage on $50,000 salary with no down payment (and perhaps a variable rate), now gambling with human life. Here was the new expanding lower middle class that didn't save, but felt "entitled"; who inflated the bubble economy; who had tempted and motivated the poor financiers who traded those mortgages bundled into collateralized debt obligations, and written each other unfulfillable insurance against their default, and threatened to blow up everything unless the government, taking over failing banks, paid up. It helped that she was a "she," the evil female consumer. Octomom was the fat spider at the center of a hanging web. Squash her!

More often, her adventures simply edged the financiers off the day's coverage. It seemed much easier to tail a woman into her lousy subdivision than to try to get an interview with the male executives, traders, and middle managers who had really devastated us—executives who lived in Wilton, Greenwich, Old Saybrook, or Stonington, Connecticut (where the news executives themselves also live)—or to explain how intelligent and well-spoken people could have immiserated so many strangers across their country.

The great recession of 2008–09 yielded up a dearth of nameable villains. Their absence seemed to reflect a terror of naming villains. Never in any catastrophe in my lifetime has the "public discourse" seemed more cowardly, more unwilling to assign responsibility to individuals. Normally I would reject scapegoating. The mainstream press couldn't even find a kid.

Thinking back, whom can you identify, by name, who fell within the sphere of responsibility at a single one of the blown-up investment banks, whose risky positions spurred the chain reaction, the credit coronary that shuttered businesses large and small and wiped out 401(k)s? Who, for that matter, simply headed the failed banks in the periods that made them fail? If you can't answer, it's not because you've forgotten. Financiers were not held up to the mass public as news figures—with photographs and life histories, interviews with relatives and neighbors— whether as villains, or just as carriers of that dread disease overconfidence (and its partner, ineptitude). Who was it, *by name,* whose overleveraging, and chopped-up risk, and faulty mortgage-backed securities, and credit default swaps, froze the credit markets? Who terrified the government with half-truths and threats—until the surviving banks and insurers drained the Treasury of billions, to keep those businesses going, while their executives bathed in the gold coins of their 2007 incomes?

If you remember Edward Liddy—the closest we ever came to seeing a visible individual in a position of responsibility on TV for more than one night's broadcast—testifying to Congress as head of AIG in March 2009, you'll remember that it was compulsory for the press to identify him as *not* the chief of the company in its bad old days. He was someone who must *not* be blamed, even as he argued for the $173 billion in tax revenues sucked out of government to prop up his new employer. The press didn't follow up this sentence with the logical next one, naming the chief of AIG in the period for which someone *should* be blamed. Who *was* the old chief?*

---

* He was Martin J. Sullivan, who led AIG for three fatal years, 2005 to 2008, after the company's notorious previous chief, Maurice R. "Hank" Greenberg, left under a cloud of accusations of misstatement of earnings. Sullivan was last known to live in Chappaqua, New York, in Westchester, if any news organizations cared to sit on his lawn. Greenberg, now CEO of the AIG-linked insurer C. V. Starr & Co. (Starr founded AIG), and currently very active in lobbying Congress to adopt more favorable policies toward

But Octomom, Octomom! And Bernard Madoff. Is it in very bad taste to point out that the two villains we gained by name in the months of deepening recession, in early 2009, were a woman and a Jew? Suleman and Madoff. That is to say, at the moment when American capitalism tottered under the mistakes, bad bets, lies, overconfidence, cupidity, and evil of its financial firms, the press groped at traditional scapegoats—and it left one blinking, dumbfounded. In the past, when people told me scapegoating works in these vulgar ways, I didn't believe them. Admittedly the anchors and editors had first stumbled around in a mode of semi-investigation for some months, September to December, seemingly unsure of whom to feature on the broadcasts, whom to wait for outside Wall Street offices (if anyone—I don't remember this happening much), so near to their own television headquarters, or which bankers to sic TV investigative teams on (none, as I recall). Then they followed the lineups of congressional hearings from Barney Frank's House Financial Services Committee, relying on the same live C-Span the rest of us were watching (but without the level of analysis mustered on any week's Monday Night Football), increasingly uncomfortable, it seemed, with anything that might be fomenting "class war." Luckily, Bernard Madoff took over the headlines in December 2008, and this fixation on one Jewish banker could not be anti-Semitism, because his prominent Jewish victims also wanted his head. Indeed, we had the sorry spectacle of Elie Wiesel, conscience of humanity, investor with Madoff, becoming the spokesman for vengefulness. "I would like him to be in a solitary cell," Wiesel said, "with only a screen, and on that screen for at least five years of his life, every day and every night, there

AIG (in which his firm still has a large financial stake), lives near Central Park. Joseph Cassano, responsible for the AIG Financial Products division whose credit-default swaps were at the center of the meltdown, lives happily and wealthily in London. Angelo Mozilo, founder of Countrywide, originator of a disproportionate quantity of troubled mortgages and responsible for massive foreclosures, lives in his mansion in Santa Monica and speculates in real estate for his own amusement. Richard Fuld, head of Lehman Brothers when it collapsed, has restarted his deal making at an investment firm called Matrix Advisors in Manhattan. You can find their addresses online. Why not write one of them a letter?

should be pictures of his victims, one after the other after the other, all the time a voice saying, 'Look what you have done to this old lady, look what you have done to that child, look what you have done,' nothing else."

Madoff had run a Ponzi scheme, which was at least easy to explain: a little money from later investors is paid to early investors to mimic great returns, the rest goes to the swindler himself, and nothing need really be "invested." This felt as if it helped make sense of the meltdown. The problem was that it had nothing to do with the meltdown. Neither metaphorically nor literally, unless you consider out-and-out fraud a useful metaphor for legal forms of self-interested recklessness and illegal abuses undertaken in collusion by hundreds of people across financial industries. Bernard Madoff couldn't affect the market because he wasn't really investing to make his returns. The portfolio was fictitious. The downturn led to Madoff's exposure as a curious side effect; as the real loss of value for investors elsewhere led them to try to withdraw cash from the fake fund, they found out their money wasn't there anymore. Yet Madoff was on my front page every day and my news broadcast at night. Then, following Madoff, we had Octomom.

I don't mean to suggest that Nadya Suleman isn't a loon, or a wrongdoer. She clearly belongs to the tradition of the great American wrecks. Sweet, self-serving, at once devious and oblivious, she seems an inheritor of Joan Didion's California "dreamers of the golden dream," who can remake reality by sheer force of their denial of contradictions, practicalities, and other people's eventual suffering. But the press followed sunkissed Nadya into its own inner California—a land of editorials that write themselves and immoral behavior everyone can hate—without squinting to see what lay beyond.

Pornographers were nimbler. Vivid Entertainment, known for its swift-footedness in releasing celebrity sex tapes (Kim Kardashian, Pamela Anderson), offered $1 million to Octomom to star in a new production. Sarah Palin had received similar treatment from Larry Flynt, though without any offers of remuneration, when he cast impersonators in the election-time release *Who's Nailin' Paylin* [*sic*]? (Straight sexism: I know of no *W.'s Wang* or *Ballin' Bush* in which W. got drilled for oil.) But one felt Flynt and Hustler Inc. put money into a hardcore film representing Palin because they correctly sensed the American male— red state or blue state—not only wanted to tear the woman down, but also wanted to guess what she'd be like in bed. It mixed hate with, say, erotic curiosity.

Vivid's Octomom offer reflected not erotic but biological curiosity. Or anatomical—as in a frog dissection. One could only imagine Nadya supine, pullulating. Perhaps America wanted to look into that womb that had housed so many, in search of a visual confirmation of the prime mover. Yet if we'd looked in, we would have seen only another of those clichés in detective shows ("Taggart, look at this!") where the two cops enter the suspect's lair and, on one crazy-quilt wall, find clipped photographs from tabloids and magazines depicting the twisted ideal the madwoman has all along been stalking. In this instance, Angelina Jolie.

For who was Nadya, progenitor of so many multiples, herself trying to mimic and double? It wasn't a *resemblance* we were all looking at, when—I remember it as just about a week into the debacle—side-by-side photos ran on the cover of *Life&Style*, with a questioning headline, and Nadya was asked about it on *Dateline NBC*. It was more like a physical impersonation: eyes shaped this way, nose turned that way, lips surgically swollen and wide. She was plainly Angelina, stretched and inflated.

And who is Angelina Jolie? Angelina, age thirty-four, actress, celebrity, humanitarian, fills many roles, but chief among them is that of America's most famous baby getter. She hasn't turned in a notable film performance since *Girl, Interrupted* at twenty-four. Yet Jolie now stands atop the celebrity journalism pyramid.

She is an unusual cover girl. Angelina, like one of the ancient gods, is able to violate all laws, then fascinate us with her selective reintroduction of them. She takes what she wants. She is the virago who acquired Brad Pitt, sexiest and emptiest of male stars, and filled his blond vacancy with her life force, stealing him away from simpering Jennifer Aniston. Her swollen lips are not so much physically engorged with blood as metaphorically covered in it. But she does love children.

After filming *Lara Croft: Tomb Raider* on location in Cambodia (where it seems her performance as a stony-faced video game character didn't engross her whole attention), she became interested in humanitarian crises. Contacting the United Nations High Commissioner for Refugees, she took on the role of UN Goodwill Ambassador. Deciding one day that she wanted a child refugee of her own, she acquired "Maddox," replacing his Cambodian name, Rath Vibol. She decreed for him the considerable fortune of an actress's legally adopted child, planted him on her hip, and, once his silky infant hair was long enough to style, gave him a Mohawk like a London conceptual artist's.

Three years later she took home a baby from Ethiopia, the daughter of a young woman who had been raped and become pregnant, then had been shamed and assaulted by her community. "I think [she] is a very fortunate human being to be adopted by a world-famous lady," said the birth mother, reportedly, of her rescued offspring. Subsequently, Jolie had three biological children with Pitt. She then adopted a boy from Vietnam.

Here is a woman who will do what we other Americans won't: redistribute wealth to the poor, directly, in fact as directly as one can, adopting the poor and making them her heirs, ending their poverty forever. She takes responsibility. It's as if she went on and added babies from her own womb just to show that she isn't taking babies because she *can't* make them. She can. Nor does she specialize in some one ethnicity that her adoptions will repurify; she picks up the kids when the spirit moves her.

Of course, there's one thing odd about this. She's also, in her way, buying the kids. An alternative might have been to help the Ethiopian Muslim woman who had been raped. So if Jolie is America's conscience, she is also a bearer of one of our less beautiful traits: the will to buy whatever we want. A news report said someone had tracked down Angelina and asked her about news of Octomom's feat and the uncanny resemblance between the two of them. Jolie was said to be "totally creeped out."

. . .

About the comparative strength of "trends" in mass media, one should always be cautious. Baby interest, however, seems to have accelerated lately. Some celebrity babies fascinate because they represent the recombination of pairs of beautiful people (Brangelina's, or TomKat's). Some because they seem so suspicious (Tom Cruise and Katie Holmes's again, what with the undying rumors of his homosexuality, their Scientology, and her look of a kidnap victim). Some because people "too young" choose to keep them, with tabloids following as they do (Jamie Lynn Spears, Bristol Palin). Some because their philanthropic celebrity adoptions seem so frivolous (Madonna's adoption of a Malawian infant in violation of Malawi law; when she finally had him brought over to the UK on British Airways, failing to go to Malawi herself to pick him up, she was accused of visiting with the new baby for only three hours before departing for Pilates class). Some because of the mystery of fertility treatment (Jon & Kate Plus 8's sextuplets and twins; Octomom's octuplets).

Americans have many reasons these days to develop renewed trouble with the old question "Where do babies come from?" This is what spills onto the magazine covers. But there are two central factors that touch a number of these celebrity births, and reach beyond them—two supercauses of interest, I'd say. On the one hand, babies have become an ever more valuable commodity as couples suffer more trouble in producing them. Under conditions of sex equality, the upper and middle classes procreate later, whenever women are led by education and careers to delay childbearing—to the age of thirty-four, or thirty-six, or forty.

On the other hand, babies' classic status as liabilities for the poor (and public funds/the public treasury/public welfare/public weal), especially in the eyes of many of the rich, has been complicated recently by the increasingly radicalized politics of abortion. Babies have long stood as the prime resource-devouring symbol of the ill-controlled profligacy of the irresponsible lower classes. (Remember the song they sing at the party in *The Great Gatsby*, "Ain't We Got Fun," with its rewritten verse: "One thing's sure and nothing's surer / The rich get richer and the poor get—children.") Nowadays, children are a liability even for the middle classes, because, had too early, they keep you from your now necessary bachelor's and graduate degrees and, in an "information economy," stunt your income growth.

Yet to choose to have a baby rather than abort is suddenly to be a certain kind of moral hero, at least for antiabortionists and the increasingly wide swath of popular media they pull in their train. The old Malthusian politics of elites (like that of George H. W. Bush, once a staunch advocate of international family planning) has been born again (like his son W.) in a politics of conservative Christian fecundity. The endless focus on the holy fetus itself, the saved (and salvational) baby who can be rescued from nonexistence—wholly unmindful of its parents' resources, the family into which it will be born, and its own likely life—has made babies qua babies additionally valuable and interesting, even when born to teenagers and the poor.

Despite extensive neoliberal deregulation of other markets since 1980, under US law it is still prohibited to sell spare babies. And domestic Caucasian babies remain a scarce and valuable commodity for "white" people of all political persuasions who are infertile, gay, or simply having trouble conceiving because of delayed efforts at childbearing, following education and a career. The major options for those with money to spend include finding legal ways to adopt a child from a poorer country, getting lucky or getting ahead in a local adoption queue, paying a surrogate to gestate an embryo you provide (either your own, or gametes purchased half or *in toto*), or submitting to IVF or intrauterine insemination (IUI) with your own scientifically monitored womb. Most of these endeavors cost quite a bit. Even getting a baby of your own through IVF can cost a ton, and even if you're using your own eggs, sperm, and womb. Though competitively advertised at ten thousand to fifteen thousand dollars per trial, four trials before success is considered normal; any particular case may require more.

In the affluent West today, babies are cheap when you don't want them, expensive when you do. This paradox of timing, unnamed, seems to have become an element indigenous to the thinking of the educated professional classes. Well beyond that stratum, however, baby having has been transformed by the recent upward redistribution of America's wealth and advances in biomedicine from being something biologically prohibitive, after a certain age, to something *economized*. I don't mean simply that a person hoping to become rich has to scrimp on babies, not having too many. Rather, Americans have been brought into a system in which they make trade-offs among earning power, individual life chances, present fertility, biomedicine, and cash, in a way that mirrors "investment" thinking, whether they are rich or poor.

For educated classes, the relative triumph of IVF, surrogacy, and adoption from overseas countries with poorer populations, providing children to affluent straight and gay couples, has now woven some consumer reassurance into the old scary narrative—but also a kind of lottery mentality. You *might* still get everything you want. Your chances improve, though, the more tickets you can afford to buy, and there is no coherent feminist or social-minded vision here of what you *should* want—or why you deserve to get it—to backstop the somewhat guilty scramble to become a parent.

The animus of the antiabortion conservative right sometimes seems, subtextually, in part a revenge on these same "new class" professional elites who are too well contracepted, and too well planned and self-controlled, to regularly need abortions themselves. And of course these antiabortion campaigns are funded and publicized by rich political and economic elites on the right. Yet cast through the prism of religion they are often embraced and undertaken by the right-wing poor. This contributes the stage-managed quality of such populism, using poorer pregnant women as subjects of a proxy war (strategized largely, of course, by men). The right-wing revenge still has to consist, though, in inducing the young and poor, whenever possible, to bring to term babies who may require state aid to eat and be housed—services that in its other efforts the same right makes haste to cut. A paradoxical effect: By promoting the fertility of the poor, the right suggests that it, and not the proabortion left, is the true ally of the poor. Just don't expect a free lunch, kiddo, once you're here.

The confidence of the liberal defense of abortion, meanwhile, has sometimes seemed, of late, to be weakened by the rhetoric of late babies—of "our" collective entitlement to, and difficulty in having, babies. I don't know how to confirm or disconfirm this, and I'm hesitant to suggest it; so call it a personal fear, or feeling, about a discourse in which I, in my mid-thirties, am increasingly a participant, with biomedical hopes on which I will likely rely as I age. If you're a "successful" woman or man who needed but didn't necessarily even use abortion rights in your early twenties, can you muster the same passion for their defense when you're desperately trying to conceive at forty?

What I see in popular culture is further paradox. Beginning in 2005, the MTV documentary division scored a hit with an anodyne reality series called *My Super Sweet 16*. An ultrarich teen plans a lavish party for her sixteenth birthday. By the end of the episode, the child will usually have cried because Daddy has paid for the totally wrong star entertainer (Usher rather than Ludacris, or vice versa), or she will have been made to dress up in a humiliating outfit, or some rank employee has scheduled the limousine too late. Five workingmen's salaries will have been thrown away on sequins, and multiple party planners will have shouted into two-way radios. All is forgiven with the presentation of a Mercedes, though the sixteen-year-old is as yet too young to drive alone in many states. In the curious way of MTV documentary, the producers play this straight. You don't know whether to envy or revile the protagonists. It is simply another ambiguous artifact of the twenty-first-century culture of excess.

Then, last year, MTV added a series called *16 and Pregnant*. What was not clear until you had watched a few episodes was that this was an exact counterpart to *My Super Sweet 16*. The girls were in much different circumstances, to be sure. They had chosen to carry their accidental pregnancies to term. They lived, and were being filmed, in other parts of the country than the coasts, where rich teens were filmed. The congruence was that the baby seemed, in its way, as much a promise of luxury for the girls, at the start of each episode, as had the expensive fête and German automotive marvel for their richer brethren. This is what these girls in Iowa, Michigan, and Tennessee were able to *have*, despite their parents' pleas that they think again. The ritual of telling the kids at school matched the invitation giving (Who should I tell I'm pregnant? Who should I not tell? How is it that I told only ten people and now *everybody* knows? Am I off the cheer team? Will they throw me a party?); visits with obstetricians come off exactly the same as those with party planners; then comes the Big Day. The two shows' rhetoric and even narrative structure were the same. At sixteen, pregnancy entailed a special power, and glamour, and if one had courage and low expectations enough to persist in it, it was better than the shit job one had after school. It was super fun to go shopping for baby clothes. Pregnancy at sixteen justified being followed by an MTV crew—no small declaration on behalf of the wider culture. This was no lame *Frontline* crew, mind you, reporting a social problem. Because a baby when you were young and energetic and fertile was what other people couldn't have. It was an odd reward for *not* being rich and upwardly mobile—a new, alternative source of media fascination. Of course, teen pregnancy didn't lead to car keys; quite the opposite, as when we saw new mother Farrah unable, despite begging and tears, to get her mom to help her lease a Ford Focus so she could get out of the house sometimes on her own. Early pregnancy was declassing. Even this unusually wealthy-ish cheerleader had to surrender plans for college, eliminate her social life, and spend her time caring for the kid. Her after-school telemarketing job, shown in the first minutes of the program, at the end seemed like a lifetime fate. Or the teen could hand the baby over to a nice wealthy couple in their mid-to-late thirties, as Catelynn did on the season finale. I don't know if either tale was cautionary. It all seems grim; yet the pregnancy series, as much as the party series, is unavoidably, unbelievably *watchable,* not in the manner of PBS-style vitamin-rich sociological documentary, but Technicolored. Did I mention the cartoon intertitles? The chirping first-person narration of each episode? It was a realization of a different social fantasy.

The adult bourgeois version of this fantasy, one that unites the extremes of rich and poor, was the overdiscussed *Juno* (2007). That dumb movie briefly generated an opinion-page debate, got four Academy Award nominations, and won one (for its screenplay). Some thought it was antiabortion (because its teen protagonist decided to carry her pregnancy to term). Some thought it encouraged teenage pregnancy. The missed point of the movie was the fantasy of a natural solidarity and reciprocity between still poorish, too-young girls, who are superfecund, and richish, too-old professional women, who can no longer easily conceive. This is why it is a romantic comedy: all men to the side, the two ages and life paths of woman must find each other. Juno finally hands off her baby to the wife in the rich thirty-or-forty-something couple that had pleaded to adopt her child. The husband, played by Jason Bateman, had turned out to be a jerk, unready for fatherhood, possibly coming on to Juno—illustration of the eternal juvenility of wealthy men, since they can conceive with younger paramours until they die. (Of a Viagra overdose, presumably.) If the American dream of mobility succeeds, the poor young girl will eventually turn into the rich middle-aged professional. Cosmic justice will then require some new teen, as yet unknown, to hand Juno a new accidental baby, once Juno has finished law school and completed her climb to the top.

Nadya Suleman infuriated everyone because she had attained the egocentric maximum at each pole. But she did not mediate. She did not solve. Blithe as a sixteen-year-old, living with her beleaguered parents, battling before the cameras with her mom, Angela, who counseled restraint ("I was really upset at the doctor. He promised not to do this again"), while Nadya made gag-me-with-a-spoon faces of adolescent disdain, she was TV's most ne'er-do-well underage mom. Yet she was as devoted to her children as any mature mother. No one ever doubted she was genuinely loving, gentle, and good with the kids; you could tell as much just from short bits of footage. Most important, she had all the gravity and purpose—and legal and professional capital—of a thirty-three-year-old from a rising middle class, calm and comfortable in the presence of authority (whether paparazzi or Child Protective Services), unintimidated by police (they exist to protect her from criminals!), knowing how, very politely, to stand on her rights.

Octomom just timed it badly. She raised fears that babies have become a rare commodity, a status item, property—at a moment when property itself was being allocated to the wrong people. There was indeed something unsavory but not unfamiliar in Nadya's defensiveness whenever she thought (often incorrectly) that someone was implying others should adopt from her fourteen. This in addition to the hysteria and 911 calls when, as will happen with fourteen kids, she misplaced one.

Rights in advanced societies have a tendency to turn into rights-to-biology once both democracy and the minimum necessities of life have been ensured. The matters on our rights agenda in 2010 are not freedom of speech at all (what would you like to say, citizen, that you can't already legally say?), but rights to the use of your body, rights to babies, rights to sex, rights to health; or battles over the correct boundaries of these things, as in the right to life, the status of fetuses, the line where therapy becomes enhancement. The space of the womb—location of "reproductive privacy," against the intrusions of the state—becomes precisely the space into which one invites medical interventions: abortions if preserving the right to choose, implantations if improving fertility.

And yet the real determinants—the means, the practical restrictions, the horizons of possibility—for all these "personal" things winds up being the old, male, mathematical, formal, realms of financial economy that the official parts of our culture are afraid to touch and will not name. Even if Nadya Suleman was a scapegoat for those who had truly done us harm, she and the financiers were also different maximizations of a complex whose separate parts are growing together. The popular print and broadcast press chose which one, of two parts, we would have steady access to and ready judgments of: the easy one, the feminine, the lower middle class, the thoughtless. Not the male, the upper class, and (as the financial instruments were routinely described) the "sophisticated" and "innovative." That choice was a moral failure and an act of cowardice. Yet the hatred and the rage that followed—the commentators' rage, the popular rage—were not entirely untrue or unrevealing. Nadya Suleman had multiplied as if by magic a class of biological assets other people had to work for, compete for. She played a version of the drama of our time in the marionette theater of her womb. The financiers multiplied treasures, the means of life, too. But we were hostage then to the financiers, and still are.

In March 2009, AIG financiers in Connecticut hired private security forces and warned of danger to their families because of "populist rage" supposedly stoked by the press. But when *The New York Times* called the police departments of the towns where the anonymous financiers lived, spokespersons reported no knowledge of any threats. "We haven't heard of it," Sergeant Carol Ogrinc of the New Canaan Police told the *Times*. "There have been no complaints made to our department."*

On April Fools' Day, a group of people snatched a child seat from Nadya Suleman's porch and smashed it through the back window of her Toyota minivan. "Obviously, this is quite a unique situation," said Lieutenant Fred Wiste of the La Habra Police. "As a matter of course we have increased patrol checks around her home."

[2010]

---

* This was during the period when AIG was under fire for $168 million in "retention bonuses," paid by the newly bailed-out company, to executives of its Financial Products division, the division that caused the disaster. The press broke the story of this use of taxpayer funds in March 2009, without identification of names, leading to congressional interest and an unusually high level of public complaint against the financiers. New York State attorney general Andrew Cuomo subpoenaed lists of the bonus recipients and threatened to make their names public. AIG top executives Edward Liddy (since retired) and Gerry Pasciucco announced that naming names would endanger the executives' families (hence the show of bodyguards) and, anyway, the recipients promised voluntarily to give the bonuses back; thus, AIG didn't need legal intervention into its salary contracts, or the replacement of the employees in question. Cuomo held back the names, and the main print and broadcast outlets stopped following the story. Nine months later, in January 2010, almost in passing, an outside contributor to *The New York Times*—Steven Brill, in a *Sunday Magazine* profile of the government pay czar Kenneth Feinberg—noted that he'd learned during his research on Feinberg that the AIG executives who promised to return the bonuses had lied. "All but two have since reneged," Brill reported.

II

THE CONCEPT OF EXPERIENCE
(THE MEANING OF LIFE, PART I)

So many conditions conspire to make life intolerable. A life is too short. You get only one of them. You find, living among other people, that every person has his own life, visible and desirable, and you can't enter it; true as well for other lives past and future.

Cursed you seem, in certain moods. You are a man and not a woman, or a woman and not a man. You were born one person rather than two, or many. You are alive now instead of then. The morbid person knows he was born to die, but even the short time until the end he doesn't know how to fill. The optimist says we were born for life, and in solitary hours fears he doesn't live. Looking around at the dumb show, you see events flying past and can't close on anything solid. Memory floats you back to days that will never be repeated, letting you know you didn't appreciate them when they occurred. You move behind the time, like a clock continually losing seconds, and despair.

The problem is experience; specifically, a *concept of experience* that gives us the feeling we are really living, but makes us unsatisfied with whatever life we obtain.

Our acceptable philosophy is eudaemonistic hedonism. It says: we act, and choose, and react, by an insatiable hunger for pleasure, and this is to be adjusted, very reasonably, by an educated taste for happiness.

Happiness is a vague bliss. Sunny and sociable, it considers the well-being of family and friends, while ordinary pleasure is immediate and private. If you say, "I live for happiness," no one will challenge you, since everyone is assured of the crumbs from your meal. The flaw of this philosophy, however, is that neither happiness nor pleasure can be put into reality directly. The pursuit of happiness has to enter occurrence, and raw occurrence can't be saved or savored. Pleasure, like pain, will be unmemorable if it exists only as immediate sensation. Neither an orgasm nor the pains of childbirth can be recalled as feeling when you're not undergoing them. So we learn to ask ourselves *what it was like* when the encounter or shock of sensation took place. You monitor the inward influence of occurrences as you undergo them, ruminating an interior object, something that can be brought up, later, to release a musty whiff of pleasure; or chewed again, to test if it's "the real thing," life; or digested some more to see if it will yield some elusive nutriment of happiness.

The new object is called "experience," in the word's most modern sense. Experience is directly attainable. It is definite and cumulative, where happiness is ambiguous and pleasure evanescent.

Any question of "the meaning of life" is usually raised as a joke. But some urge compels us to answer. "What am I living for?" The mistake commonly in our answers is that they project only a *what* and don't spell out a *how*. A monk said, "I live for God"; a modern says, "for happiness." But the meaning of life always comes down to a *method* of life. Sometimes the method follows from the goal, as religious obedience followed a God who paid attention. Often we don't know how we are living.

Face-to-face with the shortcomings of more respectable goals, we have turned large tracts of our method of life over to experience—unwittingly. Even where life appears to be lived for happiness, it is lived by and through experience. We see our lives as a collection of experiences: "the day I met those people at that party"; "the night I lost my virginity"; "the feeling I had as a tourist in Paris" or "when I stood at the lake in the woods." These snow globes and beach rocks can be held on to, compared, and appraised for quality. You put them on the shelf, and take them down; or lie awake at night, just wondering at them. They come with stories, and you put forward your experiences as rivals to the experiences others can tell. We become lifelong collectors, and count on fixed mementos to provide the substance of whatever other aims we may declare, when asked, are our real goals or reasons to live.

Give experience your energy and like any living process it divides and grows. The deliberate wish to "live" takes over from the day-to-day accident formerly called life. Experience, pursued, creates certain paradoxes.

The most memorable experiences need spontaneity, so you act "spontaneously" knowing full well that you are making memories for future time. They require surprise, so you launch yourself into situations in which surprises are likely to occur. They thrive on immediacy, so you hold yourself deliberately suspended in the most colorful and intense instants, proving immediacy by a special interruption and distance. Accident is precipitated; immediacy is studied; fate is forced.

The concept of experience attains its full dominion when it makes its own standard, dependent on sheer *quantity*—on filling up, or using up, a life. Less and less of experience can any longer be really bad or good. It can only be had or missed, life only used or wasted. Even the bad things, you become reluctant to wish undone.

All these developments together give a self-defeating quality to the concept of experience. In filling a cabinet with treasures, you feel, for the first time, your true poverty. You amass experiences, and inevitably learn they're not enough, and never will be enough. You dwell on the album of your past, and are dissatisfied. You are like the traveler, back from any trip, who has to ask, "Why didn't I take more pictures?"

You can wish your experiences had been more plentiful, or longer lasting. You can wish they had made you someone else—or that you could retell them to anyone who'd understand. But you do not wish you hadn't had them. The need to retell experiences becomes your last means to try to redeem experience from aimless, pure accumulation—

and either you cannot find a listener or you realize that you are mute, unfit to communicate the colors of this distant realm of experience in any way adequate to the wonders you found there. Thus everyone longs to tell his story today, but not as literature.

Meanwhile, the permanent conditions of human life always remain in force, and the concept of experience recasts them in its own image—chiseling all statues with the face of the new emperor. Experience reconstructs the eternal limitations of human life to make us responsible for them. Instead of fate and finitude, we think of failure and waste. And only deliberately sought experience puts itself forward as life's avenger and redeemer.

"Youth is wasted on the young," we say—but even children know their obligations. In the nursery they learn the imperative not to lose a moment of life. The adult obsession with brevity, capturing soon-to-be-lost instants of childhood in photographs, baby books, mementos, and home movies, teaches them to take a mental snapshot of a moment, so as not to lose it to time. This is the first practical lesson in the concept of experience. Kids receive the inoculation against wasting precious moments alongside the other needles that teach them fear. But consciously sought, active experience begins in the years of adolescence.

Sex and intoxication are the most famous techniques the young use to create experience. Both activities are fundamental because they exist to find out what a person *feels like* while doing them. If friends ask any of us about the major experiences of those years, even into the twenties, these encounters still come to mind, whether or not they can be spoken: flirtations, romances, sex casual or deliberate—the learning of what it was like to come in contact.

"Hooking up" is a means to knowledge. The blurred floating face behind a fringe of hair reveals a mystery, and the difference of a face seen close up, possessing qualities of the monumental and the intimate, makes a lesson without words. You would like to know how somebody particular will kiss, what a particular body looks like, what you, personally, are capable of, what the postures of bliss will be. You learn how people differ in details where they might be most the same.

In intoxication, falling into chairs, against walls, and onto friends, a person enters a realm of free experience. Liquor unlocks the innocent belief that the way you feel about anyone else should be the way he feels about you. Drugs make perception the subject of experience, by slight derangement, tuning you to the colors, outlines, and movements we take for granted. So sex and intoxication become forms of philosophy available to mindlessness. This shouldn't diminish either one. As activities, they create experiences that push past the little you can learn about other people from social interactions and conversation, into immediacies it seems you couldn't know in any other way. They point to a world a lot looser and more liberal than this one.

You could also easily say, how pointless—how uncomfortable I was, how much I disliked that person, how rotten I felt; how disappointed I was by what I learned in sex and intoxication, how ashamed of what I revealed. You can suffer hangovers in more shades of misery than the merely physical, and vow never to touch the stuff, or person, again. But somehow the experience seems definitive, for better and for worse. What was learned is not unlearned. Once you discover these earliest means to experience, of course, the question becomes how often you have to, or even can, *discover* them again, rather than repeating them with diminishing returns. So these two forms of experience may or may not have a time limit to them, associated with the feeling of youth.

One could argue that isolation is overcome in these experiences. I've said your life has to be your own: no one else can live it for you, as you can't enter anyone else's life to know how it feels. And it's true that the earliest experiences that make you say, "I'm really living," also suggest another person may be living along with you—in physical passion, by reciprocated touch, or in altered perception, when you take the same drugs and share effects.

The more serious problem of isolation in human life isn't physical or immediate in the way sex and intoxication suggest. It is general, in the frustration that no one will feel the way I do in the many various moments that affect me most deeply. No one knows "what it is like for me" by any direct chemical transaction, and I find I can't tell it in words. So experience comes to lend us a hand in being with one another, closing the gap of the inner "how it feels" by a sort of delay and exchange. You can hear it reflected in practically any intimate conversation you care to eavesdrop on: "Ah, I can't say something exactly like *that* happened to me, but it does remind me of the time that I . . ." Two commiserators use each other as transponders of their own experiences, in their best shot at empathy. Your own experiences open a door into the inside feeling of somebody else's life.

We really wish to be multiple. Because of the mobile and vicarious character of so many promised happinesses, our era tempts us to push against the boundaries of any single destiny. From middle-class hopefulness, we think we have freedom of career. From the modern hiatus of college, we think life could be a thing of play and experiment. From the narrow and desperate occupational specialization that follows, we are left to suspect that we could have done, or should have done, something else. More different lifestyles are represented to us daily, televisually, than to any previous group of people, and actual jobs are more specialized. So it's easy to feel dissatisfaction with doing any one thing.

Sought-after experience lets you multiply your possible existences; getting a piece, or a taste, of many lives, as you tell yourself you know what it would have been like. Travel becomes the main new experience people remember when sex and intoxication stop being the sole authoritative ones. What did you do last year? "Well, I took a trip to Washington"—or London, or Katmandu. While traveling somewhere else, you can simulate to yourself: "If I were another, this is how I would feel." If I had been born to royalty, I would have filled a throne in a palace like this. If I had been a peasant, my prayers would have risen in a little church like this one. If I had no job—if I had become an "artist"—I could sit all day in a café, as I'm doing now. The water-cooler conversation in which job holders have the best relief from work revolves around the places they're going or have been. Even dispatched someplace by the company, you gather the experiences that will last, for amusement, and knowledge, and the taste of another existence, through many ordinary days. Most travel is local: not only is there a Japan, but a Japanese restaurant, or Japantown in a big city. Each moment that you say to yourself, "This is how *they* do it," you feel another life, and the phantom extension of experience.

But the only-onceness of your life, mortality, may be the undercondition of all your other troubles. Old-style mortality reminded us that death lay around every corner, by disease, accident, or violence. Contemporary mortality expects a solid life span, not a premature ending, thanks to medicine; but it resents the completeness of the ending of life, a life that preserves nothing, and leaves no soul, and can never be repeated.

Sometimes the concept of experience answers mortality by encouraging a spirit of recklessness. "You only live once" is the ironic verbal preface to actions that help kill you early. Or the concept of experience pushes you to pile up new experiences even in old age, refusing an earlier meaning of "experience" as the apprenticeship or tutelage needed to reach adult knowledge. A desire for quantity, facing mortality, leads to the same perverse consequence that occurs with physical goods: if you know something will be taken away prematurely, in this case "life," the impulse is to use it up, or, sometimes, to use it roughly, and risk breaking it.

Other forms of sought experience confront mortality very differently, when you try to align yourself with immortal things and, in the presence of quick passing objects, assimilate the perception of mortality as a sort of strength. Nature is usually what we need to experience to make the trick work. The sights of trees, or mountaintops, or the sea, possess their intrinsic delights by diversity of colors, and motion, and the millions of objects in a single scene. But nature takes on its occult power for redeeming experience when it puts the human being at a middle point between the perishable and the eternal. You watch nature's decline in autumn and rebirth in spring, while you stay just as you were; half the objects in a forest clearing will die before you do, the leaves and birds and mushrooms, and yet you stay the same. Nature's beauty seems to have been made for you, since only a human being can appreciate it; but you know nature is not created for you, and this melancholy indifference of nature to your appreciation adds its own gratifying experience of superior knowledge. It's easier, finally, to have a mountain outlive you than another human being—especially when you know the mountain as it doesn't know you, and everything smaller submits to you, as the squirrels run away in fright and the leaves fall at your feet.

The downside of sought-after experiences is usually that they end.

If they don't end, it brings worse trouble. Some people never stop following the same early experiences without limit. The sex seeker evolves from an innocent voyager in uncharted seas to a bored and cynical conquistador. The drunk finds that the fun is no longer shared as his circle of drinking buddies dwindles. The traveler goes from learning to mere categorizing: he has seen so much of the world that every town is reminiscent of another.

Youthful experiences are complicated by the pressure of new people, adding to the crowd that advances at your back. Contemporary perma-adolescence—the repetition of the experiences of youth ad infinitum—far from expressing solidarity with the young, becomes an act of hostility toward them. The concept of experience makes you fear you didn't grab enough in the short time you were in the candy store. So you refuse to leave, and thereby prove that life won't be ceded to those who come after you.

Most of us just have simple dissatisfaction. The sense that each or any moment might be won for experience, but is lost to time instead, leaves a residue of perpetual loss. We find out that every situation is withdrawn from us finally, and we didn't have the will to take it far enough when we still could. When a cloud hangs over me, I think: "I was never the Casanova I meant to be: I was too slow. I was never the traveler I meant to be: I liked my comforts too much at home. I never built a cabin in the woods: I'm no carpenter. I never took the drugs I planned to take: I thought I'd lose my mind." But I am bored by Casanovas, inveterate travelers, nature lovers, and the drug-obsessed, as they speak from the narrowness of their exhaustive experience of one thing. Nor can I make anyone feel what I *did* do. Trying to get a taste of everything, besides, gave me a depth of understanding of no one thing—I missed the experience of insight for a diffuse ambition.

Truly dissatisfied persons, maybe more than anybody else, take a large proportion of their experience from books. Or they find they can double their own little experience, and make a second pass at the day-to-day, by writing it down. Poor scribblers! Such people are closest to a solution, and yet to everyone else they seem to be using up time, wasting life, as they spend fewer hours "living" than anyone, and gain less direct experience. Serious reading often starts from a deep frustration with living. Keeping a journal is a sure sign of the attempt to preserve experience by desperate measures. These poor dissatisfied people take photographs, make albums, keep souvenirs and scrapbooks. And still they always ask: "What have I done?"

Build peaks, and former highlands become flatlands—ordinary topography loses its allure. The attempt to make our lives not a waste, by seeking a few most remarkable incidents, will make the rest of our lives a waste. The concept of experience turns us into dwellers in a plateau village who hold on to a myth of the happier race of people who live on the peaks. We climb up occasionally, but only with preparation, for short expeditions. We can't stay there, and everyone is restless and unsatisfied at home.

Therefore, desperate measures *are* required. Experience could be rejected or nullified—which would lead back to a set of solutions from Stoicism and Epicureanism, which people most often discover today in American Buddhist, meditative, and yogic practice, and in aspects of Christianity. One gets out of the lust for experience by denying and controlling it.

But a different set of solutions tries to *radicalize* experience, making it so total that its internal distinctions of use and waste, special and mundane, ultimately disappear.

The radical methods expand particular kinds of experience to use them against the *concept* of experience, overcoming the desperate search for quantity by a new guarantee of endlessness and voluntary initiation. These methods find ways to free experience from the accidental arrival of special occurrences. They seek to make experience occur wherever you are, and at every moment that you live; to make "life" happen at your bidding, and not at its.

The modern era bequeathed us a pair of radical methods that work: aestheticism and perfectionism.

These solutions appeared first, I think, in the 1850s. The full syndrome of the concept of experience had emerged by then, following shortly after—perhaps just by fifty or a hundred years—the rise of happiness as an acceptable answer to the question of the goal of life.

Happiness has its own history, but by the end of the eighteenth century its dominance was reflected in the intellectual triumphs of the age. In America, Jefferson amended Locke's life, liberty, and property to enshrine among our inalienable rights "Life, Liberty and the pursuit of Happiness." Utilitarianism in Britain gave a practical cast to a life lived not only for maximizing the "greatest happiness for the greatest number" but for individual pleasurable experiences, whether Bentham's push-pin or, later, Mill's higher pleasures. The Romantics, with a poetry of "emotion recollected in tranquillity" and transports in nature, helped recast private happiness as a search for the right kinds of experience. Underlying much of the new energy for happiness was a secular version of the quest for inner experience in Protestantism, particularly an inheritance from the Puritans and Quakers—apostles of private experience-diaries and public "experience meetings"—who had made experience an exaltation that might come at any time, in any activity, as an indication of God's grace. Now the exaltation was uprooted, coming from nowhere.

The first intuitive methods to use experience to fight the new concept of experience came out of the sense that something had gone wrong in respectable living—in living for utility as happiness, or duty as happiness, or wealth or property as happiness. The two writers I most associate with the two solutions are Gustave Flaubert and Henry David Thoreau.

Their names are hardly ever put together in the same sentence, yet they were nearly exact contemporaries. Thoreau was born in 1817, Flaubert in 1821; the American published *Walden* in 1854, the Frenchman *Madame Bovary* in 1857. Sometimes the earliest individuals to face a situation get its description exactly right, since they know the shock of change, with the old condition right behind them. Nor should it be surprising that such careful observers could have laid down the early basis for resistance to problems of modern life, which, over 150 years, have only intensified.

Each man reached adulthood in a postrevolutionary middle class that let him see he could choose any one of multiple lives, without ensuring him any inherited livelihood at all. Thoreau got his Harvard degree and worked at schoolteaching, management of the family pencil factory, and finally surveying—knowing no one would pay him for the thing he wanted most, which was to discover his true life. Flaubert escaped law school only by falling down with epileptic fits until he could come home and live as he pleased. Each saw and was fascinated by a market culture, with its multiplication of goods and interchangeable items, and asked himself whether one could freely choose or acquire the good things of a life—spending "life" itself, not money.

Each knew nature deeply, but as something one had to go back to, whether in deforested and railroad-transformed Concord, where Thoreau could watch the trains running near his cabin, or in Flaubert's provincial Normandy, which looked to Rouen and Paris for instruction in the new modes of life. The random, premature, and unnecessary deaths of close siblings, at the dawn of the triumphant age of modern medicine—by tetanus from a shaving nick for Thoreau's brother John, by puerperal infection for Flaubert's sister Caroline—made the brevity of life more urgent, possibly, even than we feel it to be today. So Flaubert and Thoreau withdrew, to Croisset and to Walden, to try to figure out how to survive their time.

As doctrines, aestheticism and perfectionism have the worst names imaginable. Aestheticism is thought to be the pursuit of beauty. Perfectionism is supposed to be the pursuit of perfection. Neither idea is right. In ordinary language, perfectionism is so forgotten as a goal of life that "a perfectionist" is a neurotic who can't finish his work. Aestheticism is equally forgotten; all aesthetic philosophies are held in such low regard that, for us, an "aesthetician" is a hairdresser who also gives facials. The two solutions were not just suitable for an earlier era, however, but are equally so for now. In the nineteenth century, Flaubert and Thoreau foresaw mud where others saw a perfectly rewarding way of life. Today we're up to our eyes in it.

Aestheticism asks you to view every object as you would a work of art. It believes that art is essentially an occasion for the arousal of emotions and passions. You *experience* a work of art. You go into it. Not just a calm onlooker, you imagine the figures in the painting, and relish the colors and forms, the style becoming as much an object of experience as the content; you feel or taste everything; you lust for it, let it overwhelm you, amplify it to titillate or satisfy or disgust you; you mentally twist the canvas to wring it dry.

The discipline is to learn to see the rest of the world in just that same way. Art becomes a training for life, to let you learn how to perceive what you will ultimately experience unaided. Let anyone's ordinary face fascinate you as if it were a bust of Caesar; let the lights of a city draw your eyes like Egyptian gold or the crown jewels; let a cigarette case you find on the road evoke the whole life of its imagined owner; let your fellow human beings be bearers of plot and motivation as in a work of fiction, possessors of intricate beauty or ugliness as in a painting, objects of uniqueness and fearful sublimity as in a wonder of nature. Over time, and with practice, the work of art will become less effective at stimulating these art experiences than your renewed encounters with the world will be. Art may improve *on* life, as a painter focuses and humanizes what he sees; but art experience, learned in the aesthete's stance, applied to real objects, improves *life*.

"Look more closely" is the basic answer of the aesthete to any failure

of experience: "For anything to become interesting you simply have to look at it for a long time," wrote Flaubert. Life becomes the scene of total, never-ending experience, as long as the aesthete can muster the intensity to regard it in this way. We all have a power to find the meaningful aspect of a thing by going *onto* or *into* it; by spreading the surface world with experience, and pressing your imagination and emotions into any crack. You must let it into you, too: "External reality has to enter into us, almost enough to make us cry out, if we are to represent it properly." Flaubert became a representer because he wished to *live*.

For the adept of aestheticism, experience is not rare; it is always available. There should be nothing that can't be an object of experience. It is characteristic of Flaubertian aestheticism to make a specialty of taking experience even from the ugliest things: if you can manage it with the ugly, you'll never want for experience—beautiful things will just be a bonus. Daily life far surpasses art in its depth, its freakishness, its absurdity, its accidents, its vehemence, its way of making fancy real, or of breaking the barrier between imagination and fact. But attention to the rejected also becomes a principle of the activity of living, refusing to leave anything out, and finally preferring the despised appearances that everyone else neglects, precisely because they are despised—this is the Flaubertian aesthete's peculiar morality. "There is a moral density to be found in certain forms of ugliness." No one should dare to destroy or change them.

Since I don't want to be accused of offering a method that is no method at all, or promising a solution to the deficiencies of experience without giving a step-by-step procedure, let me list again the steps to aestheticism:

Regard all things as you would a work of art;

Understand that it is never wrong to seek in art the stimulation of desire, wonder, or lust, or to search for resemblance to things in the world. You encounter art, and the result is *experience;*

Apply this flexibility of experience, taught by art, back to all objects not considered art—practicing your skill especially on the trivial, the ugly, and the despised. You will find that your old assessment of experience as something rare and intermittent, or bought with wealth or physical effort, was too narrow. By setting an endlessly renewed horizon for experience, from the endless profusion of objects, the aesthete guarantees that life-as-experience can never be diminished—not by age, by sickness, by anything, short of death.

Perfectionism, in contrast, puts the self before everything. It charges the self with weighing and choosing every behavior and aspect of its way of living. The process of weighing—so as to "live deliberately," in Thoreau's phrase—becomes the form of experience in perfectionism. You learn to consider the people and things of the world—a farmer, a stockbroker, your friend or enemy, but also any conversation, or book, or even a pond or tree—as if each might suggest an "example" of a way you, too, could be. In becoming an example, each thing invites you to measure and change your self—and therefore change your life. Perfectionism makes you weigh every experience against the state of your self, and accept or refuse it.

Perfectionism thus makes experience total, not by viewing outside people and things as art, but by feeling how each directs its summons to your self, and letting it enter and the self respond. This is easiest to understand with other people. Your neighbor who can't stop working because he's out to make his mortgage payments, like the one who lives for his family, or politics, or observing the weather, is presenting an example of a way of life that he may or may not know he has chosen. In his habits and behaviors, he presents even finer-grained examples of the way you, too, could be. Thoreau's perfectionism sought examples in natural objects, in part to get away from people and their (to him) disappointing ways—and this can be a bit harder to understand. Because Thoreau responded to nature, it made sense that the woods and ponds should summon him and point out ways to improve his self. Because he disdained anything unnecessary to life, he tried to understand the simplest living things. He could sound Walden Pond to learn its shape and depth, and then also ask of his self whether it too was clear and deep, and its proportions equally just.

Though Thoreau was peculiar in his habit of finding so many

examples in nature, there is no reason in principle that nature needs to dominate perfectionism. For Stanley Cavell, the major philosophical exponent of perfectionism in our own time, it extended from Thoreau to the things Cavell himself knew: a twentieth-century world of the city, and talk, and especially of the relations between men and women, not men and trees. In Cavell's perfectionism, the major incitement to becoming oneself turns out to be marriage—where the self takes continuous instruction from someone who is intimate and yet different, always a little unknown.

The self that responds to each summons isn't a fixed entity in perfectionism. To each example, each person and thing, the self answers, "This is me" or "This is not me." Each response by the self constitutes an experience; each discovery of an example worthy of your self pushes forward a change toward a "next" or higher self, or opens a new aspect of "who one is." The self may only truly exist in responding and corresponding to the world, and it may in fact be a series of selves, each drawing a new circle around the objects with which it finds new correspondences.

Perfectionism, too, has its simple steps:

Regard all things as if they were *examples,* which state simply the way of life they incarnate;

Understand that each of these examples, when experienced, makes a summons to your self. Experience things in this way, always inquiring of them, "What way of life do you express? What do you say to me?" and you'll learn what it is that lives in you;

If you are called to change your life by any example, and your self responds—you must change your life. And once you change, change again.

Your next self, too, will be challenged by examples, to find a next self still waiting beyond. Thus there is no perfection in perfectionism; the process of experience and correspondence never stops. If there could be any end in view, it would only be this: that the circle of things corresponding to you grow not wider, but infinitely wide, touching everything that exists.

.　　.　　.

Whenever the steps of aestheticism and perfectionism are laid out, people want to know the result before they try them. "How will I actually live?" they ask. In principle, no one should know for you.

Certain things are hinted in the lives of those who tried the methods. It's possible that these methods make people appear to withdraw from "living." Flaubert and Thoreau seemed hermited, by the standards of their friends. Both testified explicitly that a small amount of experience, by ordinary standards, went a long way with them. Since experiences had become totally available and inhered in everything, they seemed strangely unhurried in chasing after them elsewhere, though Flaubert didn't lose his taste for sex, or Thoreau for nature.

It's also possible that the pursuit of these methods becomes confusingly connected with wanting to be an artist. Both Flaubert and Thoreau became writers. For each, their famous, finished works coexist with unusual, voluminous documentation of daily living, in letters or journals. Was the daily recording their true life, and the finished work a by-product, or was it the reverse? I want to believe in principle that one could live by aestheticism or perfectionism without accepting the need to become an artist, but we'll have no proof—since anyone who did so live would leave no public record.

The best-known idea about aestheticism is that you'll *make your life a work of art.* This isn't incorrect, and it may come close to the principle that unites perfectionism with aestheticism—since perfectionism understands life as the *work of making your self,* either by advancing to another self or by "becoming what one is." It should be obvious, though, for each solution, that the work must remain unfinished; the stress falls on the active heroism of perception or deliberation. Their common principle is the learned ability, by method, to *make* your life at every moment—and not lay yourself out on a bearskin, waiting for life to paint you.

Against the obvious criticism of these solutions as solipsistic, the effort to remake your inside world inevitably turns you outward. Mature forms of each solution return you to the community of other people, albeit in an unfamiliar way. In aestheticism, this involves the sensation that one is not only the painter of one's life and the viewer who observes it, but a figure no different from the panoply of other forms in the painting, equally subject to *their* painting and viewing. In perfectionism, it emerges from an understanding of yourself as an example in the lives of others, even a negative example. Other people will surely find that you don't correspond to their selves, and they will advance through rejection of you to a next self that leaves you behind—but your only duty is to prod and provoke, in disclosing who you truly are. You have to give yourself up partly, on both methods, to find out what you will be for others, and even invite this discovery—it will change further what you become yourself.

I hope it is obvious why these solutions are needed now—even more than when they first appeared—but maybe it needs to be said. Either you know aestheticism and perfectionism as philosophy today, or you'll get them, disfigured, in weaker attempts at the solutions to the pressures of experience. The dawn of the twenty-first century illuminates a total aesthetic environment in the rich nations of the world, where you choose your paint colors, and drawer pulls, and extreme makeovers, and facial surgery, in the debased aestheticism called *consumerism,* to make yourself by buying, when you could make yourself by seeing. The radical perception of aestheticism doesn't need always-new, store-bought beauties, and doesn't feel them cloy and fade as soon as they are owned. In the debased perfectionism called *self-help,* each struggler against the limits of life is already considered wounded by experience, deficient and lost. He is taught to try through acknowledgment of common weakness to reach a baseline level of the "normal," rather than learning perfectionism's appreciation for peculiarity and refusal. He is kept ignorant of perfectionism's hope for a next, unique, or higher self for everyone.

I mistrust any authority that is happy with this world as it is. I understand delight, and being moved by the things of this world. I understand feeling strong in oneself because of one's capabilities. I know what mania is, the lust for powers not of the ordinary run. I sympathize with gratitude for the presence of other people, and for plenty and splendor. But I cannot understand the failure to be disappointed with our experiences of our collective world, in their difference from our imaginations and desires, which are so strong. I cannot understand the failure to wish that this world was fundamentally more than it is.

Experience tries to evade the disappointment of this world by adding peaks to it. Life becomes a race against time and a contest you try to win. Aestheticism and perfectionism make a modern attempt to transcend this world by a more intense attention to it—every day and in every situation. The concept of modern transcendence admits the hope that this world could be more than this world, though it acknowledges this is the only world there is. It holds that there is nothing behind reality, above or beneath it, but that the mind inevitably wishes there were. The human capacities for thought and desire are always excessive. We can imagine everything as other than it is. And so aestheticism and perfectionism develop ways of entering an experiential world, to apply mind to it, to add excess directly to the inert matter we know. The only way beyond, to something that truly rewards the extent of our minds, is not *up and away,* but *in and onto.*

I think each of us winds up obliged to answer what would give life meaning, no matter what we do. Many of us say today we live for happiness. The defects and vagueness of happiness lead to the choice of experience as the method of our lives. Experience, when we begin to seek it self-consciously, causes its own trouble, bringing back the permanent conditions of life—brevity, isolation, multiplicity, mortality—with renewed vehemence, and making us blame ourselves for them.

By a process of mind, the completion of the search for experience in aestheticism and perfectionism, making experience always available, turns the dynamic around once more. Here, at least, we do find the transcendence of limits, in the expansion of a mind by its own powers, reaching out to the world in experience that is ceaseless, and endless in extent as the number of worldly objects themselves.

Transcendence is a result in which *what* and *how,* goal and method, are both produced. Whether or not happiness or pleasure comes from the pursuit (they can), one lives one's life for the daily goal of transcending, if only by a discipline of mind, the dull conditions that we face and that someday will kill us. You live by methods that await you, at your call. You know they can go on, even to your last view of the sky, and the final question you put to yourself. This, if not the last and best answer, certainly not the only answer, is still what we have longed to know. It is a meaning of life.

[2005]

RADIOHEAD, OR THE PHILOSOPHY OF POP

I've wondered why there's so little philosophy of popular music. Critics of pop do reviews and interviews; they write appreciation and biography. Their criticism takes many things for granted and doesn't ask the questions I want answered. Everyone repeats the received idea that music is revolutionary. Well, is it? Does pop music support revolution? We say pop is of its time, and can date the music by ear with surprising precision, to 1966 or 1969 or 1972 or 1978 or 1984. Well, is it? Is pop truly of its time, in the sense that it represents some aspect of exterior history apart from the path of its internal development? I know pop does something to me; everyone says the same. So what does it do? Does it really influence my beliefs or actions in my deep life, where I think I feel it most, or does it just insinuate a certain fluctuation of mood, or evanescent pleasure, or impulse to move?

The answers are difficult not because thinking is hard on the subject of pop, but because of an acute sense of embarrassment. Popular music is the most living art form today. Condemned to a desert island, contemporary people would grab their records first; we have the concept of desert-island discs because we could do without most other art forms before we would give up songs. Songs are what we consume in greatest quantity; they're what we store most of in our heads. But even as we can insist on the seriousness of *value* of pop music, we don't believe enough in its seriousness of *meaning* outside the realm of music, or most of us don't, or we can't talk about it, or sound idiotic when we do.

And all of us lovers of music, with ears tuned precisely to a certain kind of sublimity in pop, are quick to detect pretension, overstatement, and cant about pop—in any attempt at a wider criticism—precisely because we feel the gap between the effectiveness of the music and the impotence and superfluity of analysis. This means we don't know about our major art form what we ought to know. We don't even agree about how the interconnection of pop music and lyrics, rather than the words spoken alone, accomplishes an utterly different task of representation, more scattershot and overwhelming and much less careful and dignified than poetry—and bad critics show their ignorance when they persist in treating pop like poetry, as in the still-growing critical effluence around Bob Dylan.

If you *were* to develop a philosophy of pop, you would have to clear the field of many obstacles. You would need to focus on a single artist or band, to let people know you had not floated into generalities and to let them test your declarations. You'd have to announce at the outset that the musicians were figures of real importance, but not the "most" anything—not the most avant-garde, most perfect, most exemplary. This would preempt the hostile comparison and sophistication that passes for criticism among aficionados. Then you should have some breathing room. If you said once that you liked the band's music, there would be no more need of appreciation; and if it was a group whose music enough people listened to, there would be no need of biography or bare description.

So let the band be Radiohead, for the sake of argument, and let me be fool enough to embark on this. And if I insist that Radiohead are "more" anything than some other pop musicians—as fans will make claims for the superiority of the bands they love—let it be that this band was more able, at the turn of the millennium, to pose a single question: How should it really ever be possible for pop music to incarnate a particular historical situation?

.   .   .

Radiohead belongs to "rock," and if rock has a characteristic subject, as country music's is small pleasures in hard times (getting by), and rap's is success in competition (getting over), that subject must be freedom from constraint (getting free). Yet the first notable quality of their music is that even though their topic may still be freedom, their technique involves the evocation, not of the feeling of freedom, but of unending low-level fear.

The dread in the songs is so detailed and so pervasive that it seems built into each line of lyrics and into the black or starry sky of music that domes it. It is environing fear, not antagonism emanating from a single object or authority. It is atmospheric rather than explosive. This menace doesn't surprise anyone. Outside there are listeners-in, watchers, abandoned wrecks with deployed air bags, killer cars, lights going out and coming on. "They" are waiting, without a proper name: ghost voices, clicks of tapped phones, grooves of ended records, sounds of processing and anonymity.

An event is imminent or has just happened but is blocked from our senses: "Something big is gonna happen / Over my dead body." Or else it is impossible that anything more will happen and yet it does: "I used to think / There is no future left at all / I used to think." Something has gone wrong with the way we know events, and the error leaks back to occurrences themselves. Life transpires in its representations, in the common medium of a machine language. ("Arrest this man / he talks in maths / he buzzes like a fridge / he's like a detuned radio.") A fissure has opened between occurrence and depiction, and the dam bursts between the technical and the natural. These are not meant to be statements of thoughts *about* their songs, or even about the lyrics, which look banal on the printed page; this is what happens *in* their songs. The technical artifacts are in the music, sit behind our lips, and slide out when we open our mouths—as chemical and medical words effortlessly make it into the lyrics ("polystyrene," "myxomatosis," "polyethylene").

Beside the artificial world is an iconography in their lyrics that comes from dark children's books: swamps, rivers, animals, arks, and rowboats riding ambiguous tracks of light to the moon. Within these lyrics—and also in the musical counterpoint of chimes, strings, lullaby—an old personal view is opened, a desperate wish for small, safe spaces. It promises sanctuary, a bit of quiet in which to think.

> Such a pretty house
> and such a pretty garden.
> No alarms and no surprises,
> no alarms and no surprises,
> no alarms and no surprises please.

But when the songs try to defend the small and safe, the effort comes hand in hand with grandiose assertions of power and violence, which mimic the voice of overwhelming authority that should be behind our dread-filled contemporary universe but never speaks—or else the words speak, somehow, for us.

> This is what you get
> this is what you get
> this is what you get
> when you mess with us.

It just isn't clear whether this voice is a sympathetic voice or a voice outside—whether it is for us or against us. The band's task, as I understand it, is to try to hold on to the will, to ask if there is any part of it left that would be worth holding on to, or to find out where that force has gone. Thom Yorke, the singer, seems always in danger of destruction; and then he is either channeling the Philistines or, Samson-like, preparing to take the temple down with him. So we hear pained and beautiful reassurances, austere, crystalline, and delicate—then violent denunciations and threats of titanic destruction—until they seem to be answering each other, as though the outside violence were being drawn inside:

> Breathe, keep breathing.
>
> > We hope that you choke,
> > that you choke.

Everything
everything
everything in its right place.

>   You and whose army?

We ride—we ride—tonight!

And the consequence? Here you reach the best-known Radiohead lyrics, again banal on the page, and with them the hardest mood in their music to describe—captured in multiple repeated little phrases, stock talk, as words lose their meanings and regain them. "How to Disappear Completely," as a song title puts it—for the words seem to speak a wish for negation of the self, nothingness, and nonbeing:

For a minute there
I lost myself, I lost myself.

I'm not here. This isn't happening.

A description of the condition of the late 1990s could go like this: At the turn of the millennium, each individual sat at a meeting point of shouted orders and appeals, the TV, the radio, the phone and cell, the billboard, the airport screen, the inbox, the paper junk mail. Each person discovered that he lived at one knot of a network, existing without his consent, which connected him to any number of recorded voices, written messages, means of broadcast, channels of entertainment, and avenues of choice. It was a culture of broadcast: an indiscriminate seeding, which needed to reach only a very few, covering vast tracts of our consciousness. To make a profit, only one message in ten thousand needed to take root; therefore messages were strewn everywhere. To live in this network felt like something, but surprisingly little in the culture of broadcast itself tried to capture what it felt like. Instead, it kept bringing pictures of an unencumbered, luxurious life, songs of ease and freedom, and technological marvels, which did not feel like the life we lived.

And if you noticed you were not represented? It felt as if one of the few unanimous aspects of this culture was that it forbade you to complain, since if you complained, you were a trivial human, a small person, who misunderstood the generosity and benignity of the message system. It existed to help you. Now, if you accepted the constant promiscuous broadcasts as normalcy, there were messages in them to inflate and pet and flatter you. If you simply said this chatter was altering your life, killing your privacy or ending the ability to think in silence, there were alternative messages that whispered of humiliation, craziness, vanishing. What sort of crank needs silence? What could be more harmless than a few words of advice? The messages did not come from *somewhere;* they were not central, organized, intelligent, intentional. It was up to you to change the channel, not answer the phone, stop your ears, shut your eyes, dig a hole for yourself and get in it. Really, it was your responsibility. The metaphors in which people tried to complain about these developments, by ordinary law and custom, were pollution (as in "noise pollution") and theft (as in "stealing our time"). But we all knew the intrusions felt like violence. Physical violence, with no way to strike back.

And if this feeling of violent intrusion persisted? Then it added a new dimension of constant, nervous triviality to our lives. It linked, irrationally, in our moods and secret thoughts, these tiny private annoyances to the constant televised violence we saw. Those who objected embarrassed themselves, because they likened nuisances to tragedies—and yet we felt the likeness, though it became unsayable. Perhaps this was because our nerves have a limited palette for painting dread. Or because the network fulfilled its debt of civic responsibility by bringing us twenty-four-hour news of flaming airplanes and twisted cars and blood-soaked, screaming casualties, globally acquired, which it was supposedly our civic duty to watch—and, adding commercials, put this mixture of messages and horrors up on screens wherever a TV could only be introduced on grounds of "responsibility to know," in the airport, the subway, the doctor's office, and any waiting room. But to object was demeaning—who, really, meant us any harm? And didn't we truly have a responsibility to know?

Thus the large mass of people huddled in the path of every broadcast, who really did not speak but were spoken for, who received and couldn't send, were made responsible for the new Babel. Most of us who lived in this culture were primarily sufferers or patients of it and not, as the word had it, "consumers." Yet we had no other words besides "consumption" or "consumerism" to condemn a world of violent intrusions of insubstantial messages, no new way at least to name this culture or describe the feeling of being inside it.

So a certain kind of pop music could offer a representative vision of this world while still being one of its omnipresent products. A certain kind of musician might reflect this new world's vague smiling threat of hostile action, its latent violence done by no one in particular; a certain kind of musician, angry and critical rather than complacent and blithe, might depict the intrusive experience, though the music would be painfully intrusive itself, and it would be brought to us by and share the same avenues of mass intrusion that broadcast everything else. Pop music had the good fortune of being both a singularly unembarrassed art and a relatively low-capital medium in its creation—made by just a composer or writer or two or four or six members of a band, with little outside intrusion, until money was poured into the recording and distribution and advertising of it. So, compromised as it was, music could still become a form of unembarrassed and otherwise inarticulable complaint, capturing what one could not say in reasonable debate, and coming from far enough inside the broadcast culture that it could depict it with its own tools.

A historical paradox of rock has been that the pop genre most devoted to the idea of rebellion against authority has adopted increasingly more brutal and authoritarian music to denounce forms of authoritarianism. A genre that celebrated individual liberation required increasing regimentation and coordination. The development could be seen most starkly in hard rock, metal, hardcore, rap metal—but it was latent all along.

Throughout the early twentieth century, folk musics had been a traditional alternative to forms of musical authority. But amplification alone, it seems, so drastically changed the situation of music, opening possibilities in the realm of dynamics and the mimesis of other sounds, that it created avenues for the musical representation of liberation that had nothing to do with folk music's traditional lyrical content or the concern with instrumental skill and purism. Specifically, it gave pop ways to emulate the evils liberation would be fighting against. Pop could become Goliath while it was cheering David. One aspect of amplification by the late 1960s stands out above all others: it opened up the possibility, for the first time, that a musician might choose to actually hurt an audience with noise. The relationship of audience to rock musician came to be based on a new kind of primitive trust. This was the trust of listeners facing a direct threat of real pain and permanent damage that bands would voluntarily restrain—just barely. An artist for the first time had his hands on a means of real violence, and colluded with his audience to test its possibilities. You hear it in the Who, the Doors, Jimi Hendrix. In the 1960s, of course, this testing occurred against a rising background of violence, usually held in monopoly by "the authorities," but being manifested with increasing frequency in civil unrest and police reaction as well as in war overseas. All of which is sometimes taken as an explanation. But once the nation was back in peacetime, it turned out that the formal violence of rock did not depend on the overt violence of bloodshed, and rock continued to metamorphose. The extremity of its dynamics developed toward heavy metal during the 1970s—and some connected this to industrial collapse and economic misery. Later it was refined in punk and post-punk, in periods of political defeat—and some connected the music's new lyrical alternations of hatred of authority with hatred of the self to the political, economic, and social outlook.

Maybe they were right. But this is perhaps to give too much automatic credence to the idea that pop music depicts history almost without trying—which is precisely what is in question.

.   .   .

To leap all the way into the affective world of our own moment, of course, might require something else: electronic sounds. To reproduce a new universe, or to spur a desire to carve out a life in its midst, a band might need a limited quantity of beeps, repetitions, sampled loops, drum machines, noises, and beats. "Electronica," as a contemporary genre name, speaks of the tools of production as well as their output. Laptops, Pro Tools, sequencers, and samplers, the found sounds and sped-up breaks and pure frequencies, provided an apparently unanchored environment and a weird soundscape that, though foreshadowed in studios in Cologne or at the Columbia-Princeton Electronic Music Center, didn't automatically fit with the traditions of guitars and drums that pop knew. But the electronic blips the music used turned out to be already emotionally available to us by a different route than the avant-gardism of Stockhausen or Cage. All of us born after 1965 had been setting nonsense syllables and private songs to machine noise, and then computer noise, since the new sounds reached our cradles. Just as we want to make tick and tock out of the even movement of a clock, we wanted to know how to hear a language and a song of noises, air compressors and washer surges, alarm sirens and warning bells. We hear communication in the refined contemporary spectrum of beeps: the squall of a microwave, the chime of a timer, the fat gulp of a register, the chirrups of cell phones, the ping of seat belt alerts and clicks of indicators, not to mention the argot of debonair beeps from the computers on which we type.

Radiohead, up until the late 1990s, had not been good at spelling out what bothered them in narrative songs. They attempted it in their early work. One well-known and well-loved but clumsy song sang about the replacement of a natural and domestic world by plastic replicas ("Fake Plastic Trees"). That account was inches away from folk cliché—something like Malvina Reynolds's "Little Boxes." Its only salvation may have been the effect observed rather than the situation denounced: *"It wears you out,"* describing the fatigue human beings feel in the company of the ever-replaceable. *The Bends,* the last album produced before their major period, had this steady but awkward awareness, as the title implies, of being dragged through incompatible atmospheres in the requirements of daily life. But the band didn't yet seem to know that the subjective, symptomatic evocation of these many whiplashing states of feeling—not overt, narrative complaint about them—would prove to be their talent.

On the first mature album, *OK Computer*, a risk of cliché lingered in a song of a computer voice intoning *"Fitter, happier, more productive"*—as if the dream of conformist self-improvement would turn us artificial. But the automated voice's oddly human character saved the effect. It seemed automated things, too, could be seduced by a dream of perfection equally delusory for them. Then the new commensurability of natural and artificial wasn't a simple loss, but produced a hybrid vulnerability when you had thought things were most stark and steely. The band was also, at that time, mastering a game of voices, the interfiling of inhuman speech and machine sounds with the keening, vulnerable human singing of Thom Yorke.

Their music had started as guitar rock, but with the albums *Kid A* and *Amnesiac* the keyboard asserted itself. The piano dominated; the guitars developed a quality of an organ. The drums, emerging altered and processed, came to fill in spaces in rhythms already set by the frontline instruments. Orchestration added brittle washes of strings, a synthetic choir, chimes, an unknown shimmer, or bleated horns. The new songs were built on verse-chorus structure in only a rudimentary way, as songs developed from one block of music to the next, not turning back.

And, of course—as is better known, and more widely discussed—on the new albums the band, by now extremely popular and multimillion-selling, "embraced" electronica. But what precisely did that mean? It didn't seem in their case like opportunism, as in keeping up with the new thing; nor did it entirely take over what they did in their songs; nor were they particularly noteworthy as electronic artists. It is crucial that they were not innovators; nor did they ever take it further than halfway—if that. They were *not* an avant-garde. The political problem of an artistic avant-garde, especially when it deals with any new technology of representation, has always been that the simply novel elements may be mistaken for some form of political action or progress. Two meanings of "revolutionary"—one, forming an advance in formal technique; the other, contributing to social cataclysm—are often confused, usually to the artist's benefit, and technology has a way of becoming infatuated with its own existence.

Radiohead's success lay in their ability to represent the feeling of our age; they did not insist on being too much advanced in the "advanced" music they acquired. The beeps and buzzes never seemed like the source of their energy; rather, they were a means they'd stumbled upon of finally communicating the feelings they had always held. They had felt, so to speak, electronic on *OK Computer* with much less actual electronica. And they did something very rudimentary and basic with the new technologies. They tilted artificial noises against the weight of the human voice and human sounds.

Their new kind of song, in both words and music, announced that anyone might have to become partly inhuman to accommodate the experience of the new era.

Thom Yorke's voice is the unity on which all the musical aggregations and complexes pivot. You have to imagine the music drawing a series of outlines around him, a house, a tank, the stars of space, or an architecture of almost abstract pipes and tubes, cogs and wheels, ivy and thorns, servers and boards, beams and voids. The music has the feeling of a biomorphic machine in which the voice is alternately trapped and protected.

Yorke's voice conjures the human in extremis. Sometimes it comes to us from an extreme of fear, sometimes an extreme of transcendence. We recognize it as a naked voice in the process of rising up to beauty—the reassurance we've alluded to in the lyrics—or being broken up and lost in the chatter of broadcasts, the destroying fear. In the same song that features a whole sung melody, the vocals will also be broken into bits and made the pulsing wallpaper against which the vulnerable, pale voice of the singer stands out. Only a few other popular artists build so much of their music from sampled voice rather than sampled beats, instrumental tones, or noises. The syllables are cut and repeated. A "wordless" background will come from mashed phonemes. Then the pure human voice will reassert itself.*

A surprising amount of this music seems to draw on church music. One biographical fact is relevant here: they come from Oxford, England, grew up there, met in high school, and live, compose, and rehearse there. Their hometown is like their music. That bifurcated English city, split between concrete downtown and green environs, has its unspoiled center and gray periphery of modest houses and a disused automobile factory. Its spots of natural beauty exist because of the nearby huge institutions of the university, and if you stand in the remaining fields and parks you always know you are in a momentary breathing space, already encroached upon. But for the musically minded, the significant feature of Oxford is its Church of England chapels, one in each college and others outside—places of imperial authority, home to another kind of hidden song. The purity of Yorke's falsetto belongs in a boys' choir at evensong. And then Yorke does sing of angels, amid harps, chimes, and bells: "Black-eyed angels swam with me / . . . / And we all went to heaven in a little row boat / There was nothing to fear and nothing to doubt."

And yet the religion in the music is not about salvation—it's about the authority of voices, the wish to submit and the discovery of a consequent resistance in oneself. It is antireligious, though attuned to transcendence. The organ in a church can be the repository of sublime power: a bundling of human throats in its brass pipes, or all the instruments known to man in its stops. You can hear your own small voice responding, within something so big that it manifests a threat of your voice merely being played mechanically and absorbed into a totality. To sing with an organ (as Yorke does at the end of *Kid A*) can be to discover one's own inner voice in distinction to it; and at the same time to wish

---

* Stanley Cavell used to say that the first impulse opera evokes is to wonder where in the physical singer the immaterial song can be located. In live performance, the striking thing about Thom Yorke is how small a person he is. Not only is his voice excessive, beyond human averageness, it is moored to a smaller-than-average body and onstage persona that seem to dramatize the question, in his music, of where voices come from— from individual people or the techniques that surround and overmaster them.

to be lost, absorbed, overwhelmed within it. A certain kind of person will refuse the church. But even one who refuses the church will not forget the overwhelming feeling.

Sublime experience, the philosophical tradition says, depends on a relation to something that threatens. Classically it depended on observing from a point of safety a power, like a storm, cataract, or high sea, that could crush the observer if he were nearer. (By compassing the incompassable power in inner representation, it was even suggested, you could be reminded of the interior power of the moral faculty, the human source of a comparable strength.) Radiohead observe the storm from within it. Their music can remind you of the inner overcoming voice, it's true. But then the result is no simple access of power. This sublime acknowledges a different kind of internalization, the drawing of the inhuman into yourself; and also a loss of your own feelings and words and voice to an outer order that has come to possess them.

The way Yorke sings guarantees that you often don't know what the lyrics are; they emerge into sense and drop out—and certain phrases attain clarity while others remain behind. This de-enunciation has been a tool of pop for a long time. Concentrating, you can make out nearly all the lyrics; listening idly, you hear a smaller set of particular lines, which you sing along to and remember. It is a way of focusing inattention as well as attention.

The most important grammatical tic in Radiohead lyrics, unlike the habitual lyrical "I" and apostrophic "you" of pop, is the "we." "We ride," "We escape," "We're damaged goods," "Bring down the government / . . . they don't speak for us." But also: "We suck young blood," "We can wipe you out . . . / Anytime." The pronoun doesn't point to any existing collectivity; the songs aren't about a national group or even the generic audience for rock. So who is "we"?

There is the scared individual, lying to say he's not alone—like the child who says "We're coming in there!" so imagined monsters won't know he's by himself. There's the "we" you might wish for, the imagined collectivity that could resist or threaten; and this may shade into the thought of all the other listeners besides you, in their rooms or cars alone, singing these same bits of lyrics.

There's the "we," as I've suggested, of the violent power that you are not, the voice of the tyrant, the thug, the terrifying parent, the bad cop. You take him inside you and his voice spreads over all the others who— somewhere singing these words for just a moment—are like you. You experience a release at last, so satisfying does it feel to sing the unspoken orders out loud to yourself, as if at last they came from you. You are the one willing the destruction—like Brecht and Weill's Pirate Jenny, the barmaid, washing dishes and taking orders, who knows that soon a Black Ship will come for her town, bristling with cannons. And when its crew asks their queen whom they should kill, she will answer: *"Alle!"*

So the characteristic Radiohead song turns into an alternation, in exactly the same repeated words, between the forces that would defy intrusive power and the intrusive power itself, between hopeful individuals and the tyrant ventriloquized.

It has to be admitted that other memorable lyrics sing phrases of self-help. Plenty of these important lines are junk slogans from the culture, and of course part of the oddity of pop is that junk phrases can be made so moving; they do their work again. In a desperate voice: "You can try the best you can / If you try the best you can / The best you can is good enough." Or: "Breathe, keep breathing / Don't lose your nerve." Or: "Everyone / Everyone around here / Everyone is so near / It's holding on." On the page, these lyrics aren't impressive, unless you can hear them in memory, in the framing of the song. Again, one has to distinguish between poetry and pop. The most important lines in pop are rarely poetically notable; frequently they are quite deliberately and necessarily words that are the most frank, melodramatic, and unredeemable. And yet they do get redeemed. The question becomes why certain settings in music, and a certain playing of simple against more complex lyrics, can remake debased language and restore the innocence of emotional expression. (Opera listeners know this, in the ariose transformations of *"Un bel dì"* [One fine day] or *"O mio babbino caro"* [Oh, my dear papa]. But then opera criticism, too, has a long-standing problem with lyrics.)

In the midst of all else the music and lyrics are doing, the phrases of self-help may be the minimal words of will or nerve that you need to hear.

The more I try to categorize why Radiohead's music works as it does, and by extension how pop works, the more it seems clear that the effect of pop on our beliefs and actions is not really to create either one. Pop does, though, I think, allow you to retain certain things you've already thought, without your necessarily having been able to articulate them, and to preserve certain feelings you have only intermittent access to, in a different form, music with lyrics, in which the cognitive and emotional are less divided. I think songs allow you to steel yourself or loosen yourself into certain kinds of actions, though they don't start anything. And the particular songs and bands you like dictate the beliefs you can preserve and reactivate, and the actions you can prepare—and which songs and careers will shape your inchoate private experience depends on an alchemy of your experience and the art itself. Pop is neither a mirror nor a Rorschach blot, into which you look and see only yourself; nor is it a lecture, an interpretable poem, or an act of simply determinate speech. It teaches something, but only by stimulating and preserving things that you must have had inaugurated elsewhere. Or it prepares the ground for these discoveries elsewhere—often knowledge you might never otherwise have really "known," except as it could be rehearsed by you, then repeatedly reactivated for you, in this medium.

But is the knowledge that's preserved a spur to revolution? There is no logical sense in which pop music is revolutionary. That follows from the conclusion that pop does not start beliefs or instill principles or create action ex nihilo. It couldn't overturn an order. When so much pop declares itself to be revolutionary, however, I think it correctly points to something else that is significant but more limited and complicated. There is indeed an antisocial or countercultural tendency of pop that does follow logically from what it does. That is to say, there is a characteristic affect that follows from a medium that allows you to retain and reactivate forms of knowledge and experience that you are "supposed to" forget or that are "supposed to" disappear by themselves—and "supposed to" here isn't nefarious, it simply means that social forms, convention, conformity, and just plain intelligent speech don't allow you to speak of these things, or make them embarrassing when you do. Pop encourages you to hold on to and reactivate hints of personal feeling that society should have extinguished. Of course this winds up taking in all classes of fragile personal knowledge: things that are inarticulable in social speech because they are too delicate or ideologically out of step, and things that should not be articulated because they are selfish, thoughtless, destructive, and stupid. That helps explain how these claims for "what I learned from pop" can go so quickly from the sublime to the ridiculous and back to the sublime. It explains why we are right to feel that so much of what's promised for pop is not worth our credulity. But, again, risking ridiculousness, I think the thing that pop can prepare you for, the essential thing, is *defiance*. Defiance, at its bare minimum, is the insistence on finding ways to retain the thoughts and feelings that a larger power should have extinguished.

The difference between revolution and defiance is the difference between an overthrow of the existing order and one person's shaken fist. When the former isn't possible, you still have to hold on to the latter, if only so as to remember you're human. Defiance is the insistence on individual power confronting overwhelming force that it cannot undo. You know you cannot strike the colossus. But you can defy it with words or signs. In the assertion that you can fight a superior power, the declaration that you will, this absurd overstatement gains dignity by exposing you, however uselessly, to risk. Unable to stop it in its tracks, you dare the crushing power to begin its devastation with you.

Power comes in many forms for human beings, and defiance meets it where it can. The simplest defiance confronts nature's power and necessity. In the teeth of a storm that would kill him, a man will curse the wind and rain. He declares, like Nikos Kazantzakis's peasant Zorba, "You won't get into my little hut, brother; I shan't open the door to you. You won't put my fire out; you won't tip my hut over!" This will is not Promethean, simply human.

In all forms of defiance, a little contingent being, the imperiled man or woman, hangs on to his will—which may be all he has left—by making a deliberate error about his will's jurisdiction. Because the defiant person has no power to win a struggle, he preserves his will through representations: he shakes his fist, announces his name, shouts a threat, and above all makes the statements "I am," "We are." This becomes even more necessary and risky when the cruel power is not natural, will-less itself, but belongs to other men. Barthes gives the words of the French revolutionist Guadet, arrested and condemned to death: "Yes, I am Guadet. Executioner, do your duty. Go take my head to the tyrants of my country. It has always turned them pale; once severed, it will turn them paler still." He gives the order, not the tyrant, commanding necessity in his own name—defying the false necessity of human force that has usurped nature's power—even if he can only command it to destroy him.

The situation we confront now is a new necessity, not blameless like wind or water and yet not fatal as from a tyrant or executioner. The nature we face is a billowing atmospheric second nature made by man. It is the distant soft tyranny of other men, wafting in diffuse messages, in the abdication of authority to technology, in the dissembling of responsibility under cover of responsibility and with the excuse of help—gutless, irresponsible, servile, showing no naked force, only a smiling or a pious face. The "they" are cowardly friends. They are here to help you be happy and make fruitful choices. ("We can wipe you out anytime.")

At its best, Radiohead's music reactivates the moods in which you once noticed you ought to refuse. It can abet an *impersonal* defiance. This is not a doctrine the band advances, but an effect of the aesthetic. It doesn't name a single enemy. It doesn't propose revolution. It doesn't call you to overthrow an order that you couldn't take hold of anyway at any single point, not without scapegoating a portion and missing the whole. This defiance—it might be the one thing we can manage, and better than sinking beneath the waves. It requires the retention of a private voice.

One of the songs on *Hail to the Thief* has a peculiar counterslogan:

> Just 'cause you feel it
> Doesn't mean it's there.

To sense the perversity of the appearance of these words in a pop song, you have to remember that they occur inside an art form monomaniacally devoted to the production of strong feelings. Pop music *always* tells its listeners that their feelings are real. Yet here is a chorus that denies any reference to reality in the elation and melancholy and chills that this chorus, in fact, elicits. Yorke delivers the lines with an upnote on "feel" as he repeats them, and if anything in the song makes your hair stand on end, that will be the moment. He makes you feel, that is, the emotion he's warning you against. Next he sings a warning not to make too much of his own singing: "There's always a siren / Singing you to shipwreck." And this song, titled "There There," was the first single released off the album, pressed in many millions of copies; it was played endlessly on radio and MTV.

The purpose of the warning is not to stop feelings but to stop you from believing they always refer to something, or deserve reality, or should lead to actions, or choices, or beliefs—which is, of course, what the messages you hear by broadcast like you to make of them. The feelings evoked by a pop song may be false, as the feelings evoked by all the other messages brought to you by the same media as pop songs may be false. You must judge. If leading you to disbelieve in broadcast also leads you to disbelieve in pop, so be it; maybe you believed in pop in the wrong way. You must distinguish. The broadcast messages are impersonal in one fashion. They pretend to care about you when actually they don't know or care that you, as a single person, exist. Impersonal defiance is impersonal in another way; it encourages you to withdraw, no longer to believe that there is any human obligation owed to the sources of messages—except when they remind you, truly, of what you already have subtly sensed and already know.

You can see a closed space at the heart of many of Radiohead's songs. To draw out one of their own images, it may be something like a glass house. You live continuously in the glare of inspection and with the threat of intrusion. The attempt to cast stones at an outer world of enemies would shatter your own shelter. So you settle for the protection of this house, with watchers on the outside, as a place you can still live, a way to preserve the vestige of closure—a barrier, however glassy and fragile, against the outside. In English terms, a glass house is also a glasshouse, which we call a greenhouse. It is the artificial construction that allows botanical life to thrive in winter.

Radiohead's songs suggest that you should erect a barrier, even of repeated minimal words, or the assertion of a "we," to protect yourself—and then there proves to be a place in each song to which you, too, can't be admitted, because the singer has something within him closed to interference, just as every one of us does, or should. We'll all have to find the last dwellings within ourselves that are closed to intrusion, and begin from there. The politics of the next age, if we are to survive, will include a politics of the re-creation of privacy.

[2005]

PUNK: THE RIGHT KIND OF PAIN

Where does rock come from? "Rock": I mean the music that comes out of the sixties, the music that is hardened, toughened, accelerated, then complicated, softened, disassembled, in decades that followed. Begun again—pastiched, mashed up, mimicked, reduced, and expanded once more—even up to the present moment.

"Rock," here, is not the same as rock 'n' roll, or rock and roll, whose origins lie in the 1940s and 1950s. Rock 'n' roll came from the electrification of two previous popular musics: rhythm and blues, earlier known as "race" music (meaning African-American music), and country and western, known earlier as hillbilly music (meaning the music of poor rural whites, inheriting Scottish, Irish, and English traditions, but already possessing a significant admixture of the music of African-American slaves and former slaves). It came, too, from the new possession by whites, recording music largely for teenagers, of black music, in a contest of appropriation and racial assertion, drawing together such figures of different character as Elvis and Little Richard, Chuck Berry and Buddy Holly—but not quite Muddy Waters or Ray Charles.

How strange that to become "rock," it became in a sense *more* electrified, or re-electrified, louder and capable of distortion; with more instruments besides guitar now electrifying, too; became "white" in a different way, too, by a transit through England back to the United States. It made a transit, too, in America, through the "folk revival," thus through leftist and antiracist politics, the university, and a highbrow popular audience that otherwise respected only jazz—and lapsed back into a seemingly apolitical "children's" music associated with a musical whitewashing. *That* is why folkies were so infuriated when Dylan, their kiddie hope, "went electric" at Newport in 1965, not because they disliked the sound of electric guitars (surely they would have had Charlie Christian and Wes Montgomery records in their jazz collections).

The thing that rock could do, and did, was to engage a different realm of feelings—feelings that, for all the millions of people who have felt them, and tried to specify them, are still hard to put your finger on. Say, as a first step, that rock separated itself from rock 'n' roll in the purification of its name: taking out the looser part, the dominated part, the recoil, the reaction, the passive side, the "roll"; taking out, therefore, the part that made the name balance, promising you familiar motion, of dance, of a boat or cradle, but most of all of sexual intercourse. (I'm hearing in my head Muddy Waters's version of a common blues called by different artists "Rock Me," "Rock Me Baby," "Rockin' and Rollin'," "Rockin' Chair Blues," etc.: "Rock me baby, rock me all night long / Well I want you to rock me baby, like my back ain't got no bones.") It became a music, in its origins, of the white middle-class world, as rock 'n' roll was not. It is the music that comes from the Beatles, and their particular mutation; and from electric Dylan, and his particular mutation, too; but it is not that alone. It does not occur within the 1960s as a chronological period, but with the sixties—that world event. Something we understand as political, and emotional, and technological, and economic—when science fiction became reality, as it has been since.

And rock's advent, whatever the origins and causes, has something to do with the possibility of new emotions and satisfactions from this music, beyond those of dancing and sex, time or movement, beyond daily and imminent pleasures, beyond things that could exist outside the music. The music would no longer be concomitant with ordinary reality. It might represent something only autonomous and unfolded, radiant, inside itself—available today *uniquely* in music—which one yet wishes could be brought into the world. It began to promise something total. Something incommensurable with dailiness. What is that thing?

I have been worrying recently about something at the end of Ralph Ellison's novel *Invisible Man,* from 1952. I admire the novel. I also take it to be one of the great prophetic books of the half-century that followed the end of World War II. It knows the new rise of the United States to global supremacy, it sees the American artistic and political world we still know, and it knows the flaws and doubts and corruptions that have never left us. So I have been wondering about a small detail of its prophecy.

The novel's ending is familiar. The unnamed narrator, an African-American migrant from the South, has become embroiled in radical politics in New York City, specifically in Harlem. The official white world of Jim Crow and factory labor has misused him. So has the official black world of the university and respectability. The Brotherhood, a left-wing party not unlike the Communist Party, promised the narrator cosmopolitan antiracist fraternity but betrayed Harlem's blacks and misused the narrator, too. Ras the Exhorter, a black nationalist of the old Marcus Garvey school (evocative, too, of Malcolm X, who emerged a few years later), is out to kill the narrator as an obstacle to nationalism and the creation of a separatist racial identity. The impossible conflict of the end of the book, politically, seems to be this three-way impasse between invisibility to the white majority, the ineffectiveness (or, say, in the McCarthyite 1950s, just the ending) of organized radical left-wing parties, and the self-limitation and self-destructive purism of cultural nationalism.

The thing that haunts me is that there is, actually, one other alternative route glimpsed at the end of *Invisible Man,* which I hadn't noticed or fully understood when I first read the book as a teenager and in my twenties and didn't know enough history. Ellison was able to see something, with his incredible perspicacity, as he was composing the book at the end of the 1940s, catching it as another possible vision of the future—possibly, even, the real bearer of history out of this impasse, though it seemed almost too crazy, or trivial, for him to say openly. The narrator finds it underground, literally—down in the depths of the New York subway.

> What about those three boys, coming now along the platform? . . . Their shoulders swaying, their legs swinging from their hips in trousers that ballooned upward from cuffs fitting snug about their ankles; their coats long and hip-tight with shoulders far too broad to be those of natural western men . . . the heavy heel-plated shoes making a rhythmical tapping as they moved . . . Who knew but that they were the saviors, the true leaders, the bearers of something precious? The stewards of something uncomfortable, burdensome, which they hated because, living outside the realm of history, there was no one to applaud their value and they themselves failed to understand it. . . . From time to time one of them would look at his reflection in the [subway car] window and give his hat brim a snap, the others watching him silently, communicating ironically with their eyes. . . . One held his magazine high before his face and for an instant I saw . . . the cover of a comic book.

The people he is seeing, of course, are youths—hipsters—in their original incarnation: African-American youth, wearing zoot suits, snap-brim or porkpie hats, double soles or horseshoe taps, disappearing from legitimate society into a maze of "jive," signs and countersigns, and the subliterary arts: comic books, specifically, a sign here that stands in contrast to the kind of novel that Ellison is writing. You'll miss what Ellison is saying if you don't know the meaning of specific bizarre fashion codes, held in vernacular memory but rarely recorded in histories, of the kind that would come to mark not "culture" but "subculture." They aren't listening to music here, but we know what kind of music they'll come to be associated with—not the earlier jazz of Armstrong and Ellington, which Ellison openly admired as part of the process of collective culture creation (he was himself a skilled musician, a horn player), the "hot" jazz for dance and public display, of New Orleans and Kansas City, and the great jazz orchestras, but the new late-1940s music being developed in clubs on Fifty-Second Street or uptown at Minton's, "cool," hermetic, hostile—bebop. Though this music, too, would later be recognized for its participation in high art and high culture—not least for its technical difficulty and virtuosity—and we forget how antagonistic it was before it mellowed and attained a wider mass audience (as would also be the pattern for post-bop, free jazz, and some fusion later). The role it played at *this* moment was of a kind of withdrawal from the other cultures on offer. Call the thing as a whole by the familiar word "subculture"— signified by bizarre clothing, odd talk—but revolving around, and counting for true deep meaning and joint experience upon, some new, indigestible form of popular music.

It seems to me that Ellison may have been right about the rest of the American Century. Left-wing parties might well have been the place, previously, in which youth would have organized itself and its passions. Party politics in some form. Association. Militancy. Even violence— but violence channeled, purposeful, even into formal nonviolence. But meaningful left-wing parties, which had existed from the end of the nineteenth century through the end of the 1940s, had been trivialized or eradicated, or fallen prey to much bigger history—the history of the United States and the Soviet Union, the Cold War. Then, too, party politics among mainstream parties, in first-world constitutional states like the United States and England, also a meaningful field for youth passions from, say, the Age of Revolutions through the early postwar period, was similarly neutralized and degraded in America and England into a sterile field of television theater—and a place for people without souls, uninteresting people. Instead, real passional life gets organized by subcultures, with music as the expressive center and singers as the charismatic leaders.

There was nothing more irritating, when I was young, than complaints from elders about the loss of real politics, party politics, and the sad decline of the organized left; and paeans to the great old days of all the schismatic leftist parties (Socialist, Communist, Trotskyist, antiracist liberal, etc.)—because all those things seemed so obviously square, lifeless, compared to the feelings and commitments available elsewhere. I think of Michael Walzer's essay "A Day in the Life of a Socialist Citizen"—he's in favor of such citizenship, mind you, but he tries to reckon with the fact that an enormous part of your day, in this better society, would likely be devoted to sitting in meetings. There was nothing in my existence, when young, to suggest the passionate, erotic, violent, world-changing and world-creating possibilities of meetings. Much to my loss.

The music I had in my youth was punk, more properly post-punk—a late variant of rock. I knew it in the years across which post-punk "broke," too, as it was then said—broke again into mainstream commerce, via grunge and Britpop, and destroyed itself, while seeding new fields. Post-punk was the center of meaning, and social gatherings small and large, and organizing apart from adults and authority, and the only conduit to power, and sublimity, that we could feel and love, while also feeling its fear and destructive power. A force making clear how this world was wrong, how it was not good enough for us yet, for its future citizens. Reminding you that, as the political types say about radical movements, another world is possible.

Now, as an adult, I don't even have a plausible way to talk about the force that then disclosed everything worthwhile and unacknowledged. Nor is it obvious how to connect its childish revelation with anything in adult life.

I saw a friend recently who, I knew, had been similarly marked by post-punk, though in a different part of the country and a different local scene—in Washington, DC. As an adult he's become a historian. I think he had once been my union steward. Feeling as embarrassed as if I were asking him about a sexual disease, I wanted to know how he dealt with the puzzle of how much music had meant.

"I know this sounds dumb," I said to him, "but I sometimes say to myself, when I wonder if I could ever add anything worthwhile to the world, 'If I could just give them the equivalent, in words and arguments, of the feeling I got when I was fifteen, from one minute of the first Dinosaur Jr. album—'"

"That's what I do, too!" my friend said, unnerving me. "When I want to figure out what to do in a book or an article, I say, 'If I could just get back that feeling,' and I put on the first Dinosaur Jr. album."

It seemed backward. And, looked at coldly, disturbing.

I'd like to think a bit about the Velvet Underground.

The Velvets are, of course, one of the two bands from the sixties most often claimed as predecessors of punk. (The Stooges would be the other.) One step to the side of the major canon of rock, inaugural figures of a different canon, their influence has a different basis than initial mass popularity.

The Velvet Underground consisted in its main incarnation of four musicians. Lou Reed was the songwriter, singer, guitarist, and front man. John Cale, an initiate of the minimalist and dissonant musical avant-garde under the tutelage of New York composer La Monte Young, played viola and bass guitar. Maureen "Moe" Tucker, a self-taught teenage percussionist, drummed initially without cymbals or pedals, standing up, and remained one of the only female drummers in rock. Sterling Morrison, the band's fine second guitarist, faded back, mostly because he had little to do with the constant Reed-Cale tension and creative drama. (Post-VU he became a professor of medieval English and a tugboat captain.) Cale came from Wales. All the rest were from Long Island.

The band gigged together without outside interference for one month—December 1965. They'd begun a residency at Manhattan's Café Bizarre, when Andy Warhol, already enormously famous, arrived to put the group on retainer for his own purposes. His canny lieutenant, Paul Morrissey, seems to have known of them through Cale, and the overlap between the underground film world and the avant-garde musicians who worked as film accompanists. Andy needed rock music for his upcoming "Exploding Plastic Inevitable" sound-and-light happenings, where he hid the band behind the likes of Edie Sedgwick doing the watusi and Gerard Malanga dancing with whips. He also had them accompany his own films, and generously purchased studio time for them to record a first album, supplying the famous banana cover, prominently signed "Andy Warhol" and without the band's name. (You had to find it on the LP jacket back.) Warhol (or Paul Morrissey) also inflicted Nico upon them, a blond German model and songstress with statuesque looks and a heavily accented, Weimar-era vocal delivery. Nico had won over the Factory with her celebrity and drive. She came with European film–world credentials from a part in Fellini's *La dolce vita,* and was now determined to get into music.

From the initial Warhol embrace, the Velvet Underground managed to sneak away without utterly alienating their patron. The Velvets lasted one album with Nico, a year and a half with Warhol, two albums (nearly four years) with Cale, and four albums with Reed, who anyway wrote all the lyrics. Reed himself finally retired, to let the remaining players limp on without him, moving back to Long Island "to work as a typist for his father's accounting firm." (I know all these details from an excellent book about the band by Richard Witts.) This makes a romantic finale, but of course Reed was back in New York within the year, at St. Mark's Church in-the-Bowery, to declare himself a poet, and start reading his poetry (including song lyrics), and by the end of 1972 he had recorded and released two solo albums. The grim song cycle *Berlin* followed in 1973, and he enjoyed fame and stardom, more or less, for the rest of his life. Cale during the same period had produced and played on Nico's early solo albums (from 1967 and 1969), and Nick Drake's, and released his own solo records in 1970 and 1972 and the much-admired *Paris 1919* in 1973. The never-repudiated Warhol connection and Reed's, Cale's, and Nico's steady careers kept the Velvet Underground always in public memory.

The imagination of the Velvet Underground dwells in bedrooms and residence-hotel rooms, at parties and afterparties—or wishing for parties (alone, now, in one's bedroom). "If you close the door the night could last forever / Leave the sunshine out and say hello to never" ("After Hours"). It stakes its name on a fantasy of an underground world of S&M dungeons and shooting galleries that provides a pleasure, for the listener, on the same order as reading "underground" books from the hip-Gothic tradition of Sade, Bataille, Genet, Burroughs, and Hubert

Selby Jr. Reed rewrote such books, essentially, as songs. The literal example is his "Venus in Furs," a musical setting of a book remembered because it earned its author the honor of having masochism named for him. Reed puts in the protagonist of Sacher-Masoch's book (Severin) and its principal action (flagellation and waiting for flagellation), and the Velvets provide a drone sound track.

The unity of their work has to do with the pleasures of force, both suffering and exerting it, and a theatrical Sadeanism (different from direct sadism) that could be made *musical* as well as lyrical. This is what Cale really did bring to the band, beyond Reed's fairly conventional musical instincts. The classical avant-garde is still today mostly content to play down the pain, annoyance, boredom, and nuisance of the willed adherence to dissonance, atonality, minimalism, and clipped or extended duration that are hallmarks of many of its best effects in the twentieth century. Whereas the Velvet Underground—in Cale's revision of La Monte Young—was able to reposition avant-garde annoyance and aural pain as part of a thematics of being outside and underground. Aural pain went with overt lyrics of willed pain to make avant-garde musical gestures a sonic correlative to squalor, masochism, deviance, and drugs. The essence of the Velvet Underground's success under Cale would then be really that it provided what it promised—pain.

It would be one thing to hear the order to "kiss the boot," the "tongue of thongs, the belt that does await you" in "Venus in Furs" if the lyrics were just accompanied by folk-guitar finger-picking. It's quite another, more effective thing to listen to these lyrics against Cale's excruciating freaks of viola. The VU are a band that actually causes pain, to accompany the verbal promise of pain. They show that aural pain becomes pleasure especially when listening to it constitutes an act of affiliation with a higher, because worse and more "transgressive," way of life. The person who doesn't *like* being abused by Cale's viola, or the badly recorded trebly guitars of *White Light/White Heat,* is stupid, straight. The person who knows (or learns) the pleasure of the abuse, who will listen to the seventeen minutes of "Sister Ray" and then put it on again, has ascended to a higher sphere—or, rather, descended into the underground—simply by the act of listening, with or without actual access to works, spoon, smack, speed, tenements, whips, or leather boots.

I never felt I could understand the historical meaning of the Velvet Underground, or how it should be that such a weird, and minor, troupe should be set at the head genealogically of such a vast and various posterity, until I started noticing comparisons and uncanny connections to the band, historically, that ought to be their polar opposite—that is, the Grateful Dead. In the musical-historical imagination, with its New York-vs.-California but especially its punk-vs.-hippie oppositions, the groups are antithetical. When I was introduced to punk, people wore T-shirts of the *White Light/White Heat* album cover (which wouldn't have existed in reality, decades earlier, when the album was originally released), but the mere mention of liking the Grateful Dead was grounds for deadly ostracism. So I kept my Deadheadedness secret. In the punk-rock schema, the Velvets were Papa (and Mama) punks, while the Dead were Papa hippies. By convention, punks hate hippies.

When you look at the history of both bands at their contemporaneous founding moments in 1965/1966, I think you'll find, though, that the Velvet Underground and the Grateful Dead commenced on opposite coasts, in an odd way, as basically *the same band.* Not thanks to musical training or style, but based on a new function and new kind of emotion they promised. Both bands in fact started with the same *name* in 1965: the Warlocks. And both were quickly taken up by other cultural movements and artists from other genres to furnish "house bands" for collective projects. On the West Coast, Ken Kesey hired the Dead to provide music for his LSD parties, the Acid Tests. The Palo Alto Acid Test, the first to involve the general public, took place in November 1965, just before Warhol started staging his events. (Kesey had earlier had the Dead, then still the Warlocks, playing in a Santa Cruz living room with everyone dosed.) In New York, the Exploding Plastic Inevitable enjoyed various early incarnations between January 1966 and its first broad-public invitation in April—mostly Warhol's dancing fools, slide-projector gels, light shows, silent films, and chaos. Both house bands' music depended on a tight association with drugs, principally LSD for the Dead, heroin for the Velvets (not least because of Reed's song "Heroin"). But the musicians drew fewer distinctions in their personal lives: Reed had done plenty of acid in college, while in happy California the Dead's Ron "Pigpen" McKernan was taking heroin with Cass Elliot from the Mamas and the Papas, and Jerry Garcia would have a later, lifelong heavy-duty heroin habit. As Warhol paid for the Velvets' first album, the Dead's first album was paid for by an original benefactor from the early scene of communal presentation: Owsley Stanley, supplier of LSD for the Acid Tests. Each album seemed to make drugs part of the *sound* thematic. This was the heroin "wrapped in fur" slowdown for the VU, including the literal slowing down of the tapes in mastering (something Richard Witts seems to have proven by analyzing the pitches of the recorded tunings); for the Dead, surprisingly, it was an amphetamine-fueled recording of all the songs on their first album at ridiculously fast tempi, though things slowed down subsequently.

The strangest fact, though, is that the Velvet Underground, like the Grateful Dead, too, seem to have started as a platform for extremely long, wandering, repetitive, live improvisations, appropriate to multimedia events. All of the Velvets' principals from the early years later insisted that they were far superior as a live band than in anything captured on record, alluding to unrecorded work like "Sweet Sister Ray," a sometimes forty-minute-long improvisational *prelude* to live performances of "Sister Ray." (One wonders if this title points to the later-period jam song "Sweet Jane.") To listen carefully to the VU's members is to imagine an alternate world in which people could have listened to forty versions of "Sister Ray" as they would listen to forty performances of the Dead's "Dark Star," seeking the passages of improvisational transcendence in each, or to thirty-minute VU improvisations like "Melody Laughter," made up of feedback, guitar, organ, and vocalise from Nico. It's curious to think of the VU, progenitor of punk, as originating at the same moment and under the same conditions that yielded the much-ridiculed modern-day jam band.

Why, after all, did both bands originally imagine themselves destined for the name "the Warlocks"? Essentially because both had initial visions of sorcery underlain with darkness. (They had to change names, incidentally, because each independently discovered a third band that had put out a record as the Warlocks.) These bands offered a certain kind of alternatively experienced, rather than danced-to or sung-along-to, pop music, whose relation to the audience would be primarily hypnotic and all-encompassing. This is, I'll say again, unexpected for the Velvets, though not for the Dead. One knows that "Heroin" was supposed to capture a particular kind of experience, but not that the experience might have been infinitely expandable, or should have led to improvisation, or that perhaps it was originally *meant* to occur live, not on record. Cale claimed in his autobiography, written with Victor Bockris: "The aim of the band on the whole was to hypnotize audiences so that their subconscious would take over." This provides a rationale for the viola drone, and songs built on long vamps of two chords.

The Grateful Dead wound up providing an alternative world directly, through their unique phenomenon of a mass social affiliation built up through thirty years of steady national and international touring (with just a one-year hiatus in 1975). One could spend a year "on tour" with the Dead, following their itinerary, visiting the community in venue parking lots, and not even needing to see the shows when tickets were scarce or expensive. And they were doomed to this by their way of putting together music and lyrics. From the beginning, the words to their songs, however carelessly put together, were about roads and rivers. They drew out from American music its promise of continual rambling—with the occasional respite of dew-bejeweled meadows, barefoot promenades, or rolling in the rushes down by the riverside. It's no accident that their first single was "The Golden Road (to Unlimited Devotion)," that their signature song (apart from the tripped-out "Dark Star") was "Truckin'," and that the band matured its endless-trip LSD premise into an endless-traveling touring premise, such that both principal experiences could be crystallized in one phrase in the ultimate Dead-lyric cliché: "What a long, strange trip it's been." They had dark songs, as many songs' journeys end in death or exhaustion, but even those waver, like "Dark Star," between annihilation and beatitude. ("Shall we go, you and I, while we can / Through the transitive nightfall of diamonds?") The Dead's equivalent to classically trained avant-gardist Cale was the classically trained avant-gardist Phil Lesh, but Lesh didn't double his bass guitar with any higher-pitched string instrument like viola, so the "Phil Zone" emerged as a singularly supple, harmonic, tripped-out deep end, a register of mountainous or tidal wonder. Velvet Underground lyrics, in contrast, are mostly about not going outdoors, and the wish for pleasurable self-destruction ("thank God that I'm good as dead" in "Heroin"), and the music when you're not wriggling in ecstasy on a broken-down mattress could make you pull a pillow over your head. There is a feeling that their music really can *only* transpire in private, in places that a fan base of more than three or four couldn't fit, and in a city, and in a darkened room. The Dead were fated by their lyrics to travel. The VU were fated by their lyrics, in some sense, never to be natural to a mass live audience, but to be passed on, from hand to hand, on record, to be reenacted in private.

It also seems to matter that neither band's music, in some deep way, is very *good,* or first-class art. There's something secondhand and plain about the underlying songs, derivative of bluegrass festivals and folk-rock jamborees (for the Dead) and fifties rock and Tin Pan Alley and the most rudimentary high-school bands (for VU). You don't take any of the personnel for geniuses—unless mad geniuses. The lyrics are grand, but in the manner of Grand Guignol, and dramatic and silly. The additional factor that makes them singular comes as a kind of *extrinsic* extremity. A huge appetite for drugs plus Jerry Garcia's and Phil Lesh's endless wandering, noodling string-instrument virtuosity. Or drugs plus Reed's lyrical agony and Cale's instrumental excruciation.

This last, you could say, is what the California bands were reluctant to do in their psychedelia, deliberately hurt your ears with the newly available techniques, and match this to an ethos of pain within the lyrics. West Coast bands did hurt your ears sometimes (just listen to the Jefferson Airplane), but accidentally. The critic David Fricke recounts the story, apocryphal or not, that Bill Graham, sponsor of the Dead and plenty of other bands who experimented musically with feedback, banned the VU from the Fillmore West after they ended a performance by walking off stage leaving their guitars leaning against the speakers, generating uncontrolled feedback. The insult Bill Graham presumably took from the VU was the causing of pain deliberately and impersonally, cut off from the audience, or reconnecting with it through a gesture of hostility. I remember that by the time, decades later, I was going to see post-punk shows, this gesture of leaning guitars face-forward against an amplifier stack for feedback was the way that *every* single great band of my youth—Dinosaur Jr., Sonic Youth, Mudhoney, My Bloody Valentine—left the stage.

Punk begins in fear. Maybe that's why rock is for children, first and always. You have to be that young, and not yet know the world or be jaded by it, to feel this reduction of the world with full intensity, to hear the drumbeat strike and think it's the world reaching out to punch you.

Punk promised physical experience, a buzzing charge. It seemed to offer a kind of aggression against the listener by the band and singer, but then a much profounder resistance and battle against *everybody else*—somewhere, in the fallen world—by the band, and singer, and listener, and the whole listening audience, all together. The lyrics often seemed to know that they couldn't possibly come up to the intensity of the music, or that they gained whatever power they had only from the music behind them. Yet there isn't a lot of good instrumental punk—surprisingly little, in fact. The yoking of inchoate massive force to frustrated or powerless (or, very often, partly comic and self-satirizing) verbal expression is too important to ever leave the lyrics out. The lyrics could be comic-aggressive, or they could be abject and self-assaulting. Even the best are not complex. In lyrics ranging from "Fuck school fuck school fuck my school" (the Replacements) to "I'm a leper" (Dinosaur Jr.), you get the crude extremes of aggression and abjection—and both modes were simultaneously super-serious and made for laughter. They just *said* the thing, for better and for worse.

One of the most thriving subgenres when I was young was hardcore. It was particularly scary, because of the ultrafast repetitive drumbeat, the shouted lyrics, the chopped-up guitar, but also, at least initially, because of the shaved-headed culture surrounding the music. Shaved heads meant skinheads, and to a fourteen-year-old in the ignorant 1980s, skinheads meant neo-Nazis, young German and English Hitler-fancying hooligans who ran wild in the streets of Bremen or Leeds; National Front brutes, racists—the people *60 Minutes* ran segments on that my parents would watch. In between classes at school, it was explained to me by my peers that not all hardcore was skinhead and that anyway there were antiracist skinheads, although there *was* racist white-supremacist hardcore, too, in England especially, but that was hard to find, and . . . It seemed to me an unhealthy fixation, this focus on which skinheads were Nazis and which were not. Why not just have hair? I was told about a world called "straight edge," a subculture of shaved-headed (or crew-cut) hardcore punks who not only were antiracist but additionally forswore drugs, alcohol, and tobacco (though not necessarily violence), and who Magic-Markered X's on the backs of their hands in imitation of the policy punk clubs employed to keep underage drinkers from the bar. I didn't really care; I didn't put any X's on my hands. Assorted band cassettes came and went, and at some point my friend Becky K. gave me a tape of the complete works of the great, defunct DC hardcore band Minor Threat. To that recording, I responded. I listened, stunned, and with very little idea what to make of it, but thrilled. Minor Threat's stance combined liberal guilt with a citizen's indignation. One song acknowledged being on the wrong side of the racial divide, and the guilt of collusion with evil whiteness ("Guilty of Being White"); and the others were about being a dissenter, an opponent, when all criteria of value were themselves erroneous, not only because "good guys don't wear white," but also because they were "Out of Step":

> Don't—smoke
> I don't—drink
> I don't—fuck
> At least I can—fucking think!

> I can't keep up, I can't keep up, I can't keep up
> Out of step—with the world!

That album woke me up in a way that I still can't put into words. But I did not feel *at home* with it. It did not make me feel good. I did not feel entitled to sing along. At fourteen, I did not smoke, drink, fuck, but I eagerly looked forward to all three, and had no experience that would lead me to renounce them. Yet it felt as if these people, close to my age though older, were the only people doing something, saying something, that I wanted done or said. Preparing for something, something I could follow them in doing, though I didn't know what or how.

The successor band to Minor Threat was Fugazi, formed by its lead singer, Ian MacKaye, with a singer from the great, short-lived band Rites of Spring, Guy Picciotto. To Fugazi, I became committed, heart and soul. The rhythms were more interesting, the rage alternated with a command to stand up and fight back. The critique captured something I could feel in my own life. They spoke of a fully administered world, against apathy, passivity, against a life spent sitting in society's waiting rooms. I still think often enough of the Picciotto song "Give Me the Cure," which begins: "I never thought too hard on dying before." Face-to-face with the fear of sickness, he sings of the ways society promises it could fix it, should fix it—and then can't or won't fix it. These are the lyrics that always got to me, from when I was fourteen to now:

> But you've got to—
> Give me the shot!
> Give me the pill!
> Give me the cure
> Now what you've done to my world?

MacKaye had founded a record label, Dischord Records, which issued the Fugazi and Minor Threat recordings and those of countless other bands. Prices were always fair, little more than it cost to make the copies. When Fugazi toured, they played only All Ages shows, so that no one would be turned away, often for admission prices of less than five dollars. This kept them from clubs in many cases, and so they helped maintain the alternative network of venues in which bands play in church basements, VFW halls, squats, and community centers. They never had anything to do with the major labels, or television, or advertising. Yet people knew their music, and do still.

In 1991, they held a concert in front of the White House, in the cold and rain, to protest the first Iraq War, while the television spokesmen for the country were masturbating themselves to frenzy to green-grained film of "smart bombs" hitting targets, reports of "turkey shoots" and "shooting galleries" as planes and helicopters burned up overmatched Iraqi tanks and trucks. You can see the footage online. I don't know anything else quite like it.

That same year I saw Fugazi at a club called the Channel, next to the polluted Fort Point Channel in Boston, with a wooden deck overhanging the black water. It was a Sunday afternoon all-ages show. The joists that held the low roof seemed endangered by the bodies flying and butting each other, in the second of two "pits" of moshing, where I stood, but the columns were shielded partly by chairs and cocktail-style tables piled up irregularly. I forget who opened, but the moshers had already been at it for an hour; there were slicks of sweat on the floor, though no blood was evident. I had turned fifteen. The preparatory or votary dance of the lone adolescents, between confrontations, seducing or challenging the next comers, mesmerized me, in instants when their collisions had given way to the goat dance, knees lifting, boots thudding, cocked elbows windmilling as a survivor started a circuit of the pit perimeter. Then a new array of bodies plunged, or were pushed, in, slamming in, as violence or play, or bobbing frightened or laughing across to the other side, pulling up those who got knocked down, shoving them out of the way. Heads shaved, chests bare, ribs visible, they bobbed up and down, with soaked undershirts or flannels hanging and swinging sideways, out of rhythm, from double-pronged belts.

On the low stage, forty feet away, there was Ian, there was Guy. They were playing songs off *Repeater*. It was as I'd heard: Ian MacKaye siring and ma'am-ing his audience, polite to a fault, deliberately friendly ("Good evening, everybody. How are you this evening?"; "What the heck?"), before launching into another brutal song of resistance and noise. The conscious gentleness seemed to confirm the possibility of a music that could put this channeled eruption of violent emotions toward—what? The two pits were roiling simultaneously, like the inside workings of two mad clocks, in need of repair while still in motion, and could be captured in one view with Fugazi at their head. I watched the eyes of boys right near me, blanked, numb, as others whirled in pointless energy—personally valuable, maybe, like a martial art, a discipline, a way of conquering all fear—but I sorrowed that all this seemed unworthy of the band, the music, the unnameable it pointed to. Someday, someday, I thought. I want to do something worthy of this. One thing worthy of all this beauty, before I die.

[2007, 2009, REVISED 2015]

LEARNING TO RAP

It's a fortunate fate to have your lifetime be contemporary with the creation of a major art form. Embarrassing, then, not to have understood it, or appreciated it, or become an enthusiast, even a fanatic, from the first. Especially shameful when it could have carried you, if only in imagination, across a racial barrier in America—at least as far as you can go without kidding yourself, when you're white, and therefore approaching from the wrong side. I came of age at the same time as hip-hop. But like some other ostensibly politically minded middle-class white Americans of my generation, I made a historical mistake: I chose to believe in punk rock exclusively. This meant pledging allegiance to a minor tributary (post-punk) of a minor genre (punk), to squeeze the rind of a major genre, rock, that had been basically exhausted by 1972, instead of committing to a new world-historical form.

My mistake also meant in practical terms that I didn't learn to rap properly when my mind was supple, at an age when language is effortlessly absorbed. Not that I am completely incapable or innocent of rapping. But I had never applied myself.

I tried to make up for the deficiency, finally, last year. I vowed that I would not rap in front of anyone else, ever, and that I would not try to write my own raps. I just had the idea that I could fix myself, privately. The immediate irritant was that I can hum rock, and of course I can *sing along.* I know a good part of the lyrics to all kinds of old songs: "Sunshine of Your Love," "(How Much Is) That Doggie in the Window?" But I couldn't rap along beyond a few simple refrains, not even to hip-hop songs I thought I knew well, which seemed to be increasingly occupying my head in the first year of Obama's presidency. This disability began to seem sinister, not to say racist.

I really didn't know how hard it would be to rap along until I tried. I had projected a straightforward plan of study. I would begin with the classics. I didn't want to go around on training wheels—I'd start immediately with the best. I wanted my repertoire to include songs I could live with forever. So I started with the first track from the first Nas album, "N.Y. State of Mind," which had lived in the back of my mind as a blur for a long time.

"I think of crime when I'm in a New York state of mind"—that and other easy lines, I already possessed in memory. And the famous aphorism "I never sleep, 'cause sleep is the cousin of death," which gets quoted often enough. Plus boasts like "It's only right that I was born to use mics," which gave the title to a Michael Eric Dyson book. But I suffered the illusion that a chorus or a standout aphorism was comparable to a verse. I thought I would just start at the beginning and roll through, rewinding the song and memorizing, as if it were a classic rock song or a folk ballad. I went for a walk outside on a hazy day in July, with my headphones, and pressed play:

> Rappers, I monkey flip 'em with the funky rhythm I be
>   kickin'—

"Rappers I . . ." what?

> Rappers, I monkey flip 'em with the funky rhythm I be
>   kickin'—

"Rappers I—mubbliggithm . . ."
"Rappers I go up in 'em . . ."
"Rappers I grow up with 'em . . ."

I think what Nas is saying is that his rhythmic flow has such force that it sweeps his rivals' legs out from under them. He whirls them over and lands them on their backs, as Bruce Lee knew to judo dumb opponents. That Nas can do this just with his musical skills, he confirms in line two:

Musician, inflictin' composition

But I couldn't get past the impossibility of line one. The first line is seventeen syllables in just over two bars, across eight beats in a quick 4/4 tempo—at eighty-four beats per minute. The delivery is shifted slightly, as I hear it, so that it starts with a quarter-rest and crosses into the next two bars on the last syllable. Rather than marching in the iambs of most English versification, the meter sounds subtly trochaic, suggestive of falling rhythm. And seventeen syllables! By contrast, think of the first line, over a comparable two bars, of Elvis's "That's All Right," a kind of entry into the story of rock:

Well, that's all right, Mama

Six syllables, slowed by a caesura, delivered in the same length of time as Nas's seventeen. If that seems an unfair comparison—Elvis is just getting warmed up!—there's also "All Shook Up":

A-well-a, bless-ah my soul-a, what's wrong with me?

Twelve syllables in two bars.

Obviously it's not the number of syllables that should impress anyone about a lyric. That would be like judging opera by the number of people onstage. It's the implication of the words and, for the pleasure of the ear, the way they're laid across the rhythm and the breath. One thing that registered immediately about hip-hop, at a minimum, once I tried to accompany it, is that it's a more difficult and complex lyrical art in performance than just about anything that has ever been known to rock, and it has been so for about twenty years. I guess all hip-hop listeners already know this, and I fear they will be narrowing their eyes now with distrust. But I notice that some white people my age, but especially those a decade or two older, when they try to rap, fall into end-stopped, nursery-rhyme couplets, when such rhythms haven't been common in MCing for more than two decades. It's like thinking of rock 'n' roll exclusively as the era before solid-body electric guitars predominated— say, 1963 and earlier.

It took a week of repetition for me to get the Nas song right. I still can't point the accents correctly when I do it at full voice. My delivery is made worse by the fact that my rap voice is very much a white person's voice, therefore unappealing to me, as I suspect it would be to anyone else. Rapping involved muscular tasks my mouth was not yet practiced enough to do, plus a mental focus and precision that's hard to sustain, and simply isn't called for with rock lyrics, not even, like Bob Dylan's, the most verbose.

I should add that I had to look to the Internet to find the most plausible construction of Nas's first line. There are now countless hip-hop-lyric exegetical sites that try to resolve what is being said. Even so, interpretive disagreements persist.

I grew up Jewish in the Boston suburbs. New York was the home of my father's side of the family. If my grandmother didn't take the Amtrak from New York on the weekend to visit us, we drove to the apartment, in the co-ops for workers in the garment trades, on the Lower East Side.

The New York City Housing Authority had erected the Samuel Gompers housing projects just across Delancey Street, twenty years before. They razed half of the neighborhood to do so, including the tenement in which my grandfather had been born. This was slum clearance. It created tensions, between the low-income Orthodox Jews in workers' housing, erected by the unions, on our side of the street, and the low-income black and Puerto Rican residents of the public housing erected by the city on the other. My grandfather had managed to keep the family on the street on which he'd been born, but now looked back on it from the reverse direction, toward the new buildings that sat on top of his remembered home.

One zone of contact was underneath my grandmother's first-story window, in Sheriff Park. From its picnic tables, I heard beatboxing and rap for the first time in 1980 or 1981, when I was five and six. I hung at the window to wait for the groups that gathered around battery-powered boom boxes (at that time white people called them "ghetto blasters"). This competed with the J/Z trains on the ramp of the bridge overhead. This rolling canvas for graffiti is now nostalgized, but at the time it seemed Martian to me. My grandmother's paper was the *Daily News,* which carried a front-page report of someone pushed onto the tracks or dragged into a subway tunnel and beaten, seemingly daily—at least, every time I visited—up through 1984, the year of Bernard Goetz, the subway's white vigilante. I laid my head on the sill listening, like a spaniel, or leaned my face into the screen, at risk of tearing it, until my father would call me to Shabbos dinner.

The first song I tried to rap—learning the chorus at least—came from a K-tel compilation on cassette. K-tel was a music-repackaging service that compiled a month's radio hits on cassette for sale on nighttime television and by mail order—also in drugstores, where I got my copy of *Get Dancin',* or whatever it was called. That number was Grandmaster Flash and the Furious Five's "The Message" (1982). Lying on my bed in the suburbs, in my seven-year-old voice, I rewound and repeated, and never forgot (this is accented in slow, elementary notes, on the beat, over more complex syncopation):

> Don't—push—me—'cause—I'm—close—to—the—edge
> I'm—try—in'—not—to—lose—my—head *Ha ha ha ha*
> It's like a jungle sometimes,
> It makes me wonder how I keep from goin' under.

A cliché of hip-hop memorialization—for both fans and artists—is the anecdote of the first time one heard rapping of real duration and realized one was hearing something unknown and transformative. Kids who would later become rappers place the moment in firsthand experience, one artist watching another. So it is in Jay-Z's autobiography, *Decoded,* where he recounts child Jay seeing a teenager freestyling a capella in a circle in the Marcy housing projects—the opposite end of the Williamsburg Bridge from Delancey Street, and four subway stops away.

Even I, knowing nothing, can confirm that there really was something about hip-hop's early arrival that made it feel seismic. I guess that's what it means to be in the presence of a major new art form. And even I, as I got just a little bit older, wanted to read values into the new music to make it "real," political, an answer of rival values to the grinning pumpkin head of Ronald Reagan on the evening news, a face I had learned by 1984, and his re-election, was going to get all of us killed with an arms race and his MX missile, but was busy jailing and killing black people among us and selling out Latin America in the meantime.

I find it surprising how many musical moments in early hip-hop I *did* hear as the years passed, despite being in no sense committed as a fan. Kids notice things that aren't like everything else. I remember waiting up at night for a short-lived local video station in Boston, a free rival to MTV, to play Run-D.M.C. in 1985. I knew to procure N.W.A's *Straight Outta Compton* on cassette in 1988, with no radio airplay, because of newspaper denunciations of the songs "Fuck tha Police" and "Gangsta Gangsta"—if it made the newspapers so deranged, it had to be speaking some truth. A Tribe Called Quest's *People's Instinctive Travels and the Paths of Rhythm* I knew by heart, along with De La Soul's *3 Feet High and Rising.* White people would bring the gossip that these last were mysteriously denigrated as "hippie rap" or "backpack rap" in the black community (how did we know?). I actually saw a few golden-age acts perform, basically by accident—Black Sheep, Ice-T—as I later saw the Wu-Tang Clan, on bills with rock bands or at public events and free concerts. But this same sense of an open secret, of constant unused knowledge, is probably true for other white people my age. I had every chance to lose my heart to the music, despite barriers. I just failed to do so when the time came when everyone has to make the choice of music that will define him, or the subculture indexed to it, not for the private pleasures of bedroom listening, but by his clothes and manner and friends and public identity. At that critical moment of conversion in the teen years, I blew it.

I know the exact moment of the mistake. It was the first year of high school, and older white students started giving me tapes. This was mostly music not available in any store I had ever been to. In the decisive week, one friend handed me Minor Threat's *Minor Threat* (*Complete Discography*), and another gave me Public Enemy's *It Takes a Nation of Millions to Hold Us Back*.

Public Enemy had built a place already in my consciousness. I had heard Public Enemy the summer before I started school, in the long opening sequence to Spike Lee's *Do the Right Thing*, with Rosie Perez fly-dancing to "Fight the Power." I saw the movie at a Tuesday matinee, took the train home, knowing it was the best new movie I'd ever seen, and went back to see it again at the same time the following day. "Fight the Power" included a refrain that probably—secretly—means nearly as much to me as the national anthem, and plays over and over in my mind, though I can still only mumble it with terrible embarrassment even when I'm by myself ("Fight the power / We've got to fight the powers that be"). I recall how the verses awakened my childish mind from suburban slumbers:

> Elvis was a hero to most, but he never meant shit to me
> Is he straight out racist a sucker or simple and plain
> Motherfuck him *and* John Wayne
> Cause I'm Black and I'm proud
> I'm ready, I'm hyped plus I'm amped
> Most of my heroes don't appear on no stamp . . .

Who *were* those heroes, I wondered. Shouldn't mine be the same?

Hearing Public Enemy and Minor Threat, I was scared by both, and I knew that I wasn't wanted in the world of either one. But I gave myself up to punk, and I didn't at that moment give myself up to rap. Why? I couldn't say to myself then, "Because I'm white," though surely that's the quickest way to state the complication. Even now, I don't want to say it. Not in my head, and not out loud. What kind of resistance (in the psychoanalytic sense) or vanity is that? I want to not say it because for as long as I remember, seeing the way race divided things in my grandparents' world, I knew it was bullshit, because I could see that they wanted to be white, and they weren't. They were poor, Orthodox Jewish, and weird. My parents, in taking us out to the suburbs, had let me gain the habits and self-confidence of vanishing identity, which even they—first to go to college, first to leave the ghetto—never gained. I got to be the first in my family to be *effortlessly* white, and thereby also the first to obsess on how whiteness is bogus and unfair, not something you'd want to creep in and poison your mind. Or maybe it was the success of black education: canonical American literature, which now includes Douglass, Sojourner Truth, Du Bois, Hurston, Wright, Ellison, Dr. King, Malcolm, Baldwin, Stokely Carmichael, Ishmael Reed, Morrison, Audre Lorde, and more. To ever say "I *am* white"—even though I was reaping the rewards of being seen as white—would be like pulling a sheet over my head as a mental Klansman. On the other hand, what else am I? I wasn't minoritizing myself again; I wasn't putting on a yarmulke and tsitsith. Sometimes I worry the whitest white people of all, the most unmarked and heedless, who pay the least price and gain the most unfair freedom, are those like me who get to be both "raceless" *and* antiracist, never having to fight it out in the mud of poverty, side-stepping the system, pretending to have no skin in the game.

I think I knew, in a way, that the really courageous thing would have been to step across the line, to become a white appropriator of black hip-hop music, *if* I could still force myself really to stay wrong: to be always a white face in black crowds, to be a faker and conscious of crossing, and know it and suffer it. To acknowledge becoming an outsider and a clown, without a hope of ever belonging. Not to be one of those Caucasian hip-hop heads who took it back to the suburbs, who felt they did own it. I might have needed the thrust of compulsion and mad love. Or courage beyond what I had.

.　　.　　.

So many stupidities really stem from inexperience. As I worked on my rapping in 2009, I felt I newly understood a phenomenon of the streets of New York, Boston, every American city I'd ever lived in—why you'd run into young black men, quickstepping on the sidewalk or standing on the subway, rapping at full voice to songs that leaked out of the cups of their overloud headphones. You don't hear people singing along on subways or downtown pavements to other genres with the same degree of frequency, except for aging crazies. "Hmmm," I would have thought once upon a time, "what is the proper liberal explanation for what seems otherwise like rudeness?" At hand, I had the old explanations I learned as a kid for inner-city graffiti and suburban skateboarding: This is a way of reclaiming public space when it is segregated, owned by absentees, or dominated by adults.

But now that I had lyrical skills to acquire, I thought I could see a different truth—you had to practice! Rapping along in public was practical and necessary. The learning process is hard. The rehearsal is vitiated when you do the words under your breath and don't rap loudly enough for performance. Even the breathing is different. And there is just so much to *learn* at this point, the entire canon of previous rhymes and performances, so much to memorize, from "Rapper's Delight" to "B.O.B. (Bombs Over Baghdad)" that you really ought to be rehearsing all the time. You're like a Homeric bard, who will have fifteen thousand hexameter lines to run through before a warlord or a king someday. No doubt doing this in public, and on the subway, is part of overcoming a kind of performance fright. Perhaps it's a way of becoming scary oneself, as James Baldwin once in *The Fire Next Time* characterized the need to adapt to oneself the expectations that other people will hang on you: "One needed a handle, a lever, a way of inspiring fear." All bystanders know that the emphatic quality of rapping really can be jarring, when someone is walking up behind you or standing by you on the subway, rapping "Protect Ya Neck."

The songs I was working on after Nas were Snoop Dogg's "Tha Shiznit," from his first album, and the Notorious B.I.G.'s "Party and Bullshit." The latter is canonical, a song I felt I ought to be able to do, ostensibly a happy song:

> I was a terror since the public school era
> Bathroom passes, cutting classes, squeezin' asses
> Smokin' blunts was a daily routine
> Since 13, a chubby nigga on the scene.
> I used to have the tre-deuce and a deuce-deuce in my
>   bubble goose
> Now I got the Mac in my knapsack loungin', black . . .
>
> . . . .
>
> Honeys wanna chat, but all we wanna know
> Is where the party at? And can I bring my gat?
> If not, I hope I don't get shot
> Better throw my vest on my chest, cause niggas is a mess . . .

So: Biggie was a cutup in school; all he and his crew want to do is party and get with girls. But the rhythmically difficult lines to deliver ("I used to have the tre-deuce and a deuce-deuce in my bubble goose") focus your mind on the .32 and .22 pistols he says he hid at age thirteen in his wintertime parka, like the MAC-10 submachine gun he boasts he's moved on to now, at twenty-one—kept still in his schooldays knapsack, along with his bulletproof vest.

Maybe it was the juxtaposition of kiddie banality and too-real mortality, but this song got me worrying again. It was too strange to blithely rap through things now that had been obstructions to me twenty years earlier.

First, to start with the personal, there was the problem of making sure not to say "nigger." This has always had a curiously powerful effect for white listeners, and I think it was meant to. "Nigger" is the word that righteous whites *will not use*—to the point where whites of the civil-rights generation, grown adults in their sixties or seventies, almost literally *cannot* say it, blushing, stammering, even when quoting from history (or reading from *Adventures of Huckleberry Finn*). They will call it "the n-word"—write it on a chalkboard rather than pronounce it—clear their throats and give meaningful looks or avoid people's eyes. This was a sort of victory for antiracism. But the conspicuous theater of it, the sheer ostentation of *the one word I will not speak,* also has wound up showing off how little it can mean in comparison to all the racism white people *don't* give up, and equally won't name or speak. White people in authority are okay with seeing black people profiled, demonized, and terrorized by police. They just won't say one word, which of course they can say perfectly well. I should add, I don't think white people should be taking "nigger" back up, even to "join in" to black songs—which is part of its point in rap, because it hammers home a fundamental claim that white people shouldn't be rapping. Like other formal developments of hip-hop, the place of "the n-word" in the music, after a certain point in its history, can be thought of as a clever collective strategy to forestall white cooptation.

The comedian Richard Pryor's voice is still, if I'm identifying it correctly, a voice often quoted and sampled in the now-long tradition of hip-hop songs reflecting on the meaning and use of "nigger." He called his 1976 best-selling stand-up comedy album *Bicentennial Nigger*. I like to think of a televised exchange, transcribed later in *The New Yorker* by Hilton Als, when Pryor is being interviewed by Barbara Walters, lovable paragon of the white liberal television establishment, and she is asking him about his controversial word choice:

> WALTERS: When you're on stage . . . see, it's hard for me to say. I was going to say, you talk about niggers. I can't . . . you can say it. I can't say it.
> PRYOR: You just said it.
> WALTERS: Yeah, but I feel so . . .
> PRYOR: You said it very good.
> WALTERS: . . . uncomfortable.
> PRYOR: Well, good. You said it pretty good.
> WALTERS: O.K.
> PRYOR: That's not the first time you said it. (*Laughter.*)

I think only after 1988 did hip-hop really make use of the word "nigger" ubiquitous. I can't tell if its historians date it that way; I keep looking for a good discussion of the question. But I get the impression you can't rap along to anything of significance produced after 1988 without running across this word that whites ought not say, whereas you can do so earlier. It can't be accidental that it came at a moment when the white audience for rap was growing enormously; when in absolute numbers of record sales, whites were outpurchasing blacks in hip-hop releases, and people said so, and worried about it; when Vanilla Ice was on his way. The arrival of "nigger" was like an ingenious fail-safe. If you were a white pretender, *you could not rap for real,* as blacks did; you could not train on the official rhymes. Either you could not rap in public, period, or you could never rap right, never fully, always marked off, mildly excommunicated. But probably also, in ways I can't see, it worked as an internal rebuke over respectability, and who was getting ahead and who left behind, in those years of disputes on whether the black middle class had abandoned a black "underclass."

It must be said, "nigger" makes an extremely flexible two-beat metrical insertion in rap and wide-ranging rhyme in English. It rhymes with all sorts of terms of lyrical boasting, with "bigger," "trigger," "figure," "did her," etc. N.W.A amplified the turn with a group name that was unpublishable and unsayable except as an acronym (by reputation it stood for Niggaz With Attitude). The word appeared in titles and choruses, from the most "conscious" and peaceable rappers (A Tribe Called Quest's "Sucka nigga, nigga nigga") to the grittiest (the Wu-Tang's "Shame on a nigga who try to run game on a nigga").* The repetition itself seemed to serve a function. Jay-Z proved himself the most adept, as in so many other self-branding maneuvers: creating a primary nickname for himself ("Jigga") to multiply his own rhymes

---

* "Nigga" emerged as an alternate orthography so that rappers could write down what was being said in rap without printing the unprintable word. This spelling was supposed to speak of fraternity, not hatred, though at first it principally gave artists a way around record-company strictures for titles and track listings. It would become a word of its own, like "brother" (meaning, specifically, *a black man*). But it would remain unsayable for whites. (My *Merriam-Webster's Unabridged* resolves the problem in this way: "*nigga*—n.; by alteration; plural *niggas* also *niggaz:* AFRO-AMERICAN—used chiefly among Afro-Americans; usually taken to be offensive when used by others.")

with "nigga," and producing an unequaled run of relevant titles and choruses—"Jigga That Nigga," "Nigga What, Nigga Who," and the earliest, "Ain't No Nigga." This last, cleverly, was *not* about Jay-Z saying he was not no nigga (as in Sly and the Family Stone's 1969 "Don't Call Me Nigger, Whitey"), but rather that there is *no nigga* as great as Jay-Z. So there were formal dividends for what might also have been a class divider and an anti-cooptation strategy.

The basic justification for reviving the word was simply that racism persisted and white folks treated young black folks like shit. If white America treated them like niggers, making life in the city jobless, serviceless, and abandoned, why shouldn't they announce it? This was how N.W.A explained it at the start. "Niggaz 4 Life" is not a great lyric, but it's direct:

> Why do I call myself a nigga you ask me?
> Because police always wanna harass me
> Every time that I'm rollin'
> They swear up and down that the car was stolen
> Make me get face down in the street
> And throw the shit out my car on the concrete
> In front of a residence
> A million white motherfuckers on my back like I shot the
>   President

Another obstacle to identifying with hip-hop at the moment it was turning into an epochal art form was the lethal quality of African-American city life in the late 1980s and early 1990s. When you rapped along to lyrics about homicide twenty years ago, it felt as if you were talking about homicides that were rising beyond all limits and that nobody knew how to stop.

Pre-1988 hip-hop—again, before its truly world-historical phase—hadn't seemed to be notably about shooting people to death. Guns do turn up in lyrics, and MCs speak of planning to shoot back if shot at—inevitable details of music that started in neighborhoods that were poor and thus robbery-prone. You'd carry a gun, too. Public Enemy spoke of guns differently, in the context of revolutionary self-respect, the tradition of rifle-bearing Black Panthers.

Post-1988 hip-hop seemed increasingly concerned with boasting how many bodies one had to one's name, and some of the grandest music was developed in lyrical fantasies of shooting rivals, not for self-defense or politics, but for *business*. The conceit that the rappers were themselves drug kingpins, thugs, and murderers, "gangsters," was maintained with Dr. Dre and Ice Cube and Snoop Dogg in Los Angeles, and did not diminish in the wake of the two most tragic real-world murders in hip-hop: those of New Yorker the Notorious B.I.G. and the originally San Francisco–based Tupac Shakur. Biggie was shot to death in March 1997 in his car in LA after the Soul Train Music Awards. Tupac had been killed in September 1996 in Las Vegas following a Mike Tyson fight. If anything, the gangster persona settled in further as Tupac and Biggie became "classical" references. Their life stories were ones that television liked to retell with especial relish, until it was hard not to suspect that the white music media might like some of its black rappers best once they had been shot to death.

To be a white teenager, singing along with what were—supposedly—realistic depictions of life in a black ghetto, in the actual situation of the early 1990s, was callous and ghoulish; indifferent to what you saw on the news, which was a world of crying mothers and angry preachers who had been, in effect, abandoned by wealth, government, the economy, the justice system, and charity. If you watched nightly news in the late 1980s and early 1990s in any city in the United States, what you mostly got to see from black neighborhoods was people weeping. This was because their sons, daughters, brothers, husbands, and best friends had been victims of homicide or crossfire. (This, alongside *The Cosby Show* and *In Living Color*—twin lenses on fractured times.) By 1988, it was known that the New York murder rate had exceeded any previous known record for the city, since records were kept. Homicide became the leading cause of death for African-American men in their twenties, above heart attack, accident, etc. The murdering peaked nationally in 1991. As many as one-twelfth of each year's murders, though, were being committed in New York City alone, where hip-hop had originated and from which it mostly still emanated. The other hip-hop center was then the black ghetto of Los Angeles, which televised America took a look at finally in helicopter flyover footage of the riots of 1992. The murder rates would never be so high again, as they began dropping precipitously in 1995 and have dropped steadily since. But we didn't know that then.

"Don't ever question if I got the heart to shoot you / The answer is simply too dark for the user." "Shoot point blank, a motherfucker's sure to die." "Beef is when I see you, guaranteed to be in ICU." "Let's picnic inside a morgue/ Not pic-a-nic baskets, pic-a-nic caskets." "From the Beretta/ puttin' all the holes in your sweater." These were lines in the songs I was practicing, twenty years later.

Of course the songs were obviously a combination of street report and fantasy. But, really, what business would I have had back then, singing along? I hear the songs, now that they have just become "lyrics" again, and I wonder if my recoil then was ignorance or ethics, whether I have more depth now, or less. *Should* I be singing along? I find that when I have my headphones on, I too now practice rapping on the subway, though silently. Each time "nigger" comes up, I have to make a decision. Sometimes, I've discovered, I wind up substituting "brother"—especially when I'm in public, though no one is going to hear me. Maybe they can read lips? This is embarrassing and shameful, but so is a white person, nearing middle age, rapping. I cover my mouth with a fist as if I'm coughing, and keep it there.

In the midst of this, the Roots took over the job of backing band for *Late Night with Jimmy Fallon,* a reputable hip-hop outfit taking a key role in what is fundamentally one of the squarest and most ordinary middle-class institutions of television. The undeniable task of the late show is to make viewers feel safe and mellow enough to fall asleep.

I learned that once a month after the evening's taping they were doing a residency at the Highline Ballroom in New York. This seemed a gesture of sharing the benefits: Questlove and Black Thought were hosting a kind of variety show, after midnights, midweek, with up-and-comers and celebrated guests, and themselves as house band, in a small place, for sophisticates. I felt extremely chic as Mos Def and I went in by the same door; he was pointed backstage, while I went to coat check. As always in New York, I was shocked by the extreme plushness of music venues, at every level from high to low, contrasting with the world I'd known in the provinces, where clubs tend to be dumpy and uncomfortable. In fact, I had seen the Roots play a decade earlier under a shitty tent on a soggy lawn on a college campus, on the circuit that then brought a whole range of "conscious" acts to majority-white colleges: the Roots, the Fugees, Digable Planets, and my favorites, De La Soul. The shame I'd felt at such concerts was that there were too few black people in the audience, just as there were too few black people at the universities. It didn't necessarily make me feel better to know that white fraternity houses in the South had been key moneymaking venues that Little Richard and James Brown had played to in the fifties when not on the chitlin circuit.

Here at the Highline, I was feeling much better about myself, since the audience was majority black and I was happily at ease—which, now that I write it down, is probably just code for the recognition that the audience was middle-class. Black people were upstairs in seats too expensive for me, eating dinner. That's the America I want to live in. Then, between sets, the house started playing a now-solid canon of nineties classics—Snoop Dogg and Jay-Z and others—and this multiracial, middle-class audience started singing along. And, again, I was pulled up short. Because, as we sang of Dom Pérignon and Ferraris and La Perla and Gucci, we were once again traveling through lyrics that I couldn't do as a teen, that seemed hostile or alien to hopes for an interracial middle class of the kind I seemed to be standing in now. And the kind of hip-hop I had liked and been able to sing along to, including the Roots, the "conscious" rap that seemed more connected to middle-class aspiration, more overtly political, Afrocentric, seemed like it had been sidelined in that canon.

Can I confess that in addition to working on my rapping, I'd also been doing some reading? Specifically books by African-American sociologists like Benjamin Bowser and Mary Pattillo, about the relation to property and economic power of African-Americans in the twentieth

century. Probably the most openly discussed, overt obstacle to identification when a politicized white middle-class youth encountered a
ghetto-derived hip-hop in the early 1990s was what was then called the
"materialism" problem. (That's alongside the "misogyny" problem, which
has never quite gone away, and which scholar-critics Imani Perry and
Tricia Rose have treated with more understanding than I ever could.)
Now I could see that both "materialism" and the punk–hip-hop divide
had more to do with a historical problem about capitalism, and different
orientations to its failures.

From the end of Reconstruction to the first decades of the new century, the majority of African-Americans still lived in the South, not the
North. Six million moved north in the Great Migration between the
two world wars. They came for industrial and manufacturing jobs. Yet
starting in the years just after the great Civil Rights Act of 1964, the new
migrants—shunted initially into ghettos in the least desirable parts of
the Northern industrial cities, racing to reach the middle class—faced
the cruelest Northern joke yet, at least since the withdrawal of federal
troops during Reconstruction: sudden deindustrialization and factory
job loss in the 1960s and 1970s.

For former industrial-economy workers, the new service economy
possessed codes that discriminated powerfully against poor black men
particularly. They had been acceptable in industry, where a learned
ethos of strength and toughness was favored; but their toughness was
viewed as frightening and hostile in service jobs. The best-paid service
jobs rewarded docility, Northern white English, fake intimacy, and a
minimum of visible pride or independence. Much of the service economy followed the sprawl out of the increasingly ghostly city to white
suburbs and exurbs anyway, out of reach of urban public transportation,
and therefore hard to reach for a former working-class in cities.

At risk of repeating what everybody knows, the subsequent war on
these new jobless workers in the North came with Reagan and his war
on the poor, called a War on Drugs, expanded and continued under
Bush and Clinton. The federal power—formerly often the defender of
African-Americans against the several states—now militarized local
police, and state legislatures mandated long prison terms for simple

drug possession and personal use. (Never hard to find among unemployed people pursuing self-medication with alcohol and street drugs in the absence of middle-class psychiatry, Valium, and Prozac.) Wherever local police forces had a particular history of racism and white supremacy—as especially in Los Angeles, not that the NYPD had a stellar record—the new "antigang" initiatives looked openly terroristic and antiblack. (These were the abuses that created the LA riots.)

So, the way hip-hop changed in the late eighties involved, if you like, a double response to this Reaganite (others would call it neoliberal) challenge. The double response went under a single name: in the word of the time, the "gangster" moment. In one dimension it mirrored and emulated the privatization, oligarchical temper, and militarization of Reagan neoliberalism. Gangsterization corresponded to the Wall Street fantasy of new private wealth through market economies and an entrepreneurship of pure will, not industry and productivity. In its other dimension, of course, gangster crime was a consequence and representation of the economic abandonment of the bulk of black America, everybody who had not yet reached the institutional uplift of higher education or the stability of middle- and upper-class wealth.

Its drug was crack. Scholars have shown in the decades since the so-called crack epidemic that the instant addiction, violent madness, and "crack babies" attributed to the drug at the time were overblown or fake. Crack wasn't very different chemically from the cocaine from which it was made. Crack's significance was its business model.

This was a capitalist innovation, though one at the level of cottage industry. The crack decade, from about 1986 to 1996, was like the result of a discovery that one could take available but expensive sirloin and turn it into an enormous quantity of cheap, adulterated meatballs, for a tiny population of hardcore buyers desperate for access to meat. They would taste good for a minute and then leave you feeling hungry. The sirloin in this case was Latin American cocaine.

Less important than pent-up demand for such a lousy drug was huge pent-up pressure for an avenue of local entrepreneurship to employ jobless black and Latino youth and create a hope of wealth. Anyone ambitious, hardworking, charismatic, ruthless, and organization-minded—the same virtues in demand for all capitalism—and not too afraid of police and prison, could afford to purchase a very small initial inventory of cocaine, cook it into crack on the kitchen stove, and begin putting together a network of salespeople. In a situation of 50-percent youth unemployment, one could "hire" as many underage subdealers, lookouts, and runners as one could manage. They didn't cost much, they didn't have other opportunities, and the sheer size of one's organization could confer a competitive advantage.

These various new entrepreneurs were right on top of each other, however, in a tiny impoverished geography, selling to the same restricted markets of hardcore drug addicts; competition was experienced as constant street-to-street friction. And the product cooked up by different people was all but undifferentiable as a product. If you cut it enough to be profitable, all crack is said to be basically the same. One did not succeed, entrepreneurially, by making *better* crack. The real means of advantage, both to surpass other entrepreneurs and to forestall arrest, was the wise use of security and violence. Studies of the homicide peaks in American cities suggested that the killers and victims weren't high on the drugs, but involved in aspects of sales and protection.

I hadn't known very much of this until I encountered Craig Reinarman and Harry G. Levine's great *Crack in America: Demon Drugs and Social Justice,* itself a book of the late 1990s. But as soon as you understood the social scientists' picture of the suppressed truths of crack and its economic opportunities, you could see right away that the history matched, and surely explained, misunderstood changes to hip-hop, too.

The unexpected genius of the gangster moment and everything that came after it, from 1988–89 forward, was in effect the reorganization of the themes, metaphors, ethos, and authenticity of rap lyrics around business, property, and violence—usually from crack drama. From its mid-1970s beginnings to the late 1980s, the topics of rapping had really been boasts, partying, romance, the celebration of inexpensive luxury goods (principally clothes and sneakers, like "My Adidas," plus the occasional car), neighborhood shout-outs, and memorable, occasional state-of-the-postindustrial-city plaints like "The Message." In the late 1980s, however, the topics mutated. Why? Well, each of the changes occurred in step with changes in police violence and the new structure of drug sales. This is how and why rap truly becomes a capitalist music, and also a music so emotionally effective about the situations and dilemmas of the present day. In 1990s lyrics, crack is the source of the cash that funds the first champagne, cars, and jewels. It's also the source of the pathos of being able to enjoy these for only a short time before you are shot to death or imprisoned.

Or, really, crack is only the initial reason the metaphors and ethos turn to business and the chase for money. What soon enough supplants crack dealing for pay is *rapping*, itself, for pay, as its new grandiosity of subject matter made hip-hop, justifiably, ever more salable to white America and the world.

One of the most important things to note about the corpus of music about crack is that practically no MC smokes crack. At least, not a single MC uses crack in the limited songs I know. But Biggie sells it, Jay-Z sells it, Nas sells it, Raekwon sells it, 50 Cent sells it, and with the proceeds they relax with liquor and marijuana (drugs of choice for all classes and identities of turn-of-the-twenty-first-century Americans, black and white and rich to poor). The passage back and forth between the two activities ("If I wasn't in the rap game / I'd probably have a key knee deep in the crack game," says Notorious B.I.G.) animates the new drama since 1988. You aren't always sure any longer when an MC is talking about one activity or the other, so overlapping do the two become. The greatest MCs can authenticate elaborate and purely fictional dramas with the biographical fact that any ghetto-born MC of the period was likely to have had a chance to be, at fifteen or sixteen years of age, one of those lookouts or runners on the block. Plus, drugs do have that curious effect, because of their illegality but also their oily quality of slipping into every cranny of private life, of making everyone young, across all strata, feel like an outlaw. "I was there," the crack-selling songs declare. And while the police really are lethal—and one's competitors are lethal—the rewards are material and universally appealing. In the end, this is what made hip-hop grand, operatic, titanic, embracing ranges of emotion and expression distinct from previous popular music. Crack business made it cinematic, too, as rappers integrated the American mythologies of previous eras of gangster capitalism celebrated in the movies of Coppola and De Palma and Scorsese.

This all could escape casual white listeners at the time, I think—it certainly escaped me in the early 1990s. Only now does it seem glaring, the endless rhetorical focus in the "new" hip-hop on business, organization, "the Firm" (the name Nas chose for his collective of rappers), or "the Commission" (one of the names Notorious B.I.G. used for a hip-hop crew, along with his official crew "Junior M.A.F.I.A."). It was a way of thinking about the smallest sort of business with the trappings of the biggest, cutting out all the intervening layers and middle classes of employment and job-holding institutions. So, too, did I fail to understand the ambition evinced by successful rappers to gain places in the increasingly corporate white labels that distributed 1990s hip-hop. (Jay-Z went from his own Roc-a-fella Records to become head of Def Jam Records for a period; Def Jam had once been a black-owned independent label, but in the Jay-Z era was already a division of Universal, who own everything from hip-hop to Decca and Deutsche Grammophon). Sometimes a rationale was articulated, as by Jay-Z himself, as revenge for historic exploitation of blacks by white capital and owners and music producers, and to create new role models:

> I do this for my culture,
> To let 'em know what a nigga look like when a nigga in a
>   roadster
> Show 'em how to move in a room full of vultures
> Industry's shady, it need to be taken over
> Label owners hate me, I'm raising the status quo up
> I'm overcharging niggas for what they did to the Cold
>   Crush
> Pay us like you owe us for all the years that you hoed us
> We can talk, but money talks, so talk mo' bucks.

But the rewards of success at escaping the crack game and becoming a musician, artist, and star existed in the same exceptional, private, neoliberal framework to which "gangsterism" was, surprisingly, such an incredible compelling analogy. A hundred ordinary citizens might perish, but one "innovator" would get out and all the way to the top. The kingpin, become a rapper, would acquire and exhibit the same unattainable properties known to be the toys of a high-status equities trader or corporate CEO. He'd have a private jet, a Bentley, Louis Vuitton bags, Armani suits, top-shelf whiskeys and cognacs—the things being sold in the pages of magazines seen by all of us, but directed to the white ultra-rich, as they have pulled away from the rest of the country in America's new runaway inequality.

Another thing I've been able to see clearly only with time, however, is how much post-punk, supposedly disobedient and destructive and nihilistic, actually spoke on behalf of its own compensatory perspective on capitalism, associated with a falling but sincere long-term middle class and an older "producer ethic." The punk ethos that middle-class whites got from the early 1980s had identified Reagan-Thatcher–era neoliberal winner-take-all capitalism as the problem for everyone. Reagan's "supply-side economics" was the reason hard work sent money to the top, not the middle. Globalized corporate capitalism was the reason good jobs dried up or were sent overseas. Consumer capitalism was the reason a life of products and trivial luxuries was weightless and ultimately worthless. Racism might cause the black working class to be liquidated first. But the changes were coming for all of us eventually.

So white middle-class youth in its 1990s *No Logo* moment was against conglomeration, deregulation, upward redistribution. And the post-punk achievement, frankly, was almost less its music and more its vision of "alternative," rival systems of performance, production, and distribution. This was the meaning of DIY, too—do it yourself, that other long-lived descriptor of post-punk. Every region and city generated its own small, marginal record label: SST, Dischord, Touch and Go, Taang!, Triple X, Homestead, Sub Pop, Matador, etc. If you were a young person of good taste who cared about rock music in the 1980s and 1990s, you might listen to the Minutemen, Big Black, the Replacements, Hüsker Dü, the Butthole Surfers, Sonic Youth, or, later, Fugazi, Mudhoney, Pavement, Bikini Kill. And before 1991, not a single one of them could be purchased through official capitalism, as incarnated in the despised "major labels."

Were middle-class whites going to lecture black entertainers that brandies and consumer goods wouldn't buy happiness? I hope not. Yet the consumer exaltation in one music, and the hidden producer ethic in the other, placed a chasm between the potentially like-mindedly political post-punk and hip-hop cultures.

The white middle-class rebellion, in its political anti-corporate-globalization and anticonsumer movement, confronted a hip-hop that seemed to evince a conspicuous will to capitalism—with an extremity that no black American music, which had sometimes spoken of getting ahead in business or needing to make a buck, had quite shown before. What stood out most to non-fans was the naming of white-owned luxury products, consumer logos and brands, curiously mixed with a new and unfamiliarly textured sexism: "Life ain't nothin' but bitches and money." Women seemed to be for sale, too, in the lyrics; white rock has always been super-misogynist, directly, but somehow this lyrical equivalence of women, cash, and consumer goods could be read as alien.

But black artists, from communities that had last been economically stable in the North when tied to systems of larger capital (as workers and employees, not small owners), *had* to win big at the game of official capitalism, through its new, giant conglomerations, or have no public voice at all. They didn't necessarily come from the classes of petty-bourgeois stability and entrepreneurship. There was no backstop of middle-class-white small capital, accumulated over generations.

If the money ethos was mostly scandalous in N.W.A, and grim and ironic in the Wu-Tang's "C.R.E.A.M." of 1994 ("Cash Rules Everything Around Me / C.R.E.A.M., get the money / Dollar dollar bill y'all"), it was also becoming increasingly tragicomic as the music advanced—or gleefully comic. It reached some of its great narrative heights in the elaborate tales of the Notorious B.I.G. ("Gimme the Loot," 1994; "I Love the Dough," 1996) and acquired an absurd triumphalist flavor in Jay-Z songs like "Money Ain't a Thang" (1998) with Jermaine Dupri ("In a Ferrari, a Jaguar, switchin' four lanes / With the top down, screamin' out, 'money ain't a thang!'"). As the luxury names were worked in with always elaborate rhythmic dexterity, a highlight, after some years, was Busta Rhymes's embedding of the four-syllable cognac Courvoisier to a chorus in 2001: "Give me the Henny, you can give me the Cris / You can pass me the Remy, but pass the Cour-voi-si-er!"

The best summary I know, within hip-hop, of the paradoxical history that made the music attain such intensity of artistry and prominence, comes late—in the 2000s—from Kanye West. West belongs to a postcrack generation. He is part of the line of artists that comes after the gangster triumph, but is not entirely done with its metaphors. (This also characterizes the duo Outkast, and Lil Wayne. The hip-hop historian Jeff Chang points out how few new rappers broke through to commercial success in that short generation, when label consolidation and collapse stalled the careers of some of the most talented.) West's history comes in a song called "Crack Music" (2005). The lyrics are framed by invocations of a history of state conspiracy and deception that includes Reagan's repressive rise as governor of California in the 1960s ("How we stopped the Black Panthers? / Ronald Reagan cooked up an answer") and the Reagan–Bush–Bush II arming of Saddam's Iraq before making war against it, twice ("Who gave Saddam anthrax? / George Bush got the answers").

But the main idea Kanye conveys is of a ruse of history by which the poison of crack, addicting the black ghetto, gave rise to the serum of hip-hop, by which black artists thrived and to which they have now addicted a white listening audience. He even adds a poem, spoken at the end by Malik Yusef:

> We took that shit, measured it, and then cooked that shit
> And what we gave back was crack *music*
> And now we ooze it through they nooks and crannies
> So our mammas ain't got to be they cooks and nannies
> And we gon' repo everything they ever took from granny.
> Now the former slaves trade hooks for Grammys.
> This dark diction has become America's addiction.
> Those who ain't even black use it.
> We gon' keep baggin' up this here crack music.

.   .   .

I imagine someone could object: This isn't *really* how you listen to popular music, is it? How you choose it? How your taste works? You don't *really* put it into a blender and siphon the messages off from it and sip them like red blood cells—do you? You're inhuman! Do you really judge art by a criterion of its politics—as if you had to hear an editorial, backed with a beat?

Of course the answer is: not really. But I do sing along. When I sing along, I hear myself singing along. That is, I know I'm saying these words with my own tongue, my own spirit, that *I'm* doing it. Listening to music is *doing* something. It's important that you don't listen, with pop, without moving or singing along. There's a profound pleasure in saying, with the singer of a song, words you might never utter in real life. Sometimes the pleasure is even in part because they seem opposite to your opinions—to who people *think* you are in straight life—or because they upend all respectable norms. So I like singing along to "Okie from Muskogee" and "Stand by Your Man," and also "Run for Your Life," "I Wanna Be Your Dog," "There Is a Light that Never Goes Out," "They Saved Hitler's Cock," not to mention, apropos of hip-hop, "10 Crack Commandments" and "A Milli." But it can kill my enjoyment if I'm singing lyrics that are dumb and conformist, truly stupid and cynical—basically, lyrics that indicate, in a convincing way, that the person who created them is shallow, lazy, or untalented, or racist or corrupt, especially if they're also proud of themselves. It's a bummer—though of course it happens.

I've met real fans of pop music who tell me that they honestly never listen to the lyrics, and don't hear them. This is an entirely different phenomenon, which I respect, though it seems to me a bit like the fact that some people don't dream, or that I'm color-blind to some shades of pink and green—a loss. Anyway, it leads to a different conversation, about timbres and rhythms.

In rap, though, words *are* the music. Because it speaks in whole sentences, indeed in stanzas, with extended metaphors, quotations, puns—and especially jokes, often jokes that make you think before you laugh—hip-hop is complexly articulate in a way that separates it from the rest of popular music. This doesn't preclude trying to tease out musical genealogies: obviously, in its fund of formulae and oral tradition it is like blues and toasting; in its structure of (verbal) solos, arrangements of soloists, habits of phrasal quotation and sequential improvisations around head-tunes, it's like jazz; in its presentation and distribution, it's often like singles-based "pop" (also called Top 40). But in the wider history of the traditional arts, it seems more or less the re-eruption of the whole tradition of metrical, rhyming poetry that ended around 1920. Hip-hop develops capabilities on one side, the lyrical, beyond anything that has ever been developed in the musical arts before. It communicates as language does, because essentially it *is* language, not just song.

The pleasure in American democracy has always found expression in a pleasure in the American language. Its pleasures include its extreme promiscuity, its mixed origins, its difficulty to learn "properly," its greatness when most improper, its comic obscenity, and its redundancy and superfluity, continually renewed.

Our language is free. It is unprivatizable. The ability still to use words artfully has become the mark of poor people, minority people, everyday people, and writers and intellectuals: those who cannot afford the image, and exist in a shared older world without it, or who deliberately refuse it.

Hip-hop has its memory intact. The gat a thug pulls from his waistband reawakens the Civil War and the Gatling gun. The skrilla that Southern rappers accumulate in 2010, cash money, remembers the scrip in which blacks were paid under the sharecropping system. In the official United States, our presidents since John F. Kennedy and our public figures and broadcasters have taught themselves *not* to be able to speak the rich American language. What has come out of the mouths of recent leaders, until Obama, seemed like the result of brain damage. What is expressed on Fox or CNN, on the twenty-four-hour news, exalts the image above language. It puts the image above real news, which is, in a democracy, whatever transpires in the community of the people.

Underneath the stupefying official loss of the language, there has been an accumulation of riches kept on the wrong side of those redlines by which realtors and city developers kept blacks and whites apart. All the old American words were collected in the row houses, terraces, and projects. Here is what happens to the genius of the People when ignored.

My grandmother spoke at home an American English rich in allusion, quotation, joke, formula, words borrowed from native Yiddish and acquired from neighborhood Spanglish, brought home from popular culture and the street, a vernacular far richer than the trimmed-down English she used in her job as a switchboard operator and receptionist and the standard English her children and grandchildren learned. When she became most animated, telling a good story, her "he ain't" and "I says" were let out most, her "errors" saltier and more precise than the proprieties she knew perfectly well.

I find it tempting to imagine the old language up on shelves at the tops of closets, in bottom drawers, between bed frames and mattresses, in the bins of old lumber rooms, and the small words tangled with the screws, switches, twine, and hardware of which every household has its collection, the pins and the buttons. But of course the words must have been in constant use, in the speech and stories that don't make it onto TV: carried on in the Republic, in the world of whatever constitutes and sustains the true American People (and not the one evoked by the newscasters and spokesmen).

It may be better to think of the old language as belonging to one of those buildings one sometimes hears about, from an earlier phase of the last century, built in an era of a different conception of the People and its needs—or its deserts—or reclaimed from a rich elite who had earlier moved out. A decrepit or unassuming edifice with, in its basement, a swimming pool, there all this time, statued with classic Greek heroes and goddesses in marble, and gold-trimmed, and lapis-lazuli-lined between the pristine underwater tiles, marking the lap swimmers' lanes. A *public* pool, remnant of the old metropolis, or a forgotten property turned over to new residents.

Here, in hip-hop, is a language spoken by ingenious people who can take some earned pleasure in America, by what she has left for us, and what We the People or our ancestors have made. Why should it be that those who were least cared for, most left behind, should find their way to making and keeping something most classical, valuable, intelligent for America? Why are they alone the bearers of our language when most everything official conduces to mutism?

[2010]

I stopped practicing, in the end. I still listen, admire, and enjoy. I try to sing along, a bit (only when I'm alone, still). I could say that I listen with new ears, because I learned technical difficulties of the art. Really, I regained my old ears. Instead of it becoming easier to identify with hip-hop, I remember why it's always been complicated as well as desirable. I remember where I am, in old uncertainties. They've gained historical ballast, but no resolution.

I also knew, even as I was writing, that I was trying to comprehend a history that had reached some completion and was being superseded. I could tell that Kanye and others had blown wide open what constituted the genre. I had Drake's first EP on my iPod and didn't know what to make of it. Soon even commercial hip-hop was drawing in electronic dance music, private musing, monomania, and gloom. The verbal art evolved away from dexterity, speed, and articulation, to rediscover slowed, slurred, and processed voicings, shouts, and chants. It seemed the new openness also obliged hip-hop to have to tolerate superstardom for Macklemore and Iggy Azalea, white rappers of dubious provenance. So five years' passage have shaped a new constellation.

The hardest thing to explain is why this impulse came to me after Obama's election—what that meant. I'm one of the people who felt that Obama's presidency mattered also *because* he's black. This was a gift beyond the rightness of his politics and the undoubted greatness of the man. It seemed miraculous in part because it seemed to mean that at least one half of my fellow voters weren't as racist as I'd feared, or that racism in some places still allows advance in others.

The feeling I had at his election was that I ought to change, too. I ought to learn something. Admittedly, it took a strange form—even derisory: It doesn't sound good to ask what practicing Slick Rick's "La Di Da Di" had to do with the first American president of African descent. I hope it will take other forms. Obama's silence over these eight years has inspired other black speech, I think, unveiling what he couldn't say—in Black Lives Matter, most powerfully. Maybe I'll have new chances to learn. I have some friends who are very sophisticated political thinkers; I think I'm a simple one. For me, I often think the only real political question is "Whose side are you on?" and I have to struggle always to remember it, as everything flows from that.

[2015]

IV

GUT-LEVEL LEGISLATION, OR, REDISTRIBUTION
(THE MEANING OF LIFE, PART II)

One of the lessons of starting a magazine today is that if you pay any attention to politics you will collect a class of detractors, who demand immediately to know What and Wherefore and Whether and How. Are you to be filed next to *Mother Jones* and *Z* and *American Spectator* in the back row, or with *The Nation* and *The Weekly Standard* and the *American Prospect* up front? Is it possible you have not endorsed a candidate, or adopted a party? Within the party, a position? If not a position, an issue? The notion that politics could be served by thinking about problems and principles, rather than rehearsing strategy, leaves them not so much bemused as furious.

The furious political detractors need "responsibility," which in their hands is a fiction of power. If you question the world from an armchair, it offends them deeply. If you believe you run the world from it, it exalts them—because you have bought into the fiction that justifies their elitism. These commentators who have no access to a legislative agenda and really no more exalted basis for political action than that of their ordinary citizenship (but they do not believe they are ordinary citizens) bleat and growl and put themselves on record for various initiatives of Congress over which they have no influence and upon which they will have no effect. To be on record is to be "politically responsible" in that false sense. No rebuke is made to the process of opinionating itself—

this ritual of fomenting an opinion on everything, and so justifying the excited self-stimulation of a class of unelected arbiters who don't respect the citizens within themselves.

"What do you stand for! What will you do!" Legislatively? Are you kidding? Well, there is something one can do, without succumbing to the pundits: for the day when the Congress rolls up to our doorsteps and asks for our legislative initiatives, maybe it is up to every citizen to know what is in his heart and have his true bills and resolutions ready. Call it "political surrealism"—the practice of asking for what is at present impossible, in order to get at last, by indirection or implausible directness, the principles that would underlie the world we'd want rather than the one we have.

- *Principle*: The purpose of government is to share out money so that there are no poor citizens—therefore no one for whom we must feel guilty because of the arbitrariness of fate. The purpose of life is to free individuals for *individualism*. Individualism is the project of making your own life as appealing as you can, as remarkable as you like, without the encumbrances of an unequal society, which renders your successes undeserved. Government is the outside corrective that leaves us free for life.
- *Legislative Initiative No. 1*: Add a tax bracket of 100 percent to cut off individual income at a fixed ceiling, allowing any individual to bring home a maximum of $100,000 a year from all sources and no more.
- *Legislative Initiative No. 2*: Give every citizen a total of $10,000 a year from the government revenues, paid as a monthly award, in recognition of being an adult in the United States.

The redistribution of wealth can be unnerving whenever it comes up, and most unnerving to those who have least wealth, because they have worked hardest for every dollar and can't afford to lose it.

But redistribution comes in two steps, and when you look at the steps it's not so unnerving. The first step was already accomplished last century. It was the permanent establishment of a graduated income tax, one of the greatest triumphs of civilization. A consensus was built to grade taxation to equalize the relative pain of taxation for each income earner. A little money is as useful to a person with little money overall as a larger sum is useful to a person with lots of money—and so, for equal citizenship, they carry an equal burden. Tax them proportionately the same, and everyone pays the same stake for government with the same degree of sacrifice.

The second step is our task in this century. It is an active redistribution to help dissolve the two portions of society whose existence is antithetical to democracy and civilization, and which harm the members of each of these classes: the obscenely poor and the absurdly rich. Each group must be helped. That means not only ending poverty, but ending absurd wealth. Obscene poverty doesn't motivate the poor or please the rest of us; it makes the poor desperate, criminal, and unhappy. Absurd wealth doesn't help the rich or motivate the rest of us, it makes the rich (for the most part good, decent, hardworking, and talented people) into selfish guilty parties, responsible for social evil. It is cruel to rig our system to create these extremes, and cast fellow citizens into the two sewers that border the national road. For all of us, both superwealth and superpoverty make achievement trivial and unreal, and finally destroy the American principles of hard work and just deserts. Luckily, eradicating one (individual superwealth) might help eradicate the other (superpoverty).

True property is that which is proper to you: what you mix your hands into (Locke), what is characteristic of you and no one else, and would change state in anyone else's possession. It is your clothes, your domicile, the things you touch and use, the land you personally walk. Property is the proprium, a possession that becomes like a characteristic; it starts as if it could belong to anyone, and comes to be what differentiates you. If it wears the mark of your feet and the smudge of your fingertips, your scent and your private atmosphere, then there is indeed something special and inviolable about property, even where it has come into your hands inequitably, by inheritance or a surfeit of income. The diamond worn at the throat every evening must share a certain protection, under the law, with the torn cloak that keeps some shivering person warm.

This is distinct, however, from all wealth that is not capable of being used in the ordinary necessities of a life or even the ordinary luxuries. From any wealth that cannot be touched or worn or walked every day by its possessor, which neither comes from nor enables the mixing-in of hands but always and inevitably exists as a kind of notional accumulation of numbers, the protection of the proprium withdraws. When you have more houses than you or loved ones can live in, more cars than you can drive; more income in a year than can be spent on what you or your family can actually use, even uselessly use; then we are not speaking of property anymore, not the proprium, but of the inappropriate and alien—that which one gathers to oneself through the accident of social arrangements, exploiting them willfully or accidentally, and not through the private and the personal.

Thus the rationale for restricting *income.* Inequality will always exist, but in itself it is something different. One has to recognize that while the proprium may be passed down in nonmonetary forms, too—in the peculiarities of your genetics from your parents; in the heirloom, dwelling, tool, or decoration that wears the traces of hands and breath— income always comes as a consequence of arrangements of the community, via the shared space of trade, the discussion and rules, the systems of investment, and all the voluntary associations of society, of which the largest association is government.

A rich person—continuing to draw $100,000 a year in income— stays rich, but puts part of it into his own home and bank account and part into the needs and luxuries he may actually use. This sum will be converted reasonably into the *proper,* the personal, without any absurdity. A superrich person, however, who takes in $1 million, $10 million, or $100 million, will not and can never spend it on any sane vision of the necessities of life, at least not without a parasitic order in which normal goods (a home, a dinner) are overpriced (by the existence of those who will compete to pay for them) and other goods are made to be abnormal and bloated (like the multiacre mansion). The social system allocates the extra $9,900,000 mistakenly. Reallocated, it would do much more benefit in a guaranteed citizens' income for many individuals in households with total incomes both above and below the median (now about $45,000 per household). But this is without—and this is very important—doing any harm to the formerly superrich person; if anything, it may do him a great benefit.

(And it should also be without any person or office to decide to whom money should be allocated. The goal is an automatic mechanism and universal good, not a form of control. Everyone must be given an equal sum, the $10,000, to help him be free. And that must include the rich top earner of $100,000—to keep him free, too, with the opportunity, through all the years of his adulthood, to *change* his life.)

The threat from those who oppose this line of thought is that, without "incentives," people will stop working. The worst-case scenario is that tens of thousands of people who hold jobs in finance, corporate management, and the professions (not to mention professional sports and acting) will quit their jobs and end their careers because they did not truly want to be bankers, lawyers, CEOs, actors, ballplayers, et cetera. They were only doing it for the money! Actually they wanted to be high-school teachers, social workers, general practitioners, stay-at-home parents, or criminals and layabouts.

Far from this being a tragedy, this would be the greatest single triumph of human emancipation in a century. A small portion of the rich and unhappy would be freed at last from the slavery of jobs that aren't their life's work—and all of us would be freed from an insane system.

If there is anyone working a job who would stop doing that job should his income—and all his richest compatriots' incomes—drop to $100,000 a year, *he should not be doing that job.* He should *never* have been doing that job—for his own life's sake. It's just not a life, to do work you don't want to do when you have other choices, and can think of something better (and have a $10,000 cushion to supplement a different choice of life). If no one would choose to do this job for a mere $100,000 a year, if all would pursue something else more humanly valuable; if, say, there would no longer be anyone willing to be a trader, a captain of industry, an actor, or an athlete for that kind of money—then the job should not exist.

The supposed collapse of the economy without unlimited income levels is one of the most suspicious aspects of commonplace economic psychology. Ask yourself, for once, if you believe it. Does the inventor just not bother to invent anymore if inventions still benefit larger collectivities—a company, a society—but do not lead to a jump in his or any other inventor's already satisfactory personal income? Do the professions really collapse if doctors and lawyers work for life and justice and $100,000, rather than $1 million? Will the arts and entertainment collapse if the actors, writers, and producers work for glory and $100,000? Do ballplayers go into some other line and stop playing? If you're panicking because you can't imagine a ceiling of $100,000, well, make it $150,000. Our whole system is predicated on the erroneous idea that individuals are likely to hate the work they have chosen, but overwhelmingly love money. Presumably the opposite should be true. Even the really successful trader *must* love his work in some way—he enjoys the competition, temporarily measured in money, and the action and strategy and game of thought and organization, which are his life's calling. And all this glory could be pursued in a society in which he took home only $100,000 from this sport of kings—and he, and all of us, might be better off.

"But how can you ask other people to lower their salaries, without giving your life to charity first? Isn't it hypocrisy to call for change for everyone without turning over your own income?" Morality is not saved by any individual's efforts to do charity, a pocketful here, a handful there. Charity is the vice of unequal systems. (I'm only repeating Wilde's "The Soul of Man Under Socialism.") We shouldn't have to weigh whether our money would do more good in a destitute person's pocket, or our time do more good if we ladled soup to the hungry, or our study do more good if it taught reading to the illiterate. It always, always would.

Because it is hard to give up your money, however, when not everyone else does, and hard to give up your time when not everyone else does—and nearly impossible when you have less time, and less money, than the visibly rich and comfortable—and frankly, because it's not often a good idea to give up your true calling or your life at all, our giving is limited and fitful. It can never make a large-scale difference.

Not only decency, justice, and community but nobility, excellence, and individualism can come about only by redistribution, not charity, in a society organized against drastic monetary inequality in the first place. It would be a good society in the broadest sense, one in which life was worth living, because the good life (as a life of morality, and as a life of justified luxury) could be pursued without contradiction.

The essence of individualism is *morally relevant* inequality. The misuse of inequality occurs when it comes to be based on wealth rather than ability; on birth rather than talent; on positioning rather than genius; on alienable money (which could belong to anyone) rather than action and works (which can be done only by you). These distortions spell the end of a society of individualists. Money inequality creates a single system that corrals every person and places him above or beneath another, in a single file stretching from hell to the moon. These so-called individualists will then be led, by the common standard of the dollar, to common interests, common desires, and little that's *individual* at all.

Some say the more the rich are rich, the better off everyone will be. But really the Dick Cheneys of this world are obese because they're eating everybody else's dinner. Trickle-down economics is an alimentary philosophy: the more the rich eat, the more crusts they stuff in their maws, the more they create for the benefit of all the rest of us underneath them. Even if it worked, one could not forget that what they pass on to us is predigested, already traveling through their stomachs and fattening them first, giving excess nutriment to the undeserving. Their monuments, too, which we do marvel at, are composed of waste. Why gain the world as excrement? Why should we not take it in its morally original form—if money need not pass through the rich to reach us?

- *Legislative Initiative No.3*: It makes most sense to have
  a president and vice president who will forswear wealth
  permanently. A man who rules for the *demos* need not come
  from the *demos*. But he ought to enter it; he ought to become
  one of the people he is responsible most for helping—that means
  the rest of us.

Worst-case scenario two, if we prioritize human satisfaction instead of productivity, is de-development. For centuries, it has been at the back of the Western mind that technological development might reach a point at which a democratic community would want to stop, or change direction. So the Erewhonians, in Samuel Butler's utopia, broke their machines.

It's finally become possible to take a better view: not unlimited laissez-faire hubris, and not irrational machine-breaking, either. In a country where some portions of development have gone farther than anybody would like, because of everyone's discrete private actions (as in the liquidation of landscape and the lower atmosphere)—while other portions, as in medical insurance and preventive care, have not gone far enough—then *intentional de-development* might be the best thing that can occur. The eradication of diseases is not something you would like to see end; nor would you want to lose the food supply, transportation, and good order of the law and defense. On the other hand, more cell phones and wireless, an expanded total entertainment environment, more computerization for consumer tracking, greater concentrations of capital and better exploitation of "inefficiencies" in the trading of securities, the final throes of extraction and gas guzzling and—to hell with it. I'd rather live in a more equal world at a slower pace.

[2006]

V

THE REALITY OF REALITY TELEVISION

There is a persistent dream that television will be more than it is: that it will not only sit in every home, but make a conduit for those homes to reach back to a shared fund of life.

The utopia of television nearly came within reach in 1992, on the day cable providers announced that cable boxes would expand to five hundred channels. Back then, our utopian idea rested on assumptions both right and wrong. We assumed network-sized broadcasters could never afford new programming for so many active channels. That was right. We also assumed TV subscribers wouldn't stand for five hundred channels of identical fluff, network reruns, syndicated programs, second-run movies, infomercials, and home shopping. That was wrong.

We were sure the abundance of channels would bring on stations of pure environmental happiness, carrying into our homes the comforts everyone craves: the twenty-four-hour Puppy Channel, the Sky Channel, the Ocean Channel, the Baby Channel—showing nothing but frolicsome puppies, placid sky, tumultuous ocean, and big-headed babies. It never happened. And yet cable TV did indeed get cut up for small pleasures, in the advertisement of more utilitarian interests, on the Food Network, the Style Network, and Home and Garden Television (HGTV). (Natural beauty took hold on cable only in the pious

slideshows of the Christian channels, where Yosemite is subtitled by
1 Corinthians.)

The meaningful history of technology turns out to be a history of its
fantasized uses as much as of the shapes it actually takes. Our cable-box
dreams finally rested on one beautiful notion: the participatory broadcasting of real life. With such a ludicrous number of channels, companies would just *have* to give some of the dial over to the rest of us, the
viewers—wouldn't they? And we millions would flow into the vacuum
of content. We'd manifest our nature on channels 401 to 499 as surely
as do puppies, ocean, and sky. We'd do it marrying, arguing, staring at
the wall, dining, studying our feet, holding contests, singing, sneezing.
Hundreds of thousands of us had cameras. Well, we'd plug them in and
leave the tape running for our real life.

In this underlying dream, we were neither exactly wrong nor right.
The promise of the five hundred channels went to waste. The techno-
utopians' fantasies shifted to the Internet. Nothing like the paradise
we hoped for came to fruition on TV, that's for sure. Instead we got
reality TV.

The assessment of reality television depends first on your notion of television; second, on your idea of political community.

Here is a standard misconception: since the noblest forms of artistic
endeavor are fictional and dramatic (the novel, film, painting, plays), it
can be assumed that the major, proper products of television will be its
dramatic entertainments, the sitcom and the hour-long drama. I think
this is wrong, and very possibly wrong for a whole number of reasons.
Drama has a different meaning in a commercial medium where "programming" came into being as bacon to wrap the real morsels of steak,
the sixty-second advertisements. It means something different when it
exists in a medium we switch on to see "what's on TV" rather than to
find a given single work; when the goal is more often to watch television
than to watch a particular drama and then turn it off.

From its beginnings in the early 1950s, TV has been blamed for
encouraging overindividualism, for hastening consumer suckerdom,

for spurring passivity and couch-potatoness, and for making up the sensational bread-and-circuses of mass-culture tyranny. That pretty much covers it. And yet when opponents tried to divide the wretched things flickering inside the idiot box into categories, they made excuses for quite unnecessary forms that they felt they recognized (highbrow TV dramas) while deriding unique and far more important items that didn't suit their vision of dramatic art (game shows, local news, now reality shows).

The real principled problem ought to be with drama. The modern form of the long-standing Western philosophical argument against placing drama at the center of a republic was articulated twenty years before the American Revolution. Rousseau insisted in his *Letter to M. D'Alembert* that a republic (in his case Geneva, circa 1758) was correct to keep a theater out of its public life. To Rousseau, a republic is a political community in which each person is equal and sovereign—as it should be to us, today, living in the American republic. The citizen is not sovereign alone, but sovereign through his activity in a community of peers. The drama, when it was given too much power, crowded out the true entertainments of any republican political community— entertainments whose delights must be rooted in that self-regard and free judgment in daily activity that strengthens the bonds of citizen to citizen. (Bear in mind that Rousseau, in ancien-régime Paris, loved the theater: "Racine charms me and I have never willingly missed a performance of Molière." A corrupt order, of nobility and monarchy, could hardly be made worse by drama and might be made better. But the philosopher loved a republic more.)

Rousseau expected that a republic's civic entertainments would be displays of what people already do. Singing, building, decorating, beauty pageantry, athletics, and dancing gave pleasure and "entertainment" because the participants not only accomplished the acts but became spectacles to themselves—and to others, their equals and fellow citizens, who had done just the same activities. Republican entertainments might often take the form of the contest or the demonstration. But they might also be the special celebration of ordinary living itself— the "festival":

Plant a stake crowned with flowers in the middle of a square; gather the people together there, and you will have a festival. Do better yet; let the spectators become an entertainment to themselves; let them become actors themselves; do it so each sees and loves himself in the others so that all will be better united.

"Let the spectators become an entertainment to themselves": a part of TV has always done this. It has meant, at different times, local programming, Huntley and Brinkley, the national news at six and local news at eleven, talk shows and talent shows, *This Is Your Life* and the regional tours of *Wheel of Fortune*. Accept, though, that television's most important function might always have been to let citizens *see* each other and *be seen* in their representatives—in our only truly national-universal medium—and you're left to ask what will accomplish it best today. Reality television may furnish its dark apotheosis—a form for an era in which local TV has been consolidated out of existence, regional differences are said to be diminishing (or anyway are less frequently represented), and news, increasingly at the service of sales departments, has forfeited its authority to represent the polity.

We need myths, not only of our ideal, and our average, but of our fallen extreme. Since the establishment of informed-consent rules in the 1970s, the golden age of social psychology is gone. No more Stanley Milgram's proof that ordinary citizens will push the voltage to the red zone while the electrocuted actor screams—so long as a lab-coated tester is there to give the orders. No more Philip Zimbardo's proof that fake guards will brutalize fake prisoners if you arbitrarily split Stanford students into two groups, lock them in a basement, and leave them to their own devices. No more Harold Garfinkel's demonstrations that testers can drive strangers berserk if they stare at other riders on the elevator or if children refuse to recognize their parents. Today we are reliant on *elimiDATE, Punk'd,* and *Survivor*. Watching reality television is like walking one long hallway of an unscrupulous and peculiarly indefatigable psychology department.

The first ideal-type of reality TV is the show of the pure event. *Cops* represents one end of its spectrum, the low-budget dating shows (*Blind Date, elimiDATE, 5th Wheel, EX-treme Dating*) the other. You discern patterns in each—the effect on the watchful viewer is of a patterned repetition of wholly singular encounters. In the endless scenes of arrests, traffic stops, drive-by warnings ("OK, you ain't going to do it again"), domestic disturbances, and interviews with complainants ("Calm down, ma'am, just tell me what happened"), it becomes clear that justice, at the level of the arrest, has less to do than you might have thought with the code of law. Between cop and civilian, everything is determined by personality; each word is a step in a negotiation; the tools each side possesses seem arbitrary and confused, in the wheedling or vagueness of the suspect, the mock-authoritativeness and lack of information of the cop. So you make notes to your criminal self: never voluntarily submit to a search. But it doesn't take long to realize that, in the situation, you wouldn't remember all you'd learned watching *Cops;* politeness and hustling would take over. In the immediate interaction between two people, each staring into the other's eyes and trying to persuade him toward escape or incrimination, drugged by fear when not hazy with narcotics, you see the hidden face-to-face interactions of your countrymen.

And on *Blind Date* and *EX-treme Dating* and *5th Wheel,* with wary daters eyeing each other over pasta dinners, leglessly drunk in a hundred indistinguishable neon dives and, afterward, on the best dates, mumbling vulgar blandishments in hot tubs, you see that romance is not angelic recognition or simple animal lust but a negotiation—the same as in the *Cops* arrest. The blind date and the traffic stop become on late-night TV the two paradigmatic experiences of American encounters between strangers. Homogenous America is instantly disproved by bizarre America. It is reassuring to watch this openness and fumbling. Finally you see without intermediary dramatization the landscape of tanning salons and restaurants and aikido studios in every corner of the country, the still-distinct accents but universalized, television-influenced behaviors, the dilemma of what to say and which personality to project, as if the social relation were being rebuilt, in a cutaway scale model of our society—a great televised Ark of a changing civilization—two by two.

So even though evidently all women look for "a sense of humor" and all men want someone "I can have fun with," even though all good girls say they are "wild" and all good boys avow that they are "players," this has only an equivocal effect on individuals' relentlessly erroneous attempts to approximate trends and manners learned from TV, which seems to be what's really going on. Yo-yo-ing modesty and immodesty ("I'm a bad girl. I mean, I'm mostly bad in bed"); frank talk about penis size and boob jobs but wildly variable estimates on the morality of kissing on a first date; shy clumsiness masked under pornographic aspirations ("Have you ever had a threesome?" "No, that's more, like, a goal of mine")—*this,* the cameras prove, is the current American performing reality. Everyone tries to play someone else on TV, but still feels so many tethering strings from the prosaic, deficient, and plain polite that conformity becomes chaotic and imitation idiosyncratic.

"Voyeurism" was never the right word for what it means to watch these shows. You feel some identification with the participants, and even more sympathy with the situation. "And if I were pulled over—or if I were set up on a blind date—how would I fare?" But primarily—and this is the more important thing to say about reality TV—there is always *judgment.* You can't know the deeds your countrymen will do until you see them; and once these deeds are seen, you won't fail to judge and retell them. Reality TV is related in this respect to the demimonde of *The People's Court, Divorce Court, Judge Hatchett,* and *Judge Judy.* Classy critics hate these shows too, or claim to. I think that's a mistake. The way in which all reality TV—and much of daytime TV—can be "real" across social classes is in its capacity for judgment. The "friends" on *Friends* were an ideological group, propagandists for a bland class of the affluent in a sibling-incest sitcom. The show didn't allow you to take their idiocy to task, or ever to question the details of how they paid their rent or their hairdresser's bill, or how they acted on the "outside." If only Judge Judy could sit in judgment of them, once! If only *Cops* would break down their door and throw them against the wall! Monica, you ignorant Skeletor, eat a sandwich! Ross, you vainglorious paleontologist, read a book! *You mortuary creep!* Truly, the judge shows have a vengeful appeal: they gather every inept, chiseling, weaseling, self-focused sort of person you meet in your daily life and, counting on each one's stupidity and vanity to get him up into the dock, they yell at him.

This is one way to come to terms with your fellow citizens. Much reality TV, by contrast, communicates a relative openness of judgment, though judgment is its one constant—and does so also by its wider identity of situation between the viewer and those before the cameras. (Nearly everybody has dated, and, from rich to poor, nearly everybody fears the police when driving and will call on them when threatened.) Reality TV's judgment falls on "another oneself," however much one retains the right to disown and ridicule this nitwitted fellow citizen. Nowadays, at every level of our society, there is a hunger for judgment. Often this becomes summary judgment—not so much the wish to know the truth, but the brutal decisionism that would rather be wrong than stay in suspension. This is the will not to deliberate but to sentence. In the political realm, it has influenced the shape of the current disaster. Its soft manifestations own the therapeutic talk shows, in the sniffling and nose wiping of a *Dr. Phil,* where the expert is never at a loss. He will not say: "No, your situation is too messed up for me to advise you; I have a similar problem; think for yourself." Whereas the cheapest and rawest reality TV offers you a chance to judge people like you, people who do lots of the same things you do. It is cheap, it is amoral, it has no veneer of virtue, it is widely censured and a guilty pleasure, and it can be more educational and truthful and American than most anything else, very suitable for our great republic.

Until, that is, one began to see what the capital-rich networks would make of it. For they got into the act, like dinosaurs in an inland sea, and they made the waters heave. They developed the grandiose second ideal type of filmed reality, courtesy of bigger budgets and serial episodes: the show of the group microcosm.

The microcosms were large-scale endeavors, financed by Fox, MTV, NBC, ABC, CBS, and the WB. (The other shows had been cheaply made and served up to UHF and low-budget cable stations by syndication, or, like *Cops,* run in the early bare-bones years of Fox and retained.) MTV's *The Real World,* which put young adults in a group house with cameras, was the earliest and most incomplete example. The pun in its "real world" title meant both that you would see how nonactors interacted (initially fascinating) and that this was, for many of the children on the show, their first foray away from home (pretty boring, after the umpteenth homesick phone call). MTV's goal was to make up a "generation," not a society, as MTV is the most aggressive promoter of one version of youth as a wholesale replacement of adult life.

Subsequently the broadcast networks converted the dating "event" show into sagas of thirty suitors, peeling them away one by one until only the chosen bride or groom remained. *Big Brother* turned the house show, too, into a competition. An even more triumphant microcosm was *Survivor*—followed, in time, by *The Amazing Race.* The newer shows that defined the microcosmic reality and blended it with competition adopted the same basic forms of social discovery that had animated the birth of the English novel: the desert-island Robinsonade of *Survivor;* the at-the-ends-of-the-earth-be-dragons imperialist travelogue and quest romance of *The Amazing Race;* even, perhaps, the sentimental seductions of *The Bachelor,* where so many willing Clarissas rode squealing in limousines to a manor house to hand their hearts to Lovelace.

Yet *Survivor* never took up the society-from-nothing isolation of the desert island, which had motivated the original Robinson Crusoe. *The Amazing Race* didn't care about the Englishman-in-Lilliput foreignness of Swift or the chance meetings of picaresque or even the travelers' tall tales in Hakluyt. The shows had no interest in starting civilization from scratch. Nor for that matter were they much interested in travel—on *The Amazing Race,* you glimpse the blurred locals out the windows of speeding cars. These shows were about the spectacularization of a microcosmic America—about the reduction of society to a cross-section of our countrymen, still so very American, never "going native."

The shows put together sociable Americans, so they would have nothing left but their group interactions, their social negotiations, to keep them going. Nobody let them starve, nothing endangered them. Nominally structured as a contest of skill, skill mattered little and "alliances" much on *Survivor*. The sniping and soothing in couples and trios—forming and reforming, betraying and sticking together—were the main things of interest on that show and on *The Amazing Race,* where it was hard to tell if we were supposed to care, really, that one pair ran faster than another. How do Americans talk and how do they arrange things, in a completely minimal setting, a little like the office and a little like the home but not totally unlike a sequestered jury? So many of the contestants brought the workplace with them, and they were meant to, since they were identified at every subtitle of their names with their stateside jobs: Actor/Model, Computer Programmer, Fireman. This was our festival. Let's see if the alliance can hold between the Stock Trader, the Carpenter, and the Actress. Who will emerge as the "Survivor"? Let's race the Midget and her Cousin, so lovable, against the Bad Couple Who Should Not Marry. Let's see who our true representatives are.

The structure of each of the shows that "voted people off the island," requiring the microcosm to draw itself down each week, echoed, with static, the old idea of a republic of political equals, who despite unequal skills and endowments one by one would recuse themselves from activity to leave a single best representative behind to speak in public for their interests. If we truly all are equals in America, this would be a picture, in ideal form, of how we choose aldermen and selectmen and congressmen: using our sovereignty to withdraw our sovereignty—that is to say, to focus it in the hands, for two or four years, of individuals who act for us. By this means the microcosm programs resembled political allegories.

And yet many of the reality shows of the microcosmic community were quite deliberately, self-consciously implanted—sometimes by the rules, sometimes by the informal instructions given to players—with an original sin. That sin was the will to power by trickery, the will to deception, which puts the power-mad ahead of the natural leader. And the players did not rebel—they accepted this, knowing it too well from home, from what they would call their "real life." "That's how you play the game," each aspiring survivor explained, with the resignation of a trapped bear chewing off its leg, "you have to fool people, you can only be loyal to yourself." They had the republican ideal in their hands, and didn't use it. It got confused with the economic or Darwinian model of competition, in which antirepresentative stratagems are justified because one wins in the defeat and eradication of all others to gain a single jackpot. This, too, was an aspect of the realness of "reality" for Americans: we knew we were witnessing republics of voting or shared excellence competing, or perhaps blending, with another force in our lives.

As deception and power hunger are the sins built into the microcosm, so the *fixed norm* is the flaw introduced into shows of pure judgment. It produces the third ideal type of reality TV: the show of the industry standard.

It was latent in the grand-scale dating shows, these contests that brought in the single judge and red roses and arbitrary rules and an image of romantic love from somewhere in the minds of Hallmark: but who knows, maybe this was close enough to the values of dreamy romance to form some people's preexisting reality. In *American Idol,* though, you see the strong beginning of the reality show of the third type. *American Idol* was the best, and the most insinuating, of the industry shows because it took one of the basic categories of common endeavor that Rousseau loved well—a singing contest, the commonplace sibling of a beauty or dancing or athletic contest. Everyone sings, if only in the shower—and the footage of the worst contestants made clear that the contest *did* include all of us, that the equivalent of singing in the shower was being considered, too, on the way to the final idol. The show had "America" judge, by casting the final votes, *en masse.* Yet it used professional judges in the meantime, a panel of allegorical experts: Simon Cowell (rhymes with "scowl"—the Stern Judge; George III), Paula Abdul (the Universal Sexy Mommy; Betsy Ross), and Randy Jackson (the Spirit of Diversity). Allegorically, America would free itself from the tyranny of the English king, having learned his wisdom, pay due homage to its own diversity, and enjoy the independence to make its own choice—which the hands-tied Englishman's production company would have to live with, and distribute to record stores. Poor George III! What one really learned was that, unlike a singing contest in the high-school gym, the concern of the recording industry was not just, or no longer, whether someone could sing. It was whether a contestant was fitted to the industry, malleable enough to meet the norms of music marketing. The curtain was pulled away from the Great Oz, and the public invited to examine his cockpit and vote which lever or switch to pull next. As it turns out, it is really no less pleasant to choose a winner to suit the norms of music marketing than to choose on individual talent. One was still choosing, and the idol would still be ours. An idol of the marketplace, to be sure, but still our representative American idol.

The major new successes of the past few years have taught (or pretended to teach) the norms of other industries. *The Apprentice,* a show in which one tries to learn skill in business, teaches the arbitrariness of contemporary success in relation to skill. The winners are conditioned to meet a certain kind of norm, not really familiar from anywhere else in life, which corresponds to "the values of business" as interpreted by Donald Trump. *America's Next Top Model* shows how a beauty contest ceases to be about beauty. The real fascination of the show is learning, first, how the norms of the fashion industry don't correspond to ordinary ideas of beauty (you knew it abstractly, here's proof!), but to requirements of the display of clothes and shilling for cosmetics; second, how the show will, in the name of these norms, seek something quite different in its contestants—a psychological adhesiveness, a willingness to be remade and obey. *The Starlet* suggests the distance between the norms of TV acting and the craft of acting—and yet again, in the name of "how it's done in the industry," which provides one kind of interest, the contestants are recast psychologically, which provides the other.

And on it goes, with "how to become a chef" (*Hell's Kitchen*) and "how to be a clothing designer's minion" (*The Cut*), et cetera.*

All this is interesting and revealing in its way. But the final stage is all too familiar: that is, the flow back of norms justified by industry into norms for inner spaces—first the mind, which accepts insane instructions and modifications, then the spaces that have nothing to do with either public life or work, and should offer safety from their demands. I am thinking of the home and the integral body, underneath the skin.

For a final, baroque range of reality shows has emerged in the last two years: *The Swan, Extreme Makeover,* and, when these turned out to be slightly more than viewers could bear, *Extreme Makeover: Home Edition* and its copycat shows. *The Swan* and *Extreme Makeover* also drew on the most basic of all spectacles of excellence: the beauty contest, or "pageant," which once formed a way of seeing or understanding the country, as in the Miss America contests (when you would root for your state while admiring the flowers of the other forty-nine). And the new shows advanced a new kind of norm by re-creating it surgically, by literally rebuilding people's faces and bodies to suit, not beauty, but a kind of televisual glamour. Ordinary unattractive people, given nose jobs, boob jobs, liposuction, lip collagen, tummy tucks, and chin pulls—plus fifty minutes of therapy—looked like wax mannequins when, alone and imprisoned in a Gothic mansion, the naturally lovely host pulled the velvet drapes back from the mirror, and the rebuilt women, inevitably,

* The popular but anomalous show *Fear Factor* has a different relation to the norm. *Fear Factor* adds an outside rule to sport. All the sports we watch on TV (football, baseball, golf, tennis) were invented and enjoyed by participants before being transposed to the small screen for the benefit of spectators. *Fear Factor* seems in contrast to be a show of "sports" devised on behalf of spectators rather than participants. Its goal is the pleasure of the viewer. And its standard turns out to be a kind of norm no one would dare articulate or declare respectable—that television, playing the role here of the industry, makes spectators long to see the human body in postures and activities it would pain individuals to see in person. How could we have known that it's pleasurable to watch chiseled hardbodies and women in bikinis be forced to eat cow spleen or writhe in boxes of slugs, and that these delights of sexual sadism could go along with the wash-you-clean thrills of spinning platforms, ladders hanging from helicopters, and speedboat draggings, which end with the contestants' bodies hurled into rivers or lakes?

began to weep, shocked. Then the host spoke: "You're crying because you've never seen yourself so beautiful. You're crying because you've been transformed," intoning these words until the weeping, speechless victim nodded. If this looked like brainwashing, you hardly knew the horror of it until the camera cut to a boardroom of the delighted surgical experts who had done the work—each one of them equally off-kilter and monstrous because of surgical modifications made to his own face or teeth or eyes or hair. (Flashback to one of the famous Rod Serling–written *Twilight Zone* episodes, this one from 1960: an ordinary woman is called "ugly" and pressured into damaging facial surgery that we can't understand—until the camera pulls back to show us that everyone in her world is hideously disfigured! Yee-ikes!)

The point of these shows was not just how people would be altered, but that they *could* be altered. As the *Six Million Dollar Man* introduction used to say, "We have the technology . . ."; but what was needed was the rationale. When this transdermal insertion of the norm into average people came to seem suspect, the networks increasingly devoted episodes to already hideously ugly and disfigured people, so that the norm could be disguised as charity or medical necessity. But the greater success proved to be the subtle turn, with charitable aspect intact, to demolishing and rebuilding people's homes rather than their faces, in the adjunct called *Extreme Makeover: Home Edition,* which supersized existing home-decorating reality shows like *Trading Spaces* (on which two neighbors agree to redecorate one room in each other's homes). *Extreme Makeover* would get at privacy in one way or another; if not through the body then through the private space that shelters it. A team of experts came in to wreck your shabby domicile and rebuild it. The dwellings that resulted were no longer homes, but theme houses; instead of luxuries, the designers filled rooms with stage sets keyed to their ten-minute assessments of the residents' personalities: "Little Timmy wants to be a fireman, so we made his room look like it's on fire!" As long as the homeowners were poor or handicapped enough, anything was a step up. The show has been an enormous hit.

Whatever can be done in the name of charity or medicine or health will allow the reinsertion of the norm into further spheres of privacy.

Fox is said to be planning *Who Wants to Live Forever?*, a "program that predicts when participants will die and then helps them extend their lifespan through dieting, exercise, [and] breaking bad habits." The circle is closed, and "reality" here no longer lets us observe our real life, but its modifications in the name of a statistical life to come. The private matters we can't, or shouldn't, see flow in to replace our public witnessing of each other. And the festival is no longer of ourselves, but of phantasms projected by industries of health, beauty, home, all industries requiring our obedience: worse than the monsters of drama, because they don't admit their degree of fiction.

The reality of reality television is that it is the one place that, first, shows our fellow citizens to us and, then, shows *that they have been changed by television*. This reality is the unacknowledged truth that drama cannot, and will not, show you.

A problem of dramatic television, separate from what the corrupt characters say and do, is that it shows people who live as if they were *not* being shaped by television. On this point it profoundly fails to capture our reality. (The novel, in contrast, was always obsessed with the way consciousness was shaped and ruined by reading novels.) And this is consistent with the way in which television, more than other media, has a willingness to do the work of shaping life, and a subservience to advertising and industry, even when its creators do not understand what they're up to.

Drama says: this is harmless, fictional. In fact it pushes certain ways of life. But wherever industrial norms repenetrate the televised rendition of reality, they can *directly* push certain ways of life, no longer even needing to use the mediation of "harmless" fiction and drama.

One can sometimes fight corruption with corruption: *Blind Date* to counter *Friends*. So what in our television experience, against *Extreme Makeover*, will show the ways in which homes and faces cannot be remade? Who will make the reality to counter "reality"?

[2005]

.   .   .

Ten years later, almost all the shows I wrote about have been forgotten. Others replaced them. Formats have ebbed and flowed. Some have added novelties, yet old premises return—revived, I sometimes think, in the expression of something like a "second generation" of the form.

Cheap dating shows and isolated survival shows both had seemed to decline. Last year they finally returned in the new form of naked shows. *Naked and Afraid* staged the survival of a lone man and woman, marooned, nude, within a jungle or on an island desert, needing to live for twenty-one days unaided before they could paddle upriver (perhaps through piranhas, or those silverfish rumored to swim up the urethra), and scrape themselves scrambling into a truck, helicopter, or seaplane. *Dating Naked* revived the most bare-bones round-robin dating show imaginable, except that each couple strips to their spray-on tans before undertaking appropriate ice-breaker challenges: Twister, body painting, trampolines.

You could imagine that nudity would represent a final liquidation of the reality format—spending out the principal or selling off the machinery, so to speak, on which titillation had been minted. Instead, the naked shows seem to express a confidence in the persistence of reality TV as the dominant form of broadcast and cable television, as it has faced and fended off challenges from serial drama (*The Sopranos* on) and Internet clips. The nakedness is really a joke, I think, on the still-reigning accusation that the appeal of reality is literal voyeurism. "You watch these people, pretending to care, but you'd really be happier if you could see them naked." Truthfully, to see them naked, at least when they're dating, is to wish them clothed. The real fascinations of reality TV are things more like *appearing,* or *performing.* You find, watching a bare contestant, that you want him to possess every tool in his arsenal, clothes included. As on nude beaches and in doctors' consulting rooms, skin becomes ordinary and unseductive. Nudity is less annoying on the survival show only because it introduces interpersonal dramas connected with sunburns and hat weaving. Otherwise it is extraneous.

The sense of new confidence extends even to the revival of cosmetic-surgery shows, those seemingly compulsive but socially taboo attempts of the early days. The current version is *Botched,* a show clever in its fake moralism. The premise is not to *do* cosmetic surgery, but to *redo* it, as the show's surgeons start cutting and suctioning and breaking bone only after a previous nose or boob job has gone wrong offscreen. It's like the hunter who hangs back with a lovingly polished gun waiting to put the wounded animals out of their misery.

I've learned something else since I first took stock of reality TV. Illumination need not come to longtime viewers only by the means I described before—witnessed negotiation, microcosmic allegory, competition toward the industry standard—but, longitudinally, by changes of formats over the years. Because reality shows come and go in such fast-moving clusters, of common format or subject matter, and cost so little to produce, they dramatize underlying demographic and economic facts not acknowledged elsewhere on television or in the official outlook of the media. Before the financial crisis of 2008–09, I had watched several years of "house flipping" shows (*Flip This House,* and its rival, *Flip That House*) on which people without much means, or capital, were buying residential properties, sprucing them up slightly, and reselling them after a matter of months for a supposedly significant gain. Whether the properties were bought by other house flippers or by anyone who actually planned to live in them was not revealed. But it seemed clear that "value" for the long haul was not at stake, and the ability to do this flipping, for the protagonists of the shows, escaped all ordinary laws of lending, collateral, commitment to homes or neighborhoods, stability or ordinary variation in housing prices—prices only went up, untethered to real improvements or a need to live where the houses were. What the shows revealed, of course, was the existence of a nationwide housing bubble, inflated by loose rules and massive capital being pushed upon the dreamy and feckless, capital from elsewhere (from foreign manufacturing economies, as it turned out)—an unacknowledged bubble that, when it popped, took down the credit markets and "the economy" with it. When it popped, the shows moved on.

But while it was ongoing, the viewer didn't know what it was. I didn't, at least. But that experience made clear the necessity of trying to think *why* the strange formats of shows might be influenced by inexplicable or invisible social facts rather than, as it were, social or philosophical inquiries. Since the 2008–09 collapse, we've had nearly eight years of shows driven by bidding on abandoned storage lockers and garages, for what treasures might be in them (e.g., *Storage Wars*). I'd already been wondering why so much of the American landscape seems to have been filled up with "self-storage" buildings, at a time when warehouses and factories of all sorts have been abandoned and gone to rust. If the housing shows suggested, in hindsight, an epidemic of careless mortgage origination, the quantity of *new* junk languishing in these storage lockers—the skis, golf clubs, gas grills, televisions, plus assorted "tradeable" junk in the guise of "memorabilia"—made clear the epidemic of credit-card and consumer debt that must have financed the imported junk Americans had been buying. Then they lost a job, couldn't service a mortgage, had to allocate money elsewhere, or skipped town—whatever made them unable to keep up with the monthly payment for the storage locker and indifferent to the sunk cost of the goodies they were not bothering to retrieve.

In 2015, the house-flipping shows are starting up again, now modestly, often with bank-foreclosed properties. But I wonder more about the steady beat of shows of wealthier but still desperate-seeming American or global-English-speaking "consultants," engineers, and accountants, resettling their families in Macau or Dubai or elsewhere in the Gulf States, seeking the right rental for a few years—and we see their gated real-estate choices. What work is this diaspora actually performing? What to make of the vacation-and-retirement-house shows where Americans with one home already—not conspicuously classy, worldly, or patrician—buy a second, or third, on the shore, sometimes even a plane flight away? These shows would be our tea leaves or rabbit entrails for the next shock, if we knew how to read them.

Unquestionably, watching reality TV right now seems to show a United States of people selling one another the last remains of its past, in the form of a vast trade in junk, in which the patrimony is just the chance that something in the attic would be of value to someone else—on the coasts, or abroad—with money. PBS, our only public broadcasting entity and putative disseminator of the best in art, investigative reports, and culture, has basically turned itself into a vehicle in primetime for *Antiques Roadshow,* a cavalcade of preserved garbage masquerading as history lessons. Mostly what I have learned in a decade of happy watching is how much antique guns and furniture are worth. The dark side of *Antiques Roadshow* was A&E's *Hoarders,* a documentary of "pathological" people who piled up possessions in their houses (often dated newspapers, tin cans, glass bottles, "recyclables"), then had them forcibly taken away under the guise of a mental health intervention. This was a show so upsetting it gave several people I know nausea and nightmares (whether from the packed houses or their cruel emptying, I don't know). A more lighthearted recent success is *American Pickers,* in which two jerks from a Los Angeles kitsch emporium drive through the American interior, acquiring beloved junk from the rural poor and elderly shut-ins in Midwestern ghost towns ("I can get two hundred dollars for this bowling shirt in LA—look at the quality of the stitching on this name 'Edna' here"). This is the show for which medical help should be mobilized—people in the interior are not looking well. Meanwhile, the labor economy of reality shows elsewhere has turned to fantasies of ephemeral pinnacles of service work: you have to wonder how many people in America can really become chefs, fashion designers, and high-end cake decorators, rather than depressed people eating refrigerated cookie dough. The only nonfantasy labor exalted on reality TV in these years has been Alaskan, preferably hazardous— *Ice Road Truckers, Deadliest Catch* (commercial fishing, a nearly extinct industry), *Alaskan Bush People*—as if blue-collar labor could be imagined only for backwoods primitives with nesting songbirds peeking out of their beards.

·   ·   ·

Yet the truly new form to arise and seize the center of reality TV (insofar as it can have a center), which my original diagnosis neither encompassed nor predicted, began with the nuclear family, oriented to some celebrity family head—usually outré in some way; say, from the most flamboyant and/or drug-addled realm of stadium rock 'n' roll (as on *The Osbournes,* featuring a seemingly nerve-degenerated Ozzy Osbourne)—in which the focus swiftly shifted to the actually dominant, hold-the-family-together matriarch (on *The Osbournes,* Sharon Osbourne, the ur-type of the new star). A new era opened, more generally, of wives and mothers of wealth or celebrity: *The Real Housewives of —,* for example, visiting various new-wealth settings around the country (Beverly Hills, Atlanta, New York, Orange County) to see what cattiness and envy the wives of entrepreneurs and star athletes would manifest, and how they'd fight each other, when they'd acquired by marriage or inheritance a big pot of money. But the ultimate ruler of this range of shows could not have been anticipated, and constituted a mutation in the genre, itself—a genre that this same family continues to populate, with its amazing fertility. I'm thinking of *Keeping Up with the Kardashians.* The show makes one father absent, or, rather, dead (Robert Kardashian) and another (Bruce Jenner) neutered, at first only symbolically. It is a family born under the sign of plastic surgery. This sense of boundaries crossed—and remade—and becoming unrecognizable, impossible to remember, as ever having been boundaries for transgression, is essential to its glory and its mystery. The question about the Kardashians that first arose for people who didn't feel the enjoyment of reality TV, eons ago, was "Why are these people televised? Did they do anything notable?"

Corresponding to it was the clichéd logical paradox of people who were famous for being famous. The Kardashians take such a cliché, too, beyond all boundaries. For they *really* do nothing, even in an average episode or a week or month. It isn't just not doing anything notable. Their essence is unproductivity, leagued with an utter absence of charisma. Snooki on *Jersey Shore,* in contrast, had proven that certain undiscovered people are purely magnetic, charismatic, mad. "Whom the gods love, get reality shows." Their electric aura draws the camera's eye, whatever small awkward form it mantles. Snooki had this in common with Adolf Hitler. Kardashians, by contrast, are inert and mostly indolent. Unproductivity extends to their failure to produce rants, comic flights of oratory, witticisms, outraged megalomania. Kardashians skip the attractions of the old charismatic nonentities of reality TV. Their utterances are secondhand and flat.

To understand the Kardashians, you must dwell on the feeling they inspire and incarnate. It's possible to watch the Kardashians hour after hour and feel only calm. They are tranquilizing, and seem personally tranquilized. The suggestion of minor sedatives in such terminology is perhaps less germane than the miracle, imaginable as a parable, in which one throws stones into a still pond—*and no ripples issue.* The Kardashians are constantly announcing emotions, fights, complaints, and grievances: yet none of them seem to be felt, exactly, or not in the ordinary way. The nearly meditative pleasure of the show is a cast of seemingly variable individuals who are still hard to tell apart, their nearly identical names hard to remember, all female, all closely related (Kris, Kim, Kourtney, Khloé, Kylie, Kendall—did I miss one? does it matter?), claiming to have significant conflicts with one another about relationships and slights and things uttered and actions taken, while all conflicts seem uninvested with significance, inevitably to be resolved, and unmoving in the resolution ("I just want you to be happy. I care about you. Okay, hugs").

Keeping Up with the Kardashians is the reality success of indifference—taking the term in its widest application. It depicts a world in which the "individual" persists, insofar as each Kardashian evinces some inner narration and subjectivity (proven by how each faces her own camera, in the familiar reality "confessional" format, to record her unique perspective on the action, though using the same shared banal terms and common language), but these individuals are basically the same, hard to tell apart, interchangeable, undifferentiated. Their differences make no difference. This surprising motif of "indifference" goes for actual difference, too, in a social sense—as in the blurring of racial difference in the American context, and the eradication of gender difference in the gynocracy of the show. I'm not a believer in the idea that America is in any meaningful sense yet a "postracial" culture, but I do believe that the Kardashians depict one sort of creation of one.

I have witnessed more than one worldly conversation in which some skeptic—armed with genealogical information from Wikipedia—has tried to claim the Kardashians *should* be "white" (that vile term), only to meet fierce resistance from others. On the show, they clearly look indistinguishably *something,* racially or ethnically, not the nothing that is whiteness. No one knows quite what. Their surname is Armenian, acquired from the absent father. For the names of its clothing boutiques, the family contracts it to "Dash." Surely the easier contraction is *Kash,* and money as a universal solvent of identity. Kris Kardashian, the mother, who started it all, was apparently born Kris Houghton, an American Airlines stewardess from San Diego. She married money in the form of lawyer Robert Kardashian (deceased some years prior to the reality show's premiere). But the fact that the Kardashians can communicate so elegantly the flipped sense that tan is content, and paleness vacuity, without any explicit discussion, is really remarkable. Her daughters' matrimonial alliances have been with African-American athletes or musicians: Kim made her leaked sex tape, so important to the family's early fame, with the rapper Ray J, dated the NFL running back Reggie Bush, married the NBA star Kris Humphries (for ten weeks). Eventually, most amazingly, she married Kanye West, one of the true universal geniuses of our time. His first name, luckily, already started with K. Kim flaunts a booty of rare size, the likes of which is not possessed by waiflike "white" starlets, in our racial coding. And Kardashians, with their propensity for plastic surgery, are altogether in control of their form. The enlarged quasi-African-American lips of the youngest daughter, Kylie—which led to the shortlived online craze of the "Kylie Jenner Lip Challenge," in which children of all ancestries expanded their lips by getting them stuck in soda bottles—turned out to have been surgically enhanced. Khloé married and divorced basketball player Lamar Odom. Kylie, as of this writing, is dating the rapper Tyga.

The triumph over sexual difference, through the exclusive presence of mothers and daughters at the core of the show—with a variable roster of useless, collateral males, who are periodically expelled—may be linked to its "raced" universalism. There was ostensibly a male presence, in second husband and sometime father Bruce Jenner, who had been with the family for years. But he was exiled to the garage, the butt of jokes for most of the show's run. Jenner was a surprising presence, because he had once been a model of *training*—someone who had made his body do the utmost, become a winning Olympian. Now he was a husk, a hollow reed. There was a son, too—impossible to remember his name—who once he ceased to want to appear on the show became an object of pity, as the sisters hinted at depression, or subtle mental illness. The surprising pleasure of a biological family of all women (like a hive with four to six queens) was that it reproduced the competitive surface tensions of *The Real Housewives* and yet no conflict could divide them for long. As in kin-selection theory, any relative sacrifice of one sister ensured the success of her genes through another, and it certainly seemed as if everyone's earnings were going into a common pot. They were Olympic goddesses whose passions issued in no true battles and whose quiescence seemed only to increase their power.

And maybe this was the ultimate fantasia of the Kardashians, and the ultimate pleasure of the show's tranquilizing power: it displays the conceit of an economy in which "doing nothing," or rather the hard work of sitting, choosing a restaurant, sipping cold beverages, traveling in a car, traveling on a plane, dressing and undressing, and mostly just *being* (sedentarily, except when on vacation), and being willing to be watched, is enough. Isn't this what America will do to escape our productionlessness? We will be watched by the world. We'll apply our names to things, our personal brands. Miraculously, our mere American being, all passions spent, will *earn*. This past year, Bruce Jenner played his trump card by becoming the only sort of figure who could wield power in a Kardashian world—a woman. As he had his Adam's apple shaved down and breasts enhanced, he vowed in interviews that, after the completion of his transition, his new name wouldn't begin with K. The joke in her arrival as Caitlyn is that, as we hear it spoken, in the context of Kris, Kim, Khloé, Kourtney, this "Cait" surely does start with a K. It's not pronounced "Saitlin." *I Am Cait* is either the ultimate self-assertion of the vanished patriarchal order, of achievement, contest, whiteness, maleness—the long-ago real Olympian proving he can do what it takes to stay on top, in the driver's seat, even to the point of becoming female—or it is patriarchy's ultimate abdication. Nietzsche told us a century ago about the coming of the Last Men. I don't know if it occurred to him that the Last Men might be Kardashian.

[2015]

WETUBE

"Honey, what's good on YouTube tonight?" The dancing, for starters. I've seen bootie dancing (var. sp. of "booty dancing": belly dancing displaced). I've seen break dancing. I've seen birds dancing (the best-known a sulphur-crested cockatoo high-stepping to the Backstreet Boys). I'm not a particular aficionado of dance; this just happens to be where things lead. You go to America's most popular nonpornographic video-uploading Web site and click through the rat-maze portals meant to guide your itinerary—"Videos being watched right now," "Most popular, featured videos"—and what you see, after hours of what a friend of mine calls "click trance," is endless music and dancing. Six-year-olds dancing to hardstep. Elementary-school children performing incredible sequences to "Dance Dance Revolution" in their living rooms. Then more adults: people dancing at pool parties; dancing at Slip 'n Slide parties; dancing at New Year's Eve parties. Of course I've also seen YouTube's most popular clip, "The Evolution of Dance." This longtime holder of the title has been screened eighty-eight million times, at this writing. I can't personally account for more than ten of those viewings, I'm sure. But I do find my way back to it, often.

The utterly amateur "Evolution of Dance" has been made the single most-viewed clip of all time because it expresses the essence of most of the other fundamentally amateur content on YouTube—it incarnates the deep character of what, at least so far, viewers and especially the uploaders of videos look to YouTube to provide. I'm sure you've seen it already, but let me describe "The Evolution of Dance" for the edification of future generations. The onstage amateur being filmed is a man named Judson Laipply, who bills himself as an inspirational comedian. He is in a setting that can only be described as "talent-show minimal." He stands on a cheap-looking black stage and is filmed from far away, presumably from a seat in the audience on the floor. This is not the simulation of crappy talent-show filming: the most popular YouTube clip of all time *is*, in fact, a crappily made talent video. He has a stool, as comedians do, to one side, and a microphone also to the side. You can hear the laughter and cheers of the crowd throughout the routine along with the tinny musical sound track coming over the room's PA. Judson wears an Orange Crush T-shirt, jeans, and is a white guy with receding hair—perfectly ordinary, to all appearances, at the start. He's in a spotlight that later follows him with a slight nervous or incompetent delay when he dances to the left. Because he *is* about to dance, to do "The Evolution of Dance": what I expected when I first read the title was cavemen to Balanchine, but what transpires—from the beginning strains of a medley of music that runs from Elvis Presley and Chubby Checker to Eminem and Jay-Z—is that with super-elasticity, to every single snippet of these songs, in good synchrony and with a seamlessly choreographed transition from one posture into the next, inspirational comedian Judson, like a mannequin burst into motion, springs into a dance that perfectly fits. The incredible joy of the thing is manifold: first, seeing his Gumby-like ability to do so many different styles, to become anything and anyone; second, the ingenuity and athleticism with which such a kinetic medley was invented by which he would transform himself, recognizably to us, into everyone else; and third, shading into this, the fact of recognition that we just as instantly know each of the songs and each one of the dance moves that goes with it. For the defining feature of the music and its dances is that they cover "evolution" only through a period exactly coterminous with television:

therefore, with dances known from screens like the one we are watching. These are not folk dances. This is not the reel or the quadrille leading to the waltz. We know how to Elvis-dance because of Ed Sullivan, and the unseen pelvis, and all of those movies, from *Jailhouse Rock* to *Blue Hawaii;* we know the twist from crowd footage of that mania. Then when Judson does John Travolta's "I've got a finger in my pocket, I'd better point it" move to the Bee Gees; when he transitions to "Y.M.C.A.," as taught by the Village People on *Solid Gold* and seventies TV, the letters carved with his body, we are seeing dances that we have also converted from television into our own dances at weddings and bar mitzvahs—and when he drops down and does "the worm," it is the same effect; and again when he does "the robot" to Styx ("*Domo arigato,* Mr. Roboto!"); and when he does the "running man," and MC Hammer's "Hammer dance"—to when he definitively enters the last twenty years, getting huge laughs and cheers from the audience because the recognitions become more and more surprising, you see how much of all of our dancing is known to us now only from televised choreography, from music videos, from Michael Jackson's "Thriller," and from the marionette moves of 'N Sync.

There are many great clips on YouTube, but this is the greatest because it perfects the fusion of the two major reference points of YouTube video as it exists right now (perhaps everything will be different in a year): the talent show—the performance and display of individual talents of the most traditional kind—and bits of television pulled from elsewhere, especially that bastard form the music video, the three-minute montage set to a song, which even MTV abandoned in the 1990s. That's not to say that these two things, amateur talents and stolen professional TV, are all there is on YouTube; you could never say "all there is on YouTube," because there is always more. Someone will always be there to say to you the words "dogs pooping," and indeed on plugging that phrase into the search box there will be footage of dogs pooping: on ice, on the sidewalk, in the park. Yet the things one comes to "naturally" on YouTube, by clicking through, are heavily weighted to the following options: dancing, singing, and instrumentals (expert and inexpert), skateboarding, bike tricks, car and motorcycle accidents (caught on tape by traffic cameras), momentary *America's Funniest Home Videos* miscues and bloopers, and, finally, short bits of talking to the camera.

The strangest and most effective genre of clips—the form of video satisfying to the maximum number of people for the minimum amount of effort—may be simply this: footage of absolutely anything whatsoever, silenced and set to a sound track. For example, a car show: engine after chrome engine of open-hooded Mustangs, set to heavy metal. With a tremendous power of darkness, the music sets the mood of these V8s, so you can ignore the daytime—the happy people sitting on lawn chairs at the side, the beach balls, the barbecuing—and fully take in the automotive rock 'n' roll dread.

So, some initial theorems would be: talent = YouTube; talent + music = YouTube; practically anything + music = YouTube. All of the results are interesting and watchable. Yet here is another way to frame the new medium in an equation: Internet video – pornography = YouTube.

YouTube is in some sense created by the primary exclusion of porn. Rigorous and even ruthless policing seems to be what allows the new medium to exist at all. Pornography is a subsidiary genre in most media—the film, the novel, even photography—but somehow the Internet had to be completely saturated with porn, swimming, really, in pornographic videos, before something like YouTube could come to join it. In the very short time since the Internet's invention, Internet video by amateurs has been almost entirely, ubiquitously, of people having sex.

See if you can retrieve, in your noncomputer memory, this image: a small window on the old CRT screen of "amateur" people grainily humping. The first time you waited patiently for the upload and saw such a thing, at the end of the twentieth century, you couldn't have known you were looking at a major new video form. Especially when this crude image at first looked so much like old pornographic nickelodeons and stag films; and where it was confusingly mixed in with professional porn, broadcast through other Web sites. But on the Internet, the amateur, apparently self-produced, self-uploaded form turned out to be the fundamental genre, even when creepy professional exploiters entered to film or disseminate "amateurs" (as the lines blurred) after the huge underground pool of self-exposers was struck like a gusher of oil just beneath decorum's crust.

The classic explanation of porn's success on the Internet was that it furnished a new private medium—solitary, visual, and intimately sized—creating a special opportunity for arousal for those who could use it for a solitary and intimate activity, masturbation. There was an odd kind of isomorphism where, typing and clicking on your keyboard, especially on a laptop, it seemed the object of desire itself was put into your hands (or lap). Nakedness and humping were easy to find, access, hide, and revisit. "Sex" seemed the basic abstraction in all of this. One was viewing "sex." Yet with the amateurs, one begins to see that sex was not the only appeal, otherwise the Internet would have been completely conquered by the professionals. Something else was going on. What YouTube tells us, hit after millionth hit, is that we like watching *amateurs*. We don't necessarily just want to see them standing around, either (the twenty-four-hour nonpornographic webcams like JenniCam seem to have gone out of fashion some years ago). No, we like to see them perform, whatever the performance may be.

Amateur pornography swept the Internet not only because it was the most immediately arousing of instant genres, but because it was the performance par excellence which *requires no talent*. One only needs the willingness to be seen, or shown: one doesn't have to be especially good at humping (though of course in a wide enough selection people will make judgments on the quality of anything, and the comment-and-rating interfaces of some post-your-own porn Web sites allowed viewers to act as judges of every show).

The pornlessness of YouTube, meanwhile, is paradoxically accentuated by its ruses and teases used to lead you off-site, to where real porn exists, just a mouse click away. There seem to be countless triple-X promises made by women (well-covered in underwear) with Web addresses begging you to visit them someplace else; these videos, too, seem to exist only till they're caught, like animals loose in the zoo, and tranquilized and taken down by YouTube's vigilant monitors—professionals tasked with this work of culling, following the allegedly huge citizen-army of

YouTube viewers and deciding what isn't okay (if the *"inappropriate content"* is *"flagged for review"*). People still do search for nudity in this one place where you are guaranteed not to find it—I know I've looked—where even a video labeled "Britney Spears topless photos" does not show Britney Spears "topless" but an endlessly repeated zoom of her bare shoulders and neck. (That one has twenty-three and a half million hits.)

Remove the sex act from self-display and real old-fashioned talents return to the fore—my beloved dancing and singing, for example. But the traditional talents are, I've noticed, now mainly mediated talents: very few people break through on YouTube with songs they have written themselves, but very many garner clicks with performances of famous songs from other people. No one makes it very far with an improvised guitar solo, but there are vast webs of appreciation for people who can play (only their hands and guitar neck showing) a breakdown from Jimi Hendrix or Jimmy Page.

Sadly, the talent which has not yet emerged to my satisfaction is one of my favorites, that of talking. YouTube is full of things called v-logs, or vlogs, short for video logs, but connected in spirit to the early text blogs. They are, by and large, awful. I think they are so bad because they're monologues addressed to an audience which cannot give immediate feedback and force adjustments. Even the low-end talk shows one finds on community access television or college radio have guests and interlocutors to keep things moving, whereas vlogs usually only have a mute and infinitely patient screen-mounted webcam. The highest talent these vloggers could rise to, drawn from the non-Internet world, would seem to be stand-up comedy, and most vlogs are meant to be comic (or ranting, in the manner of talk-show ranters and talk-radio ranters). But good ranting is hard to find performed by people who are utterly alone. Talking on the Web is best when it's done in passion to someone, and taped surreptitiously or by paparazzi (as we know from TMZ.com); talking into a webcam at the top of a home monitor does not bring out the same genius performance principle that even solitary dancing or playing the guitar or stripping does. This, then, is another reason for the preponderance of music on YouTube: like at parties, it substitutes for anyone having to talk.

In fact, the talkers are at their best when they are writing satirical lyrics for the music-video parodies which are one of the newly emerging YouTube genres (professional record-company music videos have found a second life on YouTube anyway). The music already exists, ripe for parody; the three-minute format of a pop song seems to be about the length that can be managed with home editing equipment, and it conveniently matches the attention span of the viewer forced to listen to words. Indeed, the talkiest songs are the ripest for parody, which suggests that there may be ways to rehabilitate talking performance after all.

The biggest mistake you could make about YouTube would be accepting the idea that it allows individuals to make television. Television remains a capital-intensive and employee-intensive medium. It has ceded no ground. The videos on YouTube have very little to do with situation comedy or teleplay drama, and they even have surprisingly little to do with experimental or personal cinema—a form that individuals with less capital have found ways to use in the past. In fact, the single strongest intersection of YouTube with television is when people post things recorded from television. You can see the best soccer goals of the week, and gaffes in interviews, and bits of Japanese, Spanish, and Lebanese television (including Lebanese belly dancing), just as you can find Adorno from German television and assorted intellectuals debating on French talk shows and, indeed, assorted clips from talk shows and sports and game shows all over the world.

This fact points to an immense capability of YouTube: that it could become a comprehensive archive for television, the medium which has never had a publicly accessible archive. People post old commercials and theme songs and scenes from their favorite shows—I have no idea how they already possess them—and, again, musical performances by the great and gone, and we finally have contact with what has been lost and invisible to us except in fugitive memory. (I spent an evening watching ads from my childhood and have once again seen the Honeycomb Cereal commercial where André the Giant appears: memory confirmed; the great and gone revived; plus that catchy jingle!)

If YouTube begins the job of archiving television, it unfortunately also replicates the mistake of television, its memorylessness, by lacking a usable archive of its own content. Items come and go, and though it's possible to see what's *Most Popular Today, Last Week,* and *Last Month,* one cannot go back to a single day or week or month of traffic specifically to see what was popular *then.* So YouTube becomes another of these media without a recorded history—never mind that long-gone historical television clips disappear for copyright reasons as soon as the capital-rich media conglomerates discover them; never mind that there are ever more third-party companies devoted to discovering and rooting out this copyrighted material. And that is why, despite its fathomless reservoir of our talents, foibles, and entertainments, YouTube is not truly ours. YouTube will never be an accurate representation of "us" until it allows us to juxtapose in one space all copyrighted visual specimens made by Hollywood *alongside* a chronological archive of all the singing, satire, accident, and, yes, bootie dancing, done in response to Hollywood—as homage, parody, or substitution—in our millions of amateur bedrooms.

[2008]

An update: I suspect I was wrong about vlogs. Monologues, rants, tearful confessions, bad jokes. . . . I don't really like them, but plenty of people do, and I suspect they're ultimately pretty good. Seven years later, they still remain a blind spot for me. More appealing to me personally has been the previously unimaginable, vast genre of "unboxing" videos: movies made by the purchasers of brand-new power tools, car vacuums, digital cameras, DVD players, etc., for the thrill and education of others considering the same acquisition, to show what happens when you take it home and unbox the Styrofoam, tape, plastic bags, and finally the immaculate new product.

I've come to think that YouTube is curiously unvicarious, as compared to other media: you don't really watch, as you would television or a movie, for experience or pleasure inconceivable or inaccessible to you. The expectation—at least the attitude evinced—is that you, the viewer, will soon do the thing pictured, too, and enjoy the benefits displayed. And somehow you do watch and take possession even when you don't, or won't, ever really own the thing or have the experience. A funny democracy of *instruction* has really come to the fore. Clips will teach you how to disassemble the laptop on which you are watching (to replace components), how to play top hits on guitar, new patterns for a child's Rainbow Loom, how to load bullets in a magazine or film in an antique camera. Anything done with hands will be filmed, in promise that the camera's point of view will become your eyes, and yours the fingers manipulating a screwdriver onscreen. The evolution of "reaction videos," too—these YouTube clips of innumerable individual faces as they watch, for the first time, other YouTube clips which are scary, funny, or endearing—came as a surprising new genre that instantly seemed obvious. The "virality" but localism of YouTube, its small-scale feeling and nonvicariousness, *would* mean that any video you enjoyed must also be seen being enjoyed by others—after it is imaginatively understood, somehow, that you've already pressed the clip on every one of your family and friends. It emerges that the feeling of broadcast doesn't need a very big audience, or doesn't effectively distinguish between big and small audiences—between ten viewers, and ten thousand—to accomplish its same feeling of publicity, especially when reception can be shifted over time as you leave a posted video "up." One month later you have one hundred viewers, one year later either a hundred and one or those full ten thousand. Other people will eventually "find things," find everything, either through search terms or wandering byways of links through what others have looked at.

The problem for generalization is that I therefore don't really know how others use YouTube, except when I happen to encounter, in life, friends or family looking at some completely unfamiliar category of video, which they take as their norm, evincing surprise at my watching habits—as does frequently happen. "My" view of YouTube gets taken for the medium itself, but the way in which YouTube is always showing you previously unimagined uses casts doubt on the whole method of criticism, taking your individual experience as representative. I was amazed, for example, to find YouTube becoming, for me, chiefly a vehicle for music—music only, I mean, in audio form, and not footage of musicians. I fell for a while into the world of people who post videos of "needle drops," or complete plays of different rare jazz and rock LPs, singles, even 78s. The video is usually a stationary shot of the record sleeve, propped up on a stand, or the interior label, and occasionally of the vinyl record actually revolving. The wittiest collector was a Japanese "whole album" demigod who was posting rare Blue Note vinyl LPs accompanying a static shot of a kind of grandiose phonograph shrine he'd built, in which only his sleeping bulldog, at bottom left, breathed and moved as the instruments played. But I don't think using YouTube almost exclusively as a music service is the norm—is it?

Here, though, as I suspect in lots of other subworlds I don't see, the owners of YouTube kept intervening to erase things. Uploads of popular songs, variously sourced and recorded, somehow redirected searchers to the new, slick corporate universe of Vevo, a moneyed "music service" run by the studios and dense with compulsory advertisements. Supposedly YouTube possesses a music-matching service that recognizes and blocks uploads of songs that have already been eradicated at the behest of music studios.

Meanwhile, "The Evolution of Dance" was dethroned as the most-watched video of all time. Initially, I think, by another vernacular marvel, "Charlie Bit My Finger." Then, however, by one or another official major-label music video, and the most-viewed list has belonged to professional jobs from the studios ever since.

The reason does not seem to be that WeTube has lost interest in the We, but that YouTube has increasingly disclosed its true possession by the They. Each year it further consolidates its will to make money from advertising and do the bidding of conglomerates at its own level. Google bought the site in 2006, and has relied on the shortness of memory, and our inability to protest anyway, to make YouTube each year a little bit worse. And possibly nothing has changed YouTube in seven years as importantly as the ads. Unlike television, to which commercials were indigenous—the skunks, mosquitos, and snakes of that particular media ecology—the compulsory commercials preceding YouTube videos now, and now interrupting at intervals the replay of long recordings, are invasive species, purely extraneous and insulting.

So vandalism has come to be the flip side of this extraordinary Taj Mahal, or vast, architecturally promiscuous city, made by users—YouTube's, the organizer's, vandalism of what we have created. Treasured things keep disappearing even as new ones appear. Whenever a controversial or newsworthy clip is heard to be posted—as witnesses and "citizen journalists" put up footage from their camera phones, and its presence even makes it into the front-page recounting of the news, precisely the kind of thing a collective repository should exist to keep and share—one's immediate question is: "Is it still up?" Which asks, has the They gotten to it yet and removed it? The They are always disappearing things. Who knows why: taste, corporate request, government preference? Or just because of the gray Theyness of Them?

In that sense, in addition to everything that makes the site ever more frustrating, and all the things kidnapped in the night, YouTube keeps giving one piece of news that, though never novel, does stay news: what They think of us, and how we should feel about Them.

[2015]

WHAT WAS THE HIPSTER?

If I speak of the degeneration of our most visible recent subculture, the hipster, it's an awkward occasion. Someone will point out that hipsters are not dead, they still breathe, they live on my block. Yet it is evident that we have reached the end of an epoch in the life of the type. Its evolution lasted from 1999 to 2009, though it has shifted appearance dramatically over the decade. It survived this year; it may persist. Indications are everywhere, however, that we have come to a moment of stocktaking.

Novelty books on the order of *Stuff Hipsters Hate* and *Look at This Fucking Hipster* began appearing again this year, reliving the hipster's previous near-death in 2003 (titles then: *A Field Guide to the Urban Hipster; The Hipster Handbook*). Institutions associated with the hipster label have begun fleeing it. Dov Charney, CEO of American Apparel, announced in August that "hipster is over" and "hipsters are from a certain time period." Gawker proposed to substitute a new name for the hipster by fiat—approving, after some consideration, the term "fauxhemian."

Elsewhere—and especially in Europe—the deathbed scene looks more like an apotheosis. One German paper rounded up that country's most recent reports of hipster emergence: "The current issue of the magazine *Neon* sees them at a club in Moscow, the *Berlin Tagesspiegel* spotted them yet again this week in the bars on Oranienstraße, *Taz* reported that in the 'US hipster scene' it's cool to dress like Indians, the *Neue Zürcher Zeitung* knows that in Stockholm they are drawn to the district of Södermalm, *Geo Saison* had drinks with them at a bar in Prague, *Die Welt* found them in Australia from Sydney to Brisbane, the Sunday *Frankfurter Allgemeine Zeitung* knows the Parisian 'Hipster-labels,' and the weekend edition of the *Süddeutsche Zeitung* commented recently that 'big-city hipsters' are now decorating their apartments with taxidermy." The hipster has been reborn, too, in the American shopping mall, where Hot Topic sells thick-framed lensless eyeglasses to tweens and Nine West sells a "Hipster" sandal.

A key myth repeated about the hipster, by both the innocent and the underhanded, is that the word has no definition. In August, after noting that *The New York Times* had printed "hipster" as a noun or an adjective more than 250 times in the previous year, Philip Corbett, the paper's grammarian, wrote an open letter to the newsroom warning against its use. He certainly could have objected that it made for lazy headline copy, or that a derogatory term was being misused as praise. Instead, he objected that it wasn't clear enough what the word means.

We do know what "hipster" means—or at least we should. The term has always possessed adequately lucid definitions; they just happen to be multiple. If we refuse to enunciate them, it may be because everyone affiliated with the term has a stake in keeping it murky. Hipster accusation has been, for a decade, the outflanking maneuver par excellence for competitors within a common field of cool. "Two Hipsters Angrily Call Each Other 'Hipster,'" a headline in *The Onion* put it most succinctly.

The longer we go without an attempt to explain the term simply and clearly, the longer we are at the mercy of its underlying magic. In the interest of disenchantment, let me trace a history and offer some definitions. If we see the hipsters plain, maybe we'll also see where they might come undone.

·   ·   ·

When we talk about the contemporary hipster, we're talking about a subcultural figure who emerged by 1999, enjoyed a narrow but robust first phase until 2003, and then seemed about to dissipate into the primordial subcultural soup, only to undergo a reorganization and creeping spread from 2004 to the present.

The matrix from which the hipster emerged included the dimension of nineties youth culture, often called alternative or indie, that defined itself by its rejection of consumerism. Yet in an ethnography of Wicker Park, Chicago, in the nineties, the sociologist Richard Lloyd documented how what he called "neo-bohemia" unwittingly turned into something else: the seedbed for post-1999 hipsterism. Lloyd showed how a culture of aspiring artists who worked day jobs in bars and coffee shops could unintentionally provide a milieu for new, late-capitalist commerce in design, marketing, and Web development. The neo-bohemian neighborhoods, near to the explosion of new wealth in city financial centers, became amusement districts for a new class of rich young people. The indie bohemians (denigrated as slackers) encountered the flannel-clad proto-businessmen and dot-com paper millionaires (denigrated as yuppies), and something unanticipated came of this friction.

The Lower East Side and Williamsburg in New York, Capitol Hill in Seattle, Silver Lake in LA, the Inner Mission in San Francisco: this is where the contemporary hipster first flourished. Over the years, there developed such a thing as a hipster style and range of art and finally, by extension, something like a characteristic attitude and weltanschauung. Fundamentally, however, the hipster continues to be defined by the same tension faced by those early colonizers of Wicker Park. The hipster is that person, overlapping with the intentional dropout or the unintentionally declassed individual—the neo-bohemian, the vegan or bicyclist or skate punk, the would-be blue-collar or postracial twenty-something, the starving artist or graduate student—who in fact aligns himself both with rebel subculture and with the dominant class, and thus opens up a poisonous conduit between the two.

The question arises: What was it about the turn-of-the-century moment that made it so clear—as it was immediately clear—that the character had to have this name, the hipster, which was so fraught with historical meaning? Subculture has never had a problem with neologism or exploitation of slang, from emo to punk to hippie. The hipster, however, was someone else already. Specifically, he was a black subcultural figure of the late forties, best anatomized by Anatole Broyard in an essay for the *Partisan Review* called "A Portrait of the Hipster." A decade later, the hipster had evolved into a white subcultural figure. This hipster—and the reference here is to Norman Mailer's essay "The White Negro" for *Dissent* in 1957—was explicitly defined by the desire of a white avant-garde to disaffiliate itself from whiteness, with its stain of Eisenhower, the bomb, and the corporation, and achieve the "cool" knowledge and exoticized energy, lust, and violence of black Americans. ("Hippie" itself was originally an insulting diminutive of "hipster," a jab at the sloppy kids who hung around North Beach or Greenwich Village after 1960 and didn't care about jazz or poetry, only drugs and fun.)

The hipster, in both black and white incarnations, in his essence had been about superior knowledge—what Broyard called "a priorism." He insisted that hipsterism was developed from a sense that minorities in America were subject to decisions made about their lives by conspiracies of power they could never possibly know. The hip reaction was to insist, purely symbolically, on forms of knowledge that they possessed before anyone else, indeed before the creation of positive knowledge—a priori. Broyard focused on the password language of hip slang.

The return of the term after 1999 reframed the knowledge question. "Hipster," in its revival, referred to an air of knowing about exclusive things before anyone else. The new young strangers acted, as people said then, "hipper than thou." At first their look may also have overlapped enough with a short-lived moment of neo-Beat and fifties nostalgia (goatees, fedoras, *Swingers*-style duds) to help call up the term. But these hipsters were white, and singularly unmoved by race and racial integration.

Indeed, the White Hipster—the style that suddenly emerged in 1999—inverted Broyard's model to particularly unpleasant effect. Let me recall a string of keywords: trucker hats; undershirts called "wife beaters," worn alone; the aesthetic of basement-rec-room pornography, flash-lit Polaroids and fake-wood paneling; Pabst Blue Ribbon; "porno" or "pedophile" mustaches; aviator glasses; Americana T-shirts from church socials and pig roasts; tube socks; the late albums of Johnny Cash; tattoos.

Key institutions were the fashion magazine *Vice,* which moved to New York from Montreal in 1999 and drew on casual racism and porn to refresh traditional women's-magazine features ("It Happened," "Dos and Don'ts") and overcome the stigma of boys looking at photos of clothes; Alife, the hipster-branding consultancy–cum–sneaker store, also launched in 1999, staffed by employees who claimed a rebel background in punk/skateboarding/graffiti to justify why they were now in retail sportswear; and American Apparel, which launched in LA in 1997 as an antisweatshop T-shirt manufacturer and gradually changed its advertising focus from progressive labor practices to amateur soft-core porn.

These were the most visible emblems of a small and surprising subculture, where the source of a priori knowledge seemed to be nostalgia for suburban whiteness. As the White Negro had once fetishized blackness, the White Hipster fetishized the violence, instinctiveness, and rebelliousness of lower-middle-class "white trash." "I love being white, and I think it's something to be proud of," *Vice* founder Gavin McInnes told *The New York Times* in 2003.

This recalled the seventies culture of white flight to the suburbs, and the most uncanny thing about the turn-of-the-millennium hipsters is that symbolically, in their styles and attitudes, they seemed to announce that whiteness and capital were flowing back into the formerly impoverished city. They wore what they were in economic and structural terms—because for reasons mysterious to the participants, those things suddenly seemed "cool" for an urban setting.

The early White Hipster aped the "unmeltable ethnics" (Irish, Italian, Polish, and so forth), but now with the ethnicities scrubbed off. And rather than an indie or bohemian subculture, it felt like an ethnicity—with its clannishness, its claiming of microneighborhoods from other, older migrants (Chinese, Puerto Ricans, Orthodox Jews), and its total uninterest in integrating into the local populations.

.   .   .

It would be too limited, however, to understand the contemporary hipster as simply someone concerned with a priori knowledge as a means of social dominance. In larger manifestations, in private as well as on the street, contemporary hipsterism has been defined by an obsessive interest in the conflict between knowingness and naiveté, guilty self-awareness and absolved self-absorption. Consider hipster art. At the same time that hipsters were dressing like seventies-model Stanley Kowalskis, they were consuming culture that was considerably more anxious about machismo, heterosexuality, and maturity.

The most exemplary hipster artists are probably the early Dave Eggers, of *A Heartbreaking Work of Staggering Genius* (2000) and his journal *McSweeney's* (1998), and Wes Anderson, director of *Rushmore* (1998) and *The Royal Tenenbaums* (2001). These and other artists who were referred to as hipster produced a body of work that was otherwise classed more precisely as "precious" or "twee." The older Scottish band Belle and Sebastian, not a part of this system at their own genesis, stood at the head of a new soft-spoken, often anti-homophobic aesthetic in music. (Eggers tried to claim the older Flaming Lips as allies. Bright Eyes, Sufjan Stevens, and Joanna Newsom were later manifestations.)

The tensions of this art revolved around the very old dyad of adulthood and a child-centered world, but landed heavily on the side of the child. Formally, there was an aestheticization of the mode of pastiche, which Fredric Jameson identified in the early eighties as a characteristic mode of postmodern narrative. Here, however, "blank parody" gave way to a reconstruction of past techniques more perfect than the originals, in an irony without sarcasm, bitterness, or critique. Reflexivity was used as a means to get back to sentimental emotion.

In the nineties, it had become commonplace to assume that one could no longer say heartfelt, sincere things outright, because all genuine utterance would be stolen and repeated as advertising. Whatever anguish this caused seemed gone in the artifacts of the early aughts. The ironic games were weightless. The emotional expressions suggested therapy culture, but hipster art often kitschified—or at least made playful—the weightiest tragedies, whether personal or historical: orphans and cancer for Eggers, the Holocaust and 9/11 for Jonathan Safran Foer. By 2003, though, an overwhelming feeling of an end to hipsterism permeated the subculture. It seems possible that the White Hipster was born in part as a reaction to the 1999 WTO protests in Seattle—the emboldened anticapitalism that was the signal youth rebellion of the century's end. But 2003 spelled the beginning of the Iraq invasion, and a pivot in the national mood from post-9/11 mourning to patriotic aggression and violence. The wife-beater wearer's machismo no longer felt subversive, and while the more sinister strain of White Hipster style started to diminish, the artistic concern with innocence turned from human absolution to the fragile world of furry creatures, trees, and TRS-80s.

Suddenly, the hipster transformed. Most succinctly—though this is too simple—it began to seem that a "green" hipster had succeeded the white. Certainly the points of reference shifted from Midwestern suburbs to animals, wilderness, plus the occasional Native American. Best perhaps to call this the Hipster Primitive, for linked to the Edenic nature-as-playground motif was a fascination with early-eighties computer electronics and other rudimentary or superannuated technologies.

In culture, the Hipster Primitive moment recovered the sound and symbols of pastoral innocence with an irony so fused into the artworks it was no longer visible. Music led the artistry of this phase, and the period's flagship publication, the record-review Web site and tastemaker Pitchfork, picked up as *Vice* declined. Here are the names of some significant bands, post-2004: Grizzly Bear, Neon Indian, Deerhunter, Fleet Foxes, Department of Eagles, Wolf Parade, Band of Horses, and, most centrally, Animal Collective. (On the electronic-primitive side, LCD Soundsystem.) Listeners heard animal sounds and lovely Beach Boys–style harmonies; lyrics and videos pointed to rural redoubts, on wild beaches and in forests; life transpired in some more loving, spacious, and manageable future, possibly of a Day-Glo or hallucinatory brightness. It was not unheard of to find band members wearing masks or plush animal suits.

Where the White Hipster was relentlessly male, crowding out women from public view (except as Polaroid muses or Suicide Girls), the Hipster Primitive feminized hipster markers; one spoke now of headdresses and Sally Jessy Raphael glasses, not just male facial hair. Women took up cowboy boots, then dark-green rubber Wellingtons, like country squiresses off to visit the stables. Men gave up the porno mustache for the hermit or lumberjack beard. Flannel returned, as did hunting jackets in red-and-black check. Scarves proliferated unnecessarily, conjuring a cold woodland night (if wool) or a desert encampment (if a kaffiyeh). Then scarves were worn as bandannas, as when Mary-Kate Olsen sported one, like a cannibal Pocahontas, hungry enough to eat your arm.

There were also some practical technological withdrawals. As CDs declined, LP records gained sales for the first time in two decades—seemingly purchased by the same kids who had three thousand songs on their laptops. The most advanced hipster youth even deprived their bikes of gears. The fixed-gear bike now ranks as the second-most-visible urban marker of hip, and not the least of its satisfactions is its simple mechanism.

Above all, the post-2004 hipster could be identified by one stylistic marker that transcended fashion to be something as fundamental as a cultural password: jeans that were tight to the calves and ankles. As much as I've investigated this, I can't say I understand the origin of the skinny jean. Why, of many candidates for fashion statements, did it become ubiquitous? All that seems obvious is that it was an opportunity to repudiate the White Hipster moment, while still retaining the farthest possible distinction from the mainstream. The skinny jean was instant and utter inversion, attaining the opposite extreme from the boot-cut flared motorcycle jeans of the White Hipster. It proved the vitality of a hipster community. It meant that the group impulse would hold, no matter how vertiginous the changes.

Through both phases of the contemporary hipster, and no matter where he identifies himself on the knowingness spectrum, there exists a common element essential to his identity, and that is his relationship to consumption. The hipster, in this framework, is continuous with a cultural type identified in the nineties by the social critic Thomas Frank, who traced it back to Madison Avenue's absorption of a countercultural ethos in the late sixties. This type he called the "rebel consumer."

The rebel consumer is the person who, adopting the rhetoric but not the politics of the counterculture, convinces himself that buying the right mass products individualizes him as transgressive. Purchasing the products of authority is thus reimagined as a defiance of authority. Usually this requires a fantasized censor who doesn't want you to have cologne, or booze, or cars. But the censor doesn't exist, of course, and hipster culture is not a counterculture. On the contrary, the neighborhood organization of hipsters—their tight-knit colonies of similar-looking, slouching people—represents not hostility to authority (as among punks or hippies) but a superior community of status where the game of knowing-in-advance can be played with maximum refinement. The hipster is a savant at picking up the tiny changes of rapidly cycling consumer distinction.

This in-group competition, more than anything else, is why the term "hipster" is primarily a pejorative—an insult that belongs to the family of "poseur," "faker," "phony," "scenester," and "hangeron." The challenge does not clarify whether the challenger rejects values in common with the hipster—of style, savoir vivre, cool, etc. It just asserts that its target adopts them with the wrong motives. He does not earn them.

It has long been noticed that the majority of people who frequent any traditional bohemia are hangers-on. Somewhere, at the center, will be a very small number of hardworking writers, artists, or politicos, from whom the hangers-on draw their feelings of authenticity. Hipsterdom at its darkest, however, is something like bohemia without the revolutionary core. Among hipsters, the skills of hanging on—trend spotting, cool hunting, plus handicraft skills—become the heroic practice. The most active participants sell something—customized brand-name jeans, airbrushed skateboards, the most special whiskey, the most retro sunglasses—and the more passive just buy it.

Of course, there are artists of hipster-related sensibility who remain artists. In the neighborhoods, though, there was a feeling throughout the last decade that the traditional arts were of little interest to hipsters because their consumer culture substituted a range of narcissistic handicrafts similar enough to sterilize the originals. One could say, exaggerating only slightly, that the hipster moment did not produce any artists but tattoo artists, who gained an entire generation's arms, sternums, napes, ankles, and lower backs as their canvas. It did not produce photographers, but snapshot and party photographers: LastNightsParty, Terry Richardson, the Cobra Snake. It did not produce painters, but graphic designers. It did not yield a great literature, but it made good use of fonts. And hipsterism did not make an avant-garde; it made communities of early adopters.

The most confounding element of the hipster is that, because of the geography of the gentrified city and the demography of youth, this "rebel consumer" hipster culture shares space and frequently steals motifs from truly anti-authoritarian youth countercultures. Thus, baby boomers and preteens tend to look at everyone between them and say: "Isn't this hipsterism just youth culture?" To which folks age nineteen to twenty-nine protest, "No, these people are worse." But there is something in this confusion that suggests a window into the hipster's possible mortality.

True countercultures may wax and wane in numbers, but a level of youth hostility to the American official compromise has been continuous since World War II. Over the past decade, hipsters have mixed with particular elements of anarchist, free, vegan, environmentalist, punk, and even anticapitalist communities. One glimpses behind them the bike messengers, straight-edge skaters, Lesbian Avengers, freegans, enviro-anarchists, and interracial hip-hoppers who live as they please, with a spiritual middle finger always raised.

And hipster motifs and styles, when you dig into them, are often directly taken from these adjacent countercultures. The fixed-gear bike came from bike messengers and the anarchist culture of groups like Critical Mass and Bikes Not Bombs. Hipster approval of locavore food (because local cheeses and grass-fed beef are expensive, rare, and knowledge-intensive) brings elitism to the left-environmentalist campaign for deindustrialized agriculture. Even those trucker hats were familiar to those of us who first saw them on the wrong heads in 1999; they'd been worn in punk rock in the late eighties and early nineties, through the Reagan-Bush recession, as an emblem of the "age of diminished expectations."

Can the hipster, by virtue of proximity if nothing else, be woken up? One can't expect political efflorescence from an antipolitical group. Yet the mainstreaming of hipsterism to the suburbs and the mall portends hipster self-disgust. (Why bother with a lifestyle that everyone now knows?) More important, it guarantees the pollination of a vast audience with seeds stolen from the counterculture. Granted, they have been husked of significance—but couldn't a twelve-year-old with deep Google skills figure out what they originally meant? And might they still germinate?

Something was already occurring in the revivification that transpired in 2003. The White Hipster was truly grotesque, whereas within the Hipster Primitive there emerged a glimmer of an idea of refusal. In the United Kingdom, American-patterned hipsters in Hackney and Shoreditch are said to be turning more toward an ethos of androgyny, drag, the queer. In recent hipster art, Animal Collective's best-known lyric is this: "I don't mean to seem like I / Care about material things, like our social stats / I just want four walls and / Adobe slats for my girls." The band members masked their faces to avoid showing themselves to the culture of idolators. If a hundred thousand Americans discovered that they, too, hated the compromised culture, they might not look entirely unlike the Hipster Primitive. Just no longer hip.

[2010]

VI

ANAESTHETIC IDEOLOGY

A year ago, I wrote an essay about a modern crisis in experience. I defined experience as the habit of creating isolated moments within raw occurrence in order to save and recount them. Questing after an ill-defined happiness, you are led to substitute a list of special experiences and then to collect them to furnish your storeroom of memories: incidents of sex, drinking, travel, adventure. These experiences are limited in number, unreliable, and addictive. Their ultimate effect can be a life of permanent dissatisfaction and a compulsion to frenetic activity.

Since then, I've felt I paid too little attention to a phenomenon which is the opposite: the desperate wish for anti-experience. The connection between the quest for experience and the wish for anti-experience isn't chronological. You don't wake up the morning after some final orgy of experience and discover that you can't stand any more. It seems to be, instead, arbitrary and eruptive. You reach points in life at which you can no longer live like other people, though you don't want to die. Experience becomes piercing, grating, intrusive. It is no longer out of reach, an occasional throb in the dark. It is no longer a prize, though it is the goal everyone else seeks. It is a scourge. All you wish for is some means to reduce the feeling.

This *anaesthetic* reaction, I begin to think, must be associated with the stimulations of another modern novelty, the total aesthetic environment. For those people to whom a need to reduce experience occurs, part of their discomfort seems to be strongly associated with aesthetic intrusions from fictional or political drama—from the television, the newscast, the newspaper, the computer headlines, or any of the other unavoidable screens of pixels or paper. "I just had to turn the TV off. I couldn't stand it anymore." This is the plea we accept, more or less, as we mirror the strange look on the sufferer's face with an odd look of our own. We will accept it this far and no farther, because much more of the suffering comes from us—the "normal" others—who obnoxiously recount our daily lives, too, as a series of rare adventures. The anti-experiencers will want to turn the TV off; then they'll want to turn us off. There comes a point at which they will want to turn the sights and sounds of life off—if life becomes a nightmare of aestheticized, drama-tized events.

The hallmark of the conversion to anti-experience is a lowered threshold for eventfulness. You perceive each outside drama as your experience, which you could not withstand if it really were yours. It leads to forms of total vulnerability, as if the individual had been peeled or deprived of barriers. I don't know what word can connect the three levels of unavoidable strong experience, broadcast and recounted and personal, except the omnipresence of *drama*.

I also don't know why the nightmare comes for some people and not others, at some times and not others. After considering it, it surprises me that this breach, the fall into painful overexperience, isn't more com-mon. Why of a hundred seekers of experience and dwellers in the total aesthetic environment do only two, or ten, turn? Unless there are fea-tures of the aesthetic environment which are themselves also anaesthetic and that manage to regulate the experiential lives of the majority, to keep them from cracking.

Suppose you have reached that point. You no longer feel you are among those whom William James called the "healthy-minded." You can tell because you watch the healthy ones gaping with laughter at vio-lent movies or sitting calmly across from you at the table, over dinner, recounting from that day's news a sex scandal, an airplane crash, an accidental shooting. You hear from the healthy-minded the battles *they* have fought that day and the experiences they have won. You detect them questing after the things they desire, talking about them with natural spirit, nourished by hope and aggression like their natural milk. They are nature's creatures, in the full grace of modernity. The sad truth is that you still want to live in their world. It just somehow seems this world has changed to exile you.

In that previous essay, I spoke of solutions to a first crisis, the endless quest for experience, in practices that redeem experience by expanding it: aestheticism and perfectionism.* The solutions to this second crisis in experience, the wish for anti-experience—both from tradition and in the present—are the *anaesthetic ideologies.* They diminish experience's reach. They "redeem" experience by weakening or abolishing it. They are, in a sense, aestheticism's and perfectionism's inverse.

Anaesthetic ideologies are methods of philosophy and practice that try to stop you from feeling. Or they help you to reduce what you feel. Or they let you keep living, when you can no longer live, by learning partially how to "die." I preserve the word "ideologies" because of the methods' potential duplicity—and also because of our perhaps justified suspicion that such undertakings are, at some level, inhuman.

The gallery of heads in the West, marble smooth, marble eyed, begins near the entrance with Plato and Aristotle. Plato put a megaphone to the mouth of Socrates. Thus we learned of the Forms, the permanence of Justice, and the objectivity of the Good. Aristotle held the dissecting tool to nature and the yardstick to man, systematizing all the forms of

---

* Aestheticism and perfectionism work by putting experience under the control of the active individual, teaching him to make rare experience *always* and from *anything.* Aestheticism teaches its practitioners to find rarity or beauty in any object or event; perfectionism finds moral reflections upon the observer in the same sources. They turn even banal or ugly things into objects of singular aesthetic interest or into moral examples that would encourage the constant transformation and appreciation of the self, thus exploding the *quest* for experience by putting it always at hand.

matter and the forms of life. We learned man is a political being whose good lies in the fulfillment of his potential. Plato led to Aristotle as the only alternative to himself, and the two of them together gave us Western philosophy as a line of action and actualization.

In the ancient world, though, rival traditions competed with theirs. These philosophies did not lead toward our modernity, defined by the quest for experience. They created traditions of nonstimulation, nonsusceptibility, nonexcitement, nonbecoming, nonambition; also antifeeling, *anaesthesia*. Thus at the *origins* of philosophy, thoughts were devoted to the restriction of experience. These traditions were at least as central to the concerns of the West, once upon a time, as were the lines we have received as active common sense and normalcy. They can help us at least as much today as the "Eastern philosophies" that have been for many moderns the only, marginal way to attain some distance from one-sided Western ambition.

The students who followed the example of Socrates did not all join Plato's Academy. (My account of Socratic successors draws on the writings of A. A. Long, the great scholar of Hellenistic philosophy.) One of the earliest, Diogenes of Sinope, called Diogenes the Cynic, led a beggar's life, upheld the example of Socrates's insulting speech, and taught Socratic freedom from "property, fine appearance, social status," while preaching, unlike Socrates, nonallegiance to any city. Philosophy for him was the use of reason for each individual to talk himself out of the material needs that everyone else claimed, and thus to be free of the fears to which everyone else was subject. This freedom from conventional need and this freedom from fear—even when they meant a refusal of the world—came to be combined with the philosophical hedonism of Aristippus of Cyrene, one of Socrates's direct pupils. Cyrenaic hedonism said that pleasure and pain are prior to all other motivations, and *should* be, too. These views made a different founding to philosophy than the one mediated by Plato.

In moods of peaceful hopefulness, I think that Epicurus, a genius of the next Greek generation, should be our perfect philosopher now, for America. He was a hedonist, as we are today. But he would have freed us from the pain of our search for experience, our mistaking of the most valuable pleasures for the rarest and hardest to attain. He came to maturity while Aristotle was still alive, and began teaching a very different doctrine: that pleasure is the goal of life, but pleasure defined as the end and absence of pain. "For we are in need of pleasure only when we are in pain because of the absence of pleasure, and when we are not in pain, then we no longer need pleasure." The Epicurean ideal was *ataraxia,* imperturbability and mental detachment. This imperturbability couldn't be accomplished through avoidance—pain would come whether you wanted it or not—but only through the right way of thinking about all unavoidable experience.

Unsought pleasures, whatever they were—a lavish banquet, a night of erotic love—were never bad in themselves. The difficulty with most positive pleasures, however, was that "the things which produce certain pleasures bring troubles many times greater than the pleasures." Luxuries of experience involved you in uncertainties and pains—whether you would ever have them again, or whether you could sustain them. If pain is more to be avoided than positive pleasures are to be sought, it is "the freedom of the soul from disturbance" that is "the goal of a blessed life."

> Everything natural is easy to obtain and whatever is groundless is hard to obtain. . . . Simple flavours provide a pleasure equal to that of an extravagant life-style when all pain from want is removed. . . . So when we say that pleasure is the goal we do not mean the pleasures of the profligate or the pleasures of consumption, as some believe, either from ignorance and disagreement or from deliberate misinterpretation, but rather the lack of pain in the body and disturbance in the soul.

"For we [Epicureans]," the founder wrote, "do everything for the sake of being neither in pain nor in terror." Epicurus, on the outskirts of Athens, began the Garden, where his friends and followers "included household servants and women on equal terms with the men," as the scholar D. S. Hutchinson has noted—arrangements inconceivable to the rest of Athenian society. There they lived in peace and tranquility. They took their pleasure from a little wine mixed with water, and if you ever wanted Epicurus to enjoy an extravagance, he said, you could send him a little pot of cheese. Friendship mattered. Friends reminded one another that true happiness was freedom from fear, that death was meaningless and pain tolerable. They sought to help one another to resist being touched by any disturbance, to win a gentle victory over strong experience.

In more tempestuous or harsher moods, my thoughts for the hidden sufferers in America go over to the tougher anaesthetic of the late Roman Stoics. The Stoa existed in Epicurus's time as a place of conversation and teaching in Athens, like the Academy, the Garden, and Aristotle's Lyceum; but Stoicism seems to have come into its most emphatic and lasting form many generations afterward. If you want a simple program and definitive dogma, you look to Epictetus. He is a much later figure than his Greek predecessors, and much better documented. The violence of Epictetus's rhetoric can be tonic. Really, we will eradicate experience, not just learn to be happy with barley cakes and watered wine. Then we can withstand anything, the richest luxuries or the heaviest blows.

The Stoic system is not so different from Epicureanism in its methods of controlling needs. It disposes of the feeling for pleasure, however, as a root for the mind's disciplining of experience. Epictetian Stoicism tells you to divide the world into what is up to you and what is not up to you. All that is left for a person to do, then, is to master his desire and aversion—so that he will never have either desire for or aversion to anything not up to him. He must never desire what he cannot control—not honors, not events, not other people's thoughts, behavior, or reactions, not all the good experiences of his body. And he must have no mental aversion to anything that comes to him without his choice, like illness, death, or the bad experiences of his body. He can groan in illness, but he must not care about it. The fates of things are up to nature, not to you.

> In the case of everything that delights the mind, or is useful, or is
> loved with fond affection, remember to tell yourself what sort of

thing it is, beginning with the least of things. If you are fond of a jug, say, "It is a jug that I am fond of"; then, if it is broken, you will not be disturbed. If you kiss your child, or your wife, say to yourself that it is a human being that you are kissing; and then you will not be disturbed if either of them dies.

Life, Epictetus intimates at one point, is like a tourist visit to Olympia; you go because, well, who doesn't go? But it's bound to be incredibly annoying. "Do you not suffer from the heat? Are you not short of space? Do you not have trouble washing? . . . Do you not get your share of shouting and uproar and other irritations?" You will shrug it all off. "What concern to me is anything that happens, when I have greatness of soul?"

The only thing the Stoic should invest *any* emotion in is his own choice, which determines that "greatness of soul." He will feel pride when he remains absolute master of his choice and of his desire and aversion. He feels displeasure when he fails temporarily to be master of himself. Stoic reason makes a man absolute master of his judgments and eradicates everything that is bad while clarifying the only thing that is truly good: the right use of choice.

It is the denial of any meaning to immediate experience, apart from the judgment one places upon it, that is truly anaesthetic—a will to control one's judgments and minimize their effects, to make experiences not matter except for the inner experience of mastering experiences. The Stoic ideal was *apatheia,* release from passion and feeling, but it freed itself from everyone else's cares precisely in order to be able carelessly to do what everyone else did. It became supermilitant, because it continued to live in the world while denying it. "Practice, then," Epictetus teaches, "from the start, to say to every harsh impression, 'You are an impression, and not at all the thing you appear to be.'"

This meant not only not giving credence to impressions, but, in a sense, never aestheticizing them, never enjoying them as more than accidental facts or conjunctures, never investing them with any aura beyond their material constitution and fate, never giving them a place in a drama to be remembered or dwelt upon emotionally. Hence the hostility of Epictetus to the tragic drama and the epic of strong feelings. What sort of person complains and lets passion and experience get the better of him, saying, "Woe is me"?

> Do you suppose I will mention to you some mean and despicable person? Does not Priam say such things [in the *Iliad*]? Does not Oedipus? . . . For what else is tragedy but a portrayal in tragic verse of the sufferings of men who have devoted their admiration to external things? . . . If one had to be taught by fictions, I, for my part, should wish for such a fiction as would enable me to live henceforth in peace of mind and free from perturbation.

Then, typically, Epictetus washes his hands of the question of drama, to return his followers to their choice: "What you on your part wish for is for you yourselves to consider."

Epicureanism and Stoicism survived, even predominated, for centuries—centuries in which Platonism and Aristotelianism had gone into relative eclipse. (These latter were revived in the first century BC.) The anaesthetic doctrines' memories now sit under a layer of dust. They are neglected by us, and their masters sit among the unrecognizables in the hundred forgotten generations between classical and modern.

In the last essay, I spoke of some specific means of collecting the most important experiences: drugs and alcohol, sex, and travel. I suggested they are unreliable by themselves and contribute to dissatisfaction with existence by creating the need always to be searching for more.

Outside the disciplines of full anaesthetic ideologies—what we can find among Epicureans and Stoics, as life philosophies—I begin to wonder if our banal searches for experience today don't often contain a shot of anaesthetic; something that allows these activities to serve the moderation of experience as well as its collection. What's more, modern solutions to the intolerability of experience have a way of flipping back and forth between reactions to the too-painful experience of late-modern economy and adjustments to it as extensions of its reach.

With drugs and alcohol, the anaesthetic effect may seem just too obvious. Drowning your sorrows in drink is recognized to be the first and cheapest means of escaping experience. Whiskey continues to be a fine painkiller even if it is no longer used medicinally. You start drinking to look for fun, for experience. You end in another place. Alcohol is a means to collect experiences, and then, too, alcohol is abusive as well as abused, the cause of troubles with experience as well as a reaction to trouble with experience. If drinking fails us, which ideal is it failing— the life of fun, on a high, or the life of anaesthetization, shut off and protected?

Sometimes I find myself thinking about those high-school and collegiate and postcollegiate figures the "stoners." What were their futures? They might have had their only natural social existence, without penalties, while still in school. But it seemed a plausible existence, like that of a creature who had found the right ecological niche. This penaltyless stoner was someone who would rise in the morning and take a hit from the bong, smoke through the day, take all experience (classes, social interactions) with a hazy anaesthesia that made it not quite experience, yet not quite anything so positive as "fun"—then finish off a bowl before going to sleep, to start the next day in the same way. It seemed a life of anti-experience, different from physical addiction. No doubt there is something myopic in a nostalgia for what the stoner proved was possible, if only for a few short years. No one thinks it ends well. But there was something about his manner, wreathed in smoke, that made him seem not like an adventurer but a symbol of a bizarre but real reaction to something we can't name.

For the small group of people who insist on the legalization of marijuana, who can even become marijuana "activists," the logic of their movement has become ever more oriented to the wedge issue of medically recognizable anaesthetization, the anaesthesia of cancer patients and the terminally ill. That is because it is the only way to make marijuana legible to our world, a world of experience and not anti-experience: by the recognized evil of interior *bodily* pain rather than the wish for a life less acute, or the acknowledgment of a healthy physiology that could prefer, somehow, haze in experience to our supposed clarity.

Sex and the search for sex hold out the acquisition of experience, much praised and discussed in our culture, against the unspoken moderation of experience by sex as a reassuring and intimate repetition. We speak of an alternative only in marriage: *conjugality*, the repetition of sexual experience as an act of love, but also as a kind of interpersonal comforting. Conjugality repeats, it does not much change, and it never needs to change unless its participants decide on change, since it is not ever done with anyone else. It is not precisely anaesthetic, but anti-experience. The larger culture of experience, of course, suggests that sex, in some sense, should *always* be done with someone else, in a new way. Your spouse or helpmate must become continually somebody new, somebody unknown, to share new experiences with. Our culture has become pornographic at all levels of its narrative structure: it always seeks a further experience beyond the last one, with more reach and extremity, even where the human mind seems limited to repetition, and human habit seems to prefer it. It is probably the case even in the carnival of dating, switching of partners, anonymous intimacy, that in the act of seeking and acquiring the sheer bodily presence of another person, whoever he or she may be, there is self-reassurance and even near self-anaesthesis: what matters in the moment will be not only the recountable events but silent, forgettable, forgotten-in-the-moment acts of mutual oblivion.

There are, of course, better-organized ways of seeking some relief from experience—non-naive ways, modern ideologies. The "voluntary simplicity" movement of the last decade was a self-conscious plan for the reduction of possessions in order to unclot experience, to find out which experiences, of so many options, were really needful. Simplicity would limit the acquisitive instinct in favor of the retention of a small number of indispensable items. You would learn first to get rid of a closet of clothes, for the most useful; get rid of many friends, for fewer; stop attending to much foreign news, for news closer to home; eventually, in the "advanced" techniques, have one car instead of two, then no car at all, a smaller house, an easier job, and a diminished but possibly more manageable or more vivid experience. The ideology was not always precisely anaesthetic; sometimes it was purifying of experience.

But wherever it did not acknowledge its own real *opposition* to experience of the dramatic kind, and could be co-opted by aesthetics of more vivid, purified, and improved experience, simplicity had the capacity to flip. It could become a matter not just of fewer clothes but of more perfect, ideal clothes, even *new* clothes. It furnished the basis for its own lifestyle magazine, *Real Simple,* a glossy for those who wanted to organize and vary, to switch between simplicities, or to stylize their environments in "simpler" hues of eggshell and porcelain and light pastel, rather than to reduce objects or even learn to accept the old, ugly, and easy, which exist already and therefore might be less spiritually intrusive.

I think the organized spiritual system of the greatest anaesthetic use to the largest number of people in America today must be Buddhism. And yet this still recruits only a tiny minority of seekers. Buddhism is the genuine article, an ancient system, however complicatedly it makes its way to us for modern purposes. Contemporary "nonattachment," as it is sometimes described to me, sounds a good deal like Epicurean imperturbability and, in some formulations, Stoic apathy. The more I hear of "mindfulness," the more I hear traces of aestheticism and perfectionism, though in mindfulness they are removed at last from the limiting requirements of artistry or moral self-scrutiny and are made instead a function of permanent biological habits (breathing, attention, basic sensation) in a kind of hybrid aestheticism-imperturbability. The Buddhist would protest, justifiably, that his practices came first and should be judged on their own. (I am not a Buddhist myself and therefore a bad judge.) What is striking in the Americanization of Buddhism, however, as it appears in books and pamphlets and tapes and talks, is the mixture of different methods and aims. We may just be seeing a diversity of sects and practices, or we may be seeing the perennial Janus-faced quality of American autotherapeutics. Something like mindfulness will be a way to moderate experience for some and to collect and intensify it for others; a way to drop out for some and to get ahead for others; a system at odds with convention for some and an adjustment to conventional life, reducing friction, for others. We knew already that yoga could be imported to this country and, for some, retained as an interlocking series of total systems of practice, knowledge, and devotion—while it was made a form of gym exercise to slim down and improve muscle tone for others.

Then there is the promise of the New Age. It is surprising how often New Age solutions come to us from aliens: interplanetary beings, men of the fifth dimension, and oceanic tribes preserving ancient wisdom lit by the glassy filtered blues of their bubbled Atlantis. I suppose these fantasy archaisms and interstellar revelations are no different finally from our worship elsewhere of the Orient against the Occident—our idea that truth must come from our morning rather than our eve. No different, probably, from my own desire to rediscover anaesthesis in the heart of the West, among sandal-wearing Epicureans or Stoics, while I willfully reinterpret their complex doctrine. We cannot take advice from ourselves, and so we take it from men and women with very strange ways. The stranger the better, so estranged are we from our fellow citizens, who can see no problem.

Certainly, all these systems, however practiced, are better than depression—perhaps the major arena for involuntary anaesthesis in our time (with its attendant losses of pleasure, will, and caring). What is often enough said by the mildly depressed—though we suspect them of magnifying their own problems into social problems—is that their depression is a logical and reasonable response to an environment of experiences and demands that are too intrusive. From the opposite perspective, and with much more authority, the severely depressed are inclined to say that their death in life cannot be a logical or reasonable response to anything, for their sense of the negation of experience goes beyond what any human being could want or will as self-protection. Depression does not save the self, it tells it to die. This seems so extreme as to be outside the reach of cultural analysis, even though anaesthesis, in its many other organized forms, is often a way of learning to "die" without dying. One wants to say something about depression, still stopping short of the point at which generalization encroaches on the individual malady. If there is a cultural world shared between the rise of "experience," searched for as the only means to furnish happiness, and the steady creep of depression as a frequent, dominant affect for people who expected that their lives might be deserving of full happiness, then maybe there is also some causal connection. Maybe it is a sign that when experience has become intolerable, for whatever specific reasons, the mind and the body will *unideologically* attempt to solve what could only be solved with a practice, a system, and an ideology.

We do not live in an age of the arts. The novel, theatrical play, and piece of symphonic music don't matter very much. Art forms that seemed like the fruit of long lines of development, including opera, ballet, painting, and poetry, are now of interest to very few people.

We do, however, live in an aesthetic age, in an unprecedented era of total "design." The look and feel of things, designed once, is redesigned and redesigned again for our aesthetic satisfaction and interest. Design, which can reach the whole world, has superseded art, whose individual objects were supposed to differ from one another and hold a sphere apart from the everyday.

But the particular aesthetic manifestations that interest me here are *dramatic.* It interests me that there is no end of fictions, and facts made over in the forms of fictions. Because we class them under so many different rubrics, and media, and means of delivery, we don't recognize the sheer proliferation and seamlessness of them. I think at some level of scale or perspective, the police drama in which a criminal is shot, the hospital drama in which the doctors massage a heart back to life, the news video in which jihadists behead a hostage, and the human-interest story of a child who gets his fondest wish (a tourist trip somewhere) become the same sorts of drama. They are representations of strong experience, which, as they multiply, begin to de-differentiate in our uptake of them, despite our names and categories and distinctions.

We often say we watch the filmed dramas of strong experience for the sake of excitement or interest. This is true for any representation *in the singular case.* The large dramas of TV and movies, presumably, reflect back on our own small dramas. I, like the ER surgeons, have urgent tasks; I, like the detectives, try to solve things. If one watched, say, a single one-hour show once a month, the depicted experience might come across as a genuinely *strong* experience. If one watched (or carefully read) the news once a month, it might be a remarkably strong and probably an anguishing experience.

But since the spread of television, people have not, by and large, watched dramatic events singly, one a month or week. They've read more than one newspaper and magazine for longer than that. The newspaper itself was always a frame for diverse, incommensurable disasters. We watch and read in multiples. The media of the dissemination of dramas have not been substitutive, either; they have been additive. Not newspaper, then film, then radio, then TV, then the Internet, but all of the above exist today, all the time, in more places, with more common personalities and more crossover of tone, character, content, than before. The claims that fictional dramas exist to "excite," "thrill," or "entertain," like the claims that news exists to "teach," or to "let us know" or "be responsible," have become increasingly incoherent or irrelevant, modeled as they are on viewings of single, focused events. In the era of the total aesthetic environment, the individual case is not as significant as is the effect of scale. While a single drama on television may be thrilling—as it renders the strongest experiences, of life, death, blood, conflict—the aggregate of all dramas on television can hardly be said to be thrilling, since the total effect of television upon a regular viewer is above all *calming,* as any viewer-in-bulk can testify.

This is the paradox. Watching *enough* represented strong experience is associated with states of relaxation and leisure, the extreme loosening and mellowness in which we find a person deliberately "vegetating" in front of the TV—while the walls are painted with criminals' spattered blood, the muscle is pulsating between the doctors' hands, and the hostage is beheaded, and beheaded again, and again, on several competing twenty-four-hour news channels, which no longer promise "up-to-the-minute" but "up-to-the-second" coverage, and show precisely the same events. Over a lifetime, you will also see the same events and scenarios acted out with different faces, sometimes in different genres, some real and some fictional—but "excitement" will very rarely be the reason you turn on the TV.

It used to seem that the news existed as a special case. I think people would agree, at first, if I said that prime time exists for relaxation but the news exists for rigor and truth. Yet what has the news ever been if not also, in some way, calming—or why would one watch the eleven o'clock news before going to bed, as other people take sleeping pills or sip warm milk; why would one watch the six o'clock news, which is even more brutal, more "serious," while eating dinner—when we know in human life that the desire to eat and the ability to sleep are two activities that vanish with genuine disquiet?

With the rise of twenty-four-hour channels, news has become the core and most general case of the total aesthetic environment, because twenty-four-hour news does not play the old game of pretending you can choose to turn it off. Rather, it uses the conceit that there is always something "happening," an experience—though somebody else's— that you must also know about, and the TV is only connecting you transparently to phenomena that should be linked to you anyway. This lie is predicated on notions of virtue, citizenship, responsibility.

I say I watch the news to "know." But I don't really know anything. Certainly I can't do anything. I know that there is a war in Iraq, but I knew that already. I know that there are fires and car accidents in my state and in my country, but that, too, I knew already. With each particular piece of footage, I know nothing more than I did before. I feel something, or I don't feel something. One way I am likely to feel is virtuous and "responsible" for knowing more of these things that I can do nothing about. Surely this feeling is wrong, even contemptible. I am not sure anymore what I feel.

What is it like to watch a human being's beheading? The first showing of the video is bad. The second, fifth, tenth, hundredth are—like one's own experiences—retained, recountable, real, and yet dreamlike. Some describe the repetition as "numbing." "Numbing" is very imprecise. I think the feeling, finally, is of something like envelopment and even satisfaction at having endured the worst without quite caring or being tormented. It is the paradoxically calm satisfaction of having been enveloped in a weak or placid "real" that another person endured as the worst experience imaginable, in his personal frenzy, fear, and desperation, which we view from outside as the simple occurrence of a death.

The old philosophies of aesthetics were based on the experience of a single drama, going back to Aristotle's pity and fear in the witnessing of just one tragedy. Tragedies were presented in small clusters on a special festival day at a rare time of the year. We do not now encounter dramas on designated days of the year. The old aesthetics increasingly slip away when it is not one, or a few, doctors' dramas we watch once a year, but five thousand episodes of a hundred dramas over the course of a lifetime, amid ten thousand other renderings of dramas of equally strong experience; not one representation of a beheading but the same one run a hundred times, followed by a thousand other atrocities themselves rerun. The scale of drama can become a training in how not to relate the strong emotions of representations back to your own experience, not so that they unnerve or paralyze you, while you still learn to fashion your own experiences in the narrative manner and style of dramatic representations.

Then, too, with the change of scale, more of our strictly personal experiences are likely to be experienced *simultaneously* with outer dramas, whether "fiction" or "news." The screens continue to proliferate. Televisions play silently with closed captions in the restaurants where I go to dinner. (I remember they used to be only in bars.) They play with sound in the waiting rooms for visitors to the hospital; they play in the waiting rooms for emergency patients. One played in the garage where I had a flat tire repaired, where I saw the drama of a Florida man shot by air marshals. A wide-screen played by the men's changing rooms at Macy's. Flat-screens are on the machines at the gym and on the elevators in office buildings. Airport terminals are full of televised news, and it follows you to the screens on the backs of the seats on planes. Screens are promised on the subway, where the public rationale will be that they will only show news (to justify the remaining minutes of paid advertising)—the drama of the necessary news, which so mendaciously justifies all other drama. A few offices may have TVs on the work floor, where they are redundant, since the drama comes through on the work space itself, the screen of the computer. When I read my e-mail on Yahoo, it is accompanied by headlines of distant events, fifty-six killed, a hundred killed; video clips from movies; ads for the dating sites that will find me a new mate and reconstruct my own life as drama.

Happiness has wound up in an ideology of the need for experiences. Very well. This is our "health" and our quest. But is this happiness-by-experience itself then regulated and moderated by the constant chatter of strong represented experiences, whose effect is not, finally, to stimulate strong experience in their viewers, but to make up some hybrid of temporary relaxation and persistent desire? Does the total aesthetic environment, that is, become anaesthetic as well as aesthetic? We know its advertisements channel desire toward particular products—and don't much mind. That's just advertising. Its dramas also create and channel desire. Suppose those dramas were capable of a paradoxical, anaesthetic attenuation or deferral of all this desire, to the point where desire could be mobilized ceaselessly without pain to the viewer and without personality destruction. This would forestall the conversion to anti-experience—never causing the full and radical crisis that might occur to an unhabituated and unanaesthetized individual, facing all of these dramas and horrors and strong renderings and commercial demands and new needs as single instances, for the first and only time.

I want to think this is partly right; then the system, and its perilousness, make sense. The trouble then would be that for some people the drama-induced anaesthetic might *wear off.* Their form of experiential illness would represent a breakthrough, in other words, of aesthetic events to their original, singular effects—so that they disturb the person who is supposed to be protected, soothed, and regulated, as if he were now encountering each instance *singly,* at full strength.

If individuals in our society are afflicted suddenly with the inability to take represented experiences in a ceaseless flow, but instead undergo each and every event as if it were happening to *them*—as if fiction were real, and the real (the news networks' medical horrors, beheadings, thousands of deaths) *doubly* real, because publicly attested to and simultaneously experienced as somehow one's own—then no wonder they withdraw. If they feel every outside representation, from however far away it comes, as if it belonged to the context of their private lives and individual drama, then no wonder they tremble. And they may in part have been *asked* to feel things that way—by a system of representations that doesn't truly believe, or wish, that anyone *will.*

("If one had to be taught by fictions," said Epictetus, "I, for my part, should wish for such a fiction as would enable me to live henceforth in peace of mind and free from perturbation. What you on your part wish for is for you yourselves to consider.")

I see: Severed heads. The Extra Value Meal. Kohl-gray eyelids. A holiday sale at Kohl's. Red seeping between the fingers of the gloved hand that presses the wound. "Can you save him, Doctor?" The room of the renovated house, done in red. The kids are grateful for their playroom. The bad guy falls down, shot. The detectives get shot. The new Lexus is available for lease. On CNN, with a downed helicopter in the background, a peaceful field of reeds waves in the foreground. One after another the reeds are bent, broken, by boot treads advancing with the camera. The cameraman, as savior, locates the surviving American airman. He shoots him dead. It was a terrorist video. They run it again. Scenes from ads: sales, roads, ordinary calm shopping, daily life. Tarpaulined bodies in the street. The blue of the sky advertises the new car's color. Whatever you could suffer will have been recorded in the suffering of someone else. Red Lobster holds a shrimp festival. Clorox gets out blood. Advil stops pain fast. Some of us are going to need something stronger.

I don't know why anyone cracks, and the reasons, each time, will be different, deep, and personal. The aesthetic presentations, which seem to be everywhere, as dramas, playing out the strongest experiences—which others can receive in a manner relaxed or blasé—become intolerable. If there was indeed something formerly anaesthetic about this ceaseless flow of strong sensations, then it has just worn off, worn off for oneself *alone* as it often seems, and it is terrifying. The baffled sufferer can't understand what has happened to him.

So he tries to recover the anaesthetic. He may try first the double-dealing strategies, those that add experience in some modalities and preserve you from it in others: alcohol, sex, or another kind of plunge. There are the horrible depressions, ambiguous and painful. There is medicine. There are organized practices and systems, from Buddhism through the many traditions of the East, from Epicureanism and Stoicism back to the origins of the West. Each stands ready to be retrofitted for today. There is organized religion. There is staying in your house and never coming out.

There is also the dream of an alternate aesthetic, of a world in which aestheticized experience worked only on things that were *ordinary,* local, small, repetitive, and recalcitrant, on things that really did happen to most of us in the everyday. This would imply a challenge to drama as we know it. Would it be too much to ask for books in which there is no conflict and no disaster but mere daily occurrences, strung together by the calm being who notices them; television shows on which people sit around silently noticing one another, watch sunsets, type, chat, cook meals without teaching the viewer how, and go about their business in the dull but reassuring knowledge that nothing is going to be very different than the day before? Could there be repetition in a state of grace? Could there be "aesthetic" representation, for those for whom the worldly anaesthetic had worn off, while the systematic ideologies seemed too inhuman and restrictive? Could people live a life in the garden, in our world with its many technologies?

What would remain would not be drama, or "experience," but life. Perhaps there is a way back to life, in people's tentative steps in the interstices of this world, if they cannot live on its grid. Circling life from the cluttered outside, one asks its meaning again and again. How to get back to it: by aestheticizing everything, as before, to explode the questing aesthetic? By anaesthetic efforts, as imagined in this essay, to cut down experiences to neutral occurrences incapable of being made over as drama? Meaning starts to seem a perverse thing to ask for, when what we are really asking is what life is when it is not already made over in forms of quest or deferral. Could *this* life be reached—unmediated? Would there be anything there when we found it?

[2006]

VII

MOGADISHU, BAGHDAD, TROY,
OR HEROES WITHOUT WAR

Early this year, on March 31, 2004, two SUVs carrying American contractors for Blackwater Security Consulting drove into an ambush in Fallujah. Four were shot dead. All were ex-military men, at least two from the US special forces. Insurgents had staged the ambush. A local crowd mutilated the bodies. Cheering and chanting "Fallujah is the graveyard of Americans"—some holding up computer-printed signs that said the same thing—the locals did the opposite of burying them. They burnt the bodies with gasoline. They beat and tore them. One body was tied with a yellow rope and dragged behind a car down a main street. Another was hauled by the legs by a group of teenagers. Two bodies were tied and hung from a green iron bridge that spans the Euphrates River

Deaths by ambush occur every day now in Iraq. The Saddam Hussein regime lost a three-week war to the overwhelming force of the United States, in which our military conquered a nation of twenty-four million people, slightly larger in land mass than California, and left behind a partly relieved, partly dismayed population, who have since given birth to a variety of resistance factions.

The mutilations were unusual, though. The violation of dead bodies is against Islamic law. The dead are to be buried as soon as possible.

Other American dead whose bodies were lost during the war were buried by locals.

The incident led to a massive and bloody US Marine offensive in Fallujah in the month of April, which we tried to understand from what we could read in our newspapers and the fragmentary footage on the television. We were told that clerics had ruled that the mutilations were an offense against Islam, and yet a Marine officer reported that a videotape of the mutilations was still selling well in many Fallujah shops.

History works by analogies. Eleven years earlier, a similar set of mutilations occurred in Mogadishu, Somalia. After a firefight with Somali militias, the bodies of three US soldiers—again, from the special forces—were captured by a local crowd. These American corpses were tied by hands or feet; one was splayed over a wheelbarrow. They were mutilated by dragging, in the dusty city streets.

The Mogadishu populace, too, adhered to Islam, and the mutilations were not sanctioned by religion. Saudi Arabian troops, stationed in Mogadishu, witnessed what local crowds were doing to the captured American bodies, and were appalled. "If he is dead, why are you doing this?" they shouted.

A last analogy. Three millennia earlier, the origins of our Western way of war unfolded in the battles between Greek and Trojan warriors on the plains of Troy. Homer recorded and embellished their story in the *Iliad*. A feature of their way of fighting was the mutilation of the bodies of heroes. Achilles defeated Hector, killing him. And we know, from book 22, what he did next, defiling the body by dragging its head in the dust: "Piercing the tendons, ankle to heel behind both feet, / he knotted straps of rawhide through them both, / lashed them to his chariot . . . And a thick cloud of dust rose up from the man [he] dragged."

Whenever one compares modern war to ancient war, there is the danger that a simple continuity will be argued for, between all forms of war, across history. Warfare is not continuous, however; methods change. American commentators have already invoked the Mogadishu mutilations multiple times—in the days and months following the spectacle in Fallujah—and this analogy, in their hands, has been obscurantist. Their implication was that we were witnessing a continuity of savagery, rather than civilization; an effort to throw Americans off their mission in Iraq, rather than a reflection on the character of the American military mission itself; a manifestation of terror, irrationality, or "mob mentality," rather than the orderly policies of war, which should be available to reason.

The purpose of the comparison should have been to ask why a repetition occurred—why a scene of the mutilation of the most visible and valuable American fighters, these special forces and elite security contractors, must be restaged compulsively each time the United States fights its contemporary ground wars. What do we know of the meaning of past warfare in which such spectacles were paramount? The answers reside in the logic of the fighting itself. I do not mean to excuse the mutilators, or say that they have become Homeric. It is American fighters who have become Homeric—a small set of our frontline fighters, who have attained a kind of value and visibility unlike that of any enemy they face, or anyone else in the recent history of modern war. Mutilation is an invisible population's response to such power—making themselves visible the only way they know how, by entering the system of American bodies and American lives that our country counts so dear.

Theories of postmodern war, and recent military histories and popular battlefield narratives, make equal and opposite errors about the nature of contemporary US combat.

War theorists only care about the new. To them, everything we see is wholly unprecedented and revolutionary. Before September 11, 2001, and the three years of continuous war that have followed it, a decade or more of thought on postmodern war declared that we were coming into the presence of a new formation in the history of the world. The human body would disappear from the scene of war, and it would become a kind of video game for those people who would do the new "postmodern" killing. Paul Virilio predicted the disintegration of the personality of the warrior. Jean Baudrillard spoke of wars that didn't take place. Michael Ignatieff analyzed "virtual war." Edward Luttwak argued for "post-heroic war." Even in the Pentagon—most importantly there—the generals dreamt of a revolution in military affairs, and network-centric warfare, information warfare, and a possibility of killing without risking US life, to make the loop between sensing and killing an opponent increasingly autonomous and automatic. It has partly come true.

Popular military historians promote the misconception that wars are all the same, in all times, and that contemporary US fighters, despite their technology, are actually continuous with ancient warriors. "As with Xenophon's hoplites, the engine driving the campaign was not mechanical. Instead, it was a spirit, an unbroken code—" they write, and so on. These commentators remember the past, but they paper over the strangeness of today.

In the battles the United States has fought on the ground in the last decade, we've seen something different from what both the dissipation theorists and the warrior traditionalists describe. In Mogadishu; at Mazar-i-Sharif or Tora Bora; in Nasiriyah, Najaf, Baghdad, and now Fallujah, we've seen what had been hidden since Vietnam—the way the US military currently trains and arms its best soldiers to fight on the ground, especially in urban or unconventional surroundings. Human bodies still do the face-to-face work of killing for the United States, just as in so many spheres of the postindustrial economy small populations are still needed to do the skilled or filthy work that machines cannot reach. The military becomes reliant on a small number of frontline fighters, heavily equipped with technology, who are rewarded with a special kind of status.

And unfamiliar trappings do surround them. US soldiers wear body armor of great technical ingenuity, flexible, miraculous. They fight with powerful, almost preternatural weapons, in episodes of virtuosic slaughter, until they withdraw to safety. Eyes circle overhead to guide them, superiors to whom they can appeal in times of trouble. Medicine makes more wounds repairable, so long as they are not instantly fatal. And when a military action takes a wrong turn, jeopardizing overwhelming US supremacy, or when any soldier is killed, the military may pause or even stop the operation, as if the primary goal of warfare were to preserve US lives rather than win at any cost.

The oddity of this mode of fighting isn't quite that it marks a new formation in the history of the world, or comes unknown to us. It's that we thought we would never see it again. We are witnessing a temporary reconvergence with an ancient bit of history, caused by technology and the superior value the United States can now afford to put on the lives of its citizens and soldiers. In contemporary US warfare, the hero returns, in the manner of the *Iliad*, and "hero" has here a purely technical definition. He is the lone fighter, who takes the stage amidst a sea of mere mortal beings—one of only a few other heroes who are comparable to him in abilities and significance. The hero may kill or be killed, but he is always absolutely visible and valuable; owner of a social status, among the princes, *aristoi*, and in the front lines, *promachoi*, one among the select fighters who are by their method of life *hērōes*.

If we can see the relation of today's fighter to his Homeric predecessor, it will give us a window onto what is so strange in contemporary US fighting—and from that base, the new conditions will unfold that have made our situation so confusing in the "War on Terror," the war in Afghanistan, and the war and occupation in Iraq. Only once the terms are set is it possible to understand that if postmodern conditions re-create the hero, of a sort we haven't seen in several thousand years, the same features may prohibit what our civilization has sometimes understood as the condition of war.

The changes in the US military go back to the Vietnam War, but the place to start to understand today's warfare is Mogadishu. On October 3, 1993, US special forces troops entered the Black Sea neighborhood of the Somali capital. They engaged local belligerents in the longest sustained firefight since Vietnam. The operation had been intended to take an hour. A journalistic account—*Black Hawk Down*, by Mark Bowden—details step-by-step the fourteen hours of fighting by US Army Rangers and Delta Force commandoes that followed.

The American humanitarian mission to Somalia was meant originally to safeguard food aid during a famine. It turned into a campaign against the Habr Gidr clan and its obstructionist leader, Mohamed Farrah Aidid. By autumn of 1993, US troops had become accustomed to speedy arrests (or kidnappings) of clan officials. On October 3, soldiers landed in helicopters and captured two of Aidid's lieutenants. After that capture, however, a set of unanticipated events extended the fighting. A soldier fell from a helicopter. A helicopter was shot down by Habr Gidr militia—a feat not thought possible by Pentagon planners. A rescue convoy got lost in the streets. A second helicopter fell to a rocket. Repeated rescue sorties went out, returned, or were pinned down. Eighteen Americans were killed by sunrise and seventy-three injured. Americans killed five hundred Somalis and injured another thousand.

To anyone acquainted with the *Iliad* and its battle of Greeks and Trojans, this description of the fight in Mogadishu may make a comparison to Troy seem arbitrary. All that I have failed to indicate, perhaps, is how strange the details of contemporary combat practices feel to anyone accustomed to modern war in its twentieth-century guise. This does not look like war. It is odd to find today's US soldiers inserted and extracted for the briefest acts of violence, whisked away at the first sign of injury. It is unsettling to see a military offensive of sorts turn into a continuous rescue mission. It alters our picture of war, as the contemporary surgeries in which the heart is deliberately stopped and restarted after the completion of the procedure alter our picture of life. But the thrust of the comparison depends less on the circumstances of the conflict, and more on the status of the fighter.

What does a Homeric hero look like? He armors himself. Well-made greaves defend his legs, a breastplate burnishes his chest; a massive shield, slung on his arm, turns away spears with its layers of leather and bronze. The modern warrior of the Argonne Forest or D-day had been nowhere so well protected except for his metal helmet. But the technology of armoring has radically improved: US forces now suit up fully. Fighters don body armor, helmets, and goggles. They wear Kevlar vests, formed of layers of shielding to turn away bullets, and tough Kevlar helmets. They tuck bulletproof ceramic breastplates into their flak vests, cushion their legs with kneepads, fight with personal sniper rifles, rocket launchers, super-precise and powerful weapons.

And how does the Homeric hero fight? The Achaean or Trojan wades into the slaughter, sending the shadow of his spear hurtling over the ground, killing as many as he can before he himself is wounded or withdraws. The structure of the battle follows a steady pace of attack and withdrawal. With Diomedes's advance, or Agamemnon's, or Achilles's, Greek warriors drive their foes far back across the plain toward the gates of Troy. One peculiarity of this ancient method was that each army retained a steady place of rest. As chariots whisked them forward and back, soldiers attacked when angry and withdrew when wounded.

And today, the postmodern speed of helicopters and land vehicles recovers the ancient method from centuries of disuse. US troops maintained a secure camp on the beach in Somalia, unmolested, three miles from the center of Mogadishu—a broken-down Troy, with its burning tires and dung, its maze of littered streets and untouched mosques. American fighters "rope" in, rappelling from helicopters hovering fifty or seventy feet above the fray. With weapons blazing, they kill anyone who crosses their path. The dead fall around them until they themselves—by mischance or fate—are wounded. As injuries occur, US fighters are "extracted"—by speedy vehicles on the ground, or by small, agile helicopters that can land in the narrow streets.

Nor does any injury, in the *Iliad* or today, stop the hero but the one that kills. Men like the Homeric heroes are never half-men, never maimed or in-between. An arrow in the foot or shoulder is cause to go home temporarily in a chariot. The puncture is healed by a medic or, occasionally, the succor of a god. When a US soldier is shot, anyone can make a quick calculus to know the significance of the wound. In the face or beneath a joint of armor, it will be fatal. Any other injury will be reparable, practically, as long as the mechanisms of extraction work successfully to take a soldier off the field. Even a frightened soldier can work out his chances, as Ranger Sergeant Raleigh Cash did in Mogadishu: "He had thought it through methodically. He was wearing body armor, so if he got shot, it would probably be to the arms or legs and there were medics who would take care of him. It would hurt, but he had been hurt before. If he was shot in the head, then he would die. If he died then that was what was meant to happen." The invocation of fate by this soldier is tempered by the sense that fate has but a slim margin within which to do its grisly work.

And substitute gods watch over the troops in their desert camou-flage and flak vests just as the Olympians watched the furious mortals in their sport, bronze helmets flashing, on the plains of Troy. OH-58 observation helicopters pass over Mogadishu with cameras; a high-flying P-3 Orion spy plane regards the fighting from the clouds. Sat-ellites watch from above earth's atmosphere. A command-and-control helicopter hovers within range of the active soldiers, poised to give bat-tlefield directions. The cameras also stream images in color video, plus infrared and heat display, to senior officers in a control room miles away, who watch until—very rarely—they attempt to intervene; or to more senior generals in Tampa, Florida; or, if necessary, to Washington, DC, where higher echelons may contemplate the mayhem.

But the importance of the eye above a contemporary soldier at all times—just as it was with the eye looking down on the ancient soldier—is not really the efficacy of these gods, in pulling out wounded fighters or sending in bursts of terrible fire. It is, rather, the knowledge that someone is always up there, a peculiar reliance by the soldier on the sense that he is always, in some way, beneath the hovering US heli-copter, under the range of the satellite, under the eye. He matters as a subject for attention. Even his agony registers in a higher consciousness.

All these practical features confer superior value. This is the attribute that unites the Homeric to the American hero. Other words capture subsidiary senses of the quality that adheres to the armored, murderous, god-monitored fighter: singularity, irreplaceability, distinctness, visibil-ity. The real uniqueness of the US fighter is located in his being seen and counted, monitored and protected, simply *worth* more than any enemy he could face. The maintenance of his life seems more important than any goal he could achieve.

One is also struck by two deep differences between Homeric and con-temporary war. The first is that US postmodern fighters, unlike Greeks and Trojans, do not expect to die. The second is that US postmodern battle is one-sided—a fight against no other commensurable force.

Contemporary US fighters, regardless of their military goals, will go to great lengths to avoid the deaths of any of their own personnel. They nearly aborted the Mogadishu mission, releasing the men they had arrested, the whole point of their mission, when it looked as if these captives might slow down the soldiers' own rescue. Rescue becomes the ruling angel of warfare; rescue and bare survival.

And so the United States begins to fight on a strategy of survival. The Mogadishu firefight as it is recounted in *Black Hawk Down* includes killings of civilian noncombatants glimpsed just out of the corner of one's eye. If you keep a list, you can gradually develop a picture of what such fighting must mean to anyone not a US soldier, or reporter, or citizen. As the assault begins, US fighters kill a few Somalis by accident. They shoot an innocent woman. They shoot a few boys. Their "rules of engagement" dictate they "shoot only at someone who pointed a weapon at them." But as risk accelerates, US soldiers and attack helicopters stop shooting civilians by mistake and start shooting them deliberately. They shoot anyone advancing on the troops, then anyone suspicious in the vicinity, then any groups in the city moving in the *direction* of the pinned-down troops, then anyone at all. They gun down crowds on purpose.

Somali fighters, of course, are killed with just the same lack of registration as the crowds. Visible—they must be spotted, to be shot—but invisible. As the heroes occupy their peculiar haloes of bodily safety, a strategy of survival makes it harder to gaze out through this glare to identify anyone who might inhabit a different, more traditional order of life, such as these low-tech Somali fighters—a grim, unromanticizable bunch—who nevertheless cannot be extracted by helicopters, who cannot be remade by medicine, who fight as modern war taught them to, aiming at goals, expecting to die, and wiped out by American fighters in extraordinary numbers.

The Somalis become a natural or biological menace, a menace made of men. And this licenses any degree of killing of combatants or noncombatants. Again, that death toll: in fourteen hours, Somalis had fifteen hundred casualties, a third of whom were killed. Fewer than one hundred American casualties occurred, of whom only eighteen were killed. We can remind ourselves that Americans' abstract moral beliefs are second to none. Whenever things go right, our adherence to certain conventions of war, at the level of planning and training especially, is admirable. But whenever things go wrong, a different order obtains. The strategy of survival bleeds into a reality of extermination, and a form of warfare in which, for the Americans, there may be an enemy group, but there is no equal other side.

The analogy to the *Iliad* is an aid to thought. Homer's poem is an example of warfare everyone knows. It is so different from what our warfare is supposed to be like now that it jogs the mind.

The long-term trend of recent US military planning, however, is to expand and accelerate the features of ground combat that were most startling in Mogadishu. This has gone along with a particular line of military thought, now dominant in the Bush administration, which seeks to remodel all of the United States military on the example of special operations forces. The US Army's "I am an army of one" advertising campaign, before September 11, already recruited on the basis of the new model, picturing individual soldiers, alone, wearing futuristic armor, almost unrecognizable as human beings, or accomplishing extraordinary feats by themselves. As Secretary of Defense Donald Rumsfeld has sold his idea of "transformation" of the armed forces—which was originally more a matter of corporate-style "downsized" military organization, budgeting, and goals—by concrete examples from the special forces, and by their conspicuous recent successes.

The conventional wisdom on the 2001–02 war in Afghanistan was that it was won almost entirely by a tiny number of special forces soldiers who called in massive air power. US heroes mobilized the "proxy fighters" of the Northern Alliance, target-spotted for precision bombing, and overthrew the government of a vast country—leaving a large ground force to be called in only later, when there was little left for it to do.

Pentagon planners love this model because it is quick, requires less funding to manpower and more to technology, and is more free from public scrutiny and national opinion than the use of the regular military. Journalists have fallen in with it, too. The hagiographic literature of special forces in Afghanistan is both unilluminating and extensive. Many of the Afghan engagements are classified, but the few that are not resemble storybook tales. Heroes come roaring out of a curtain of precision explosions—as at Mazar-i-Sharif—on horseback, surrounded by faithful Northern Alliance fighters, to overwhelm a Taliban stronghold. Or heroes radio home the GPS coordinates for targets, or paint them with lasers, and moments later the enemy vehicles, or houses, or men, are vaporized by munitions dropped from Stealth bombers; the heroes melt back into the landscape, creeping among the native population. Rumsfeld himself, in a policy article in *Foreign Affairs,* likened the new forces of transformation to an opportunity to take an M-16 back to the Middle Ages. You wouldn't joust with the knights you met; you'd machine-gun them. Such was the curious charm of the special forces in Afghanistan.

The far more important development, however, may be that the armor and tracking devices which belonged to only the highest-value fighters in 1993 have been made increasingly available to a wider, though still relatively small, cadre of frontline fighters, in the regular infantry and Marines. A Marine rifleman now wears a ceramic plate in his SAPI vest, like a Delta operator ten years ago; an Army infantryman can be watched by drone planes, and his vehicle followed on the "Blue Force tracker" at headquarters. This is what we saw in Iraq, during our brief war.

Iraq—we now are coming to understand it better and better, as commentators relive our twenty-one-day war, then ask what went wrong. Iraq is the real test for the new conditions of combat.

New accounts of last year's war are arriving at a steady pace. We have David Zucchino's *Thunder Run: The Armored Strike to Capture Baghdad,* Rick Atkinson's *In the Company of Soldiers: A Chronicle of Combat,* Bing West and Major General Ray L. Smith's *The March Up: Taking Baghdad with the 1st Marine Division,* Williamson Murray and Major General Robert H. Scales Jr.'s *The Iraq War: A Military History,* and

John Keegan's *The Iraq War,* among others. Each of the accounts by "embedded" journalists adds something new. The military histories mostly confirm the larger picture that the journalists sometimes can, sometimes cannot, see.

In Iraq, the trends toward the making of "heroes" continued. The heroic aspects of monitoring, armor, and medicine appear in these books in familiar form. During the war, the death of any US soldier from hostile fire is rare and shocking. Operations pause, to evacuate wounded soldiers by armored vehicle or helicopter. Medics see the benefits of the new personal armor: in one firefight recounted by Zucchino, twenty men were wounded but "there were no head wounds, no sucking chest wounds, no wounds to vital organs."

And the United States fought another low-casualty war, with few personnel killed during the actual campaign; and remarkable numbers of Iraqi deaths whenever US forces encountered resistance. Murray and Scales cite one engagement west of the Baghdad International Airport on April 3, 2003. It began in late afternoon: "By early morning the bodies of nearly 500 fedayeen littered the ground in front of American positions." West and Smith recount an engagement at Diwaniyah: "In six hours, the battalion estimated two hundred Iraqi soldiers and fedayeen had died, not an unusual number, for the length of the battle and the panoply of weapons applied."

Zucchino gives figures for some of the dead in the fighting around Baghdad—where the massed dead can be counted in one-mile stretches of highway, and intersection by intersection. In a morning-long engagement on April 5, "the Desert Rogues [tank] battalion had just killed between eight hundred and a thousand enemy soldiers. . . . It had cost them one dead." On April 7, at one intersection, US forces may have "killed as many as two hundred and had destroyed at least forty-five vehicles. The company had not lost a man." At another: "Hubbard figured his men had killed up to four hundred enemy fighters and had destroyed eighty vehicles. A single American soldier had been injured—a minor shrapnel wound."

The strategy of the US ground campaign in Iraq was simple. The United States had two large forces, both of which left Kuwait at the same time, pursuing roughly parallel paths north to Baghdad. The main force was the Army V Corps. It included the Third Infantry (Mechanized)—a powerful force of tanks and fighting vehicles—the paratroopers of the 101st and 82nd Airborne, and the commandoes of the Special Operations Command. The I Marine Expeditionary Force had a comparable mix of tanks, helicopters, fixed-wing air support, artillery, and infantry. The Army struck along a western route, on highways and briefly through the desert on the far side of the Euphrates. The Marines fought their way north on an eastern route, between the Euphrates and the Tigris. The two forces converged on Baghdad.

At the battle for Baghdad, they reached what could have been the most elaborate and dangerous ground engagement the United States had fought in decades. The original US strategy was to conquer Baghdad by making raids from stable bases outside the city, using the relatively small cadres of the 101st and 82nd Airborne and the special forces, backed with every kind of firepower and support imaginable. This would have been like Mogadishu. Perhaps as late as April, official war plans called for these troops, who are transported in Black Hawks and closely supported by Apache attack helicopters, to strike into Iraq's capital city and clear neighborhoods day by day, in raids of attack and withdrawal.

The US forces made a discovery during the earlier campaign, however, which changed all this. In the unique Iraqi environment, tanks could perform urban warfare as well as fight traditional open-field engagements in the desert. Because Iraq had maintained a full highway system—with road signs in Arabic and English—tanks could move as swiftly as they liked. Because the monumental architecture of Saddam's Baghdad, not unlike the Mall in Washington, DC, gave tanks room to maneuver at the heart of the capital, they could drive to the center of Baghdad and collapse the city's defenses from the inside. Because the Baath defenses included fixed roadside bunkers, light gun-mounted pickup trucks, and suicide cars—all easy targets for tank guns—the tanks were lethal and unstoppable. The armed hero found a new way to "walk" into a hostile city, in other words, with an even lower risk of injury—clad in even more invincible armor and more unimaginable firepower, looking at the enemy streets over the sill of a turret, wearing the skin of a tank.

On April 5 and then April 7 and 8, 2003, Third Infantry tanks led so-called thunder runs into the city of Baghdad, killing all the fighters they encountered along the way. Nothing went wrong this time. The US forces killed, and killed, and killed. The main worry for the Americans, in the hottest engagements, was only that they would run out of ammunition.

And one sees the same ethos, the same super-power and super-value, among the frontline fighters as in Mogadishu. The one-sidedness of this mode of battle is, again, dramatic. The tankers use thermal sights to find enemy targets by their body heat, and vehicles by their engines and exhaust. The regular optical day sights are also good enough to hit standing Iraqis who, relying on the naked eye, may not even know there's a tank in view. As Zucchino paraphrases his protagonists: "Some of the dismounts would stand up right in the open. Gibbons would cut them in half with the coax and he and Booker would shake their heads and mutter, 'What the hell are these guys *thinking*?'"

The US heroes are consistently mystified by what the Iraqis are thinking, as they stick up their heads and have them blown off. Don't they know we have thermal sights? The Iraqis aim wildly, but the US machine guns, used properly, can't miss: "their computers corrected for range, lead, temperature, wind, munitions temperature, and barometric pressure. The tanks knocked down the fedayeen one or two at a time as they ran across open spots." The Iraqis continue to fight in the only way they know how—on their feet, with small arms, breathing and therefore generating heat images. They die as they are glimpsed. "They were not giving up. It seemed suicidal—men with nothing more than AK-47s or wildly inaccurate RPGs were charging tanks and Bradleys. It was like they *wanted* to die, or worse, they didn't care," the tankers think. This is simply the logic of a higher form of life regarding a lower.

A large part of the apparatus of the US military is of course still oriented to preventing US deaths. Colonel David Perkins, the commander of the 2nd Brigade tank force that made the final "thunder run," had to instruct his officers *specifically* that the primary goal of the mission was not to avoid the loss of American life: "He told his commanders that the mission's main goal was *not* to avoid getting anyone killed. It was to force the collapse of Saddam Hussein's regime."

Yet the strategy of survival reappears, in the usual ways. When a tank battalion's commander learns that some enemy soldiers are playing dead, standing up to shoot after the tanks' main guns have passed, he decides to have his men "double-tap" all visible bodies—that is, to shoot the wounded and the dead, lest they prove to be a threat later. His officers and gunners put it into practice: "Anyone in an Iraqi uniform was going to die. It didn't matter that they were wounded or pretending to be dead." Because the US forces make their assault using a capital city's highways in the early morning, civilian cars are also on the highway's on and off ramps, and when they can't be differentiated from enemy "technicals" and suicide cars, they must be destroyed. Zucchino again, paraphrasing his interviewees: "Deep down, [the tankers] knew they were inadvertently killing civilians who had been caught up in the fight. They just didn't know how many. They knew only that any vehicle that kept coming at the column was violently eliminated."

John Keegan takes note of the problem, blaming the civilians for not staying home:

> Such incidents had proliferated throughout the campaign. Civilian vehicles had time and again driven at high speed into firefights, as if their occupants were oblivious to the dangers of war all about them. . . . One of the most bewildering characteristics of this strange war was the apparent refusal of civilians to accept that a war was indeed going on. They drove about, in vehicles easily mistaken for the "technicals" used by fighters, as if the Americans should understand that they were on a family outing or on their way to market, as they often were. The result was the spectacle of dead fathers or slaughtered children in bullet-riddled cars skewed across the roadway.

As in Mogadishu, when real danger presents itself, US methods turn truly annihilative. During the Baghdad fighting, Iraqi forces mounted counterattacks at three crucial highway cloverleafs on Highway 8. The US fighters fired tens of thousands of rounds of ammunition, but still more attackers appeared, and the commanders began to fear the enemy might break their perimeters and overrun their positions So they lowered their restraints. Residential buildings bordered the highway. It became necessary not only to shoot the visible enemy inside the windows, but to take down the buildings. Zucchino:

> Hornbuckle was concentrating on four- and five-story buildings to the northeast and the southwest, where RPG teams were able to fire straight down on his men dug into the cloverleaf. They were civilian buildings in a residential neighborhood, but under the rules of engagement they were now legitimate targets because they were being used by the enemy to attack American forces. Hornbuckle had first ordered his Bradley crews to fire high-explosive Twenty-five Mike Mike straight through the windows, where he could see the RPG teams firing and moving. . . .
>
> The captain had his mortar team fire. . . . The mortars chopped the buildings down, floor by floor.

With the threat continuing from neighborhoods along the route, the commander of China Battalion, Lieutenant Colonel Stephen Twitty, gives an order to stop asking for orders, and just bring mortar fire down on the residential neighborhoods. If you sense a threat, he orders, "just level it. Take it down. Call artillery." He will end any threat to his men—no matter who may be in those neighborhoods.

My concern, however, is actually mostly with the enemy fighters, however loathsome a portion of them are, however grateful we are when American lives are protected, however necessary it was that the Saddam regime lose, and lose as quickly as possible.

Why should it matter when killing is as one-sided as this? It may seem a perverse exercise to say which specimens of military killing qualify as war, and which others do not. I know it will seem equally perverse to militarists and pacifists.

Some people claim that war is just the application of force to another group or nation until it submits. Ideal war then tends toward a totality of violence. Clausewitz began the tradition of modern thinking in this vein. Though he understood war's motives to be based in state policy, he believed war's prosecution to tend inevitably toward the "extreme," toward "limitlessness." This is often called a "realist" position.

The first thing you have to believe, to view war differently, is simply that war is a distinct long-standing human enterprise, bound by rules, and that it's a conflict between populations, rather than mere combat by soldiers or conquest by mighty rulers. Our ordinary language holds to this, in retaining such distinctions as those between war and massacre. The rules of war, too, grant immunity from violence to those who surrender, are wounded, or are taken prisoner. The rationale is simple—anyone who cannot provide a threat is no longer subject to killing.

Certain actions which seem morally allowable along the progress toward their perfection, when their goal is possible rather than actual, may became disallowable if they ever reach that goal, arriving at a perfected state. Every general in history may have dreamed of a war in which he killed all of his enemies without a single death among his own men. But the dreamed-of situation was never attainable, and its unattainability was crucial to war's ethical acceptability. Once the United States can annihilate large percentages of our foes in war with minimal losses to ourselves, we have entered a different moral universe.

One of the peculiarities of the newest US technologies of war is that they make enemy soldiers resemble disarmed persons or prisoners of war. At the start of the war in Afghanistan, the United States quickly destroyed all Taliban defenses against high-altitude aerial assault. The United States then began bombing Taliban soldiers. We killed Taliban soldiers sitting in "frontline" positions. We destroyed personnel in rear supply positions. The United States at no time stood to the front or rear: only above. Our pilots stood out of range of any threat these soldiers could present them. A ground force had not entered Afghanistan. It is a paradox of technology to make armed combatants as helpless before our weapons as the categories of disarmed soldiers whom it would be unlawful to kill.

Elaine Scarry once defined war as a reciprocal contest of injuring. Behind any military conflict—she agrees with Clausewitz—lies a crisis of policy, as one group wants to compel another to accept its will. But how should it be, Scarry asked, that wars can be won or lost *between populations* in a way that prepares each side to consent to rewrite its deepest ideologies, or remake the constitution of its society—and all because of an action so uncivilized and terrible as the maiming and killing of soldiers in war? As occurred in Japan and Germany in 1945, and as we are hoping will occur in Iraq in 2004 (also, we should note, as occurred in the United States at the end of the Vietnam War), societies wind up changing their beliefs and self-conceptions because of the outcome of a contest that seems to "realists" to have to do only with killing power.

This kind of war requires minimum mechanisms of consent by which a population can support or isolate its fighting representatives. In a liberal democracy like the United States, those are the mechanisms of a free press and representative government. In any loose or undemocratic state, they may simply be the power of the populace to provide or withdraw shelter, to respect fighters' secrecy or hand them over to the enemy.

But it also may be the case that any war which produces a lasting settlement might require two-sidedness—require, that is, the sense that a *war* actually occurred, a contest of representatives, with the real power to hurt each other, and recognize and count their losses, and equally be subject to the odd combination of skill, strength, and blind luck that means the battle is not always to the strong. It might also require time for campaigns to be drawn out, as two populations observe the carnage and ask themselves if the deaths are worth it—whether, that is, the ideas and principles incarnated in the fighters are worth the loss and pain, or whether to change ideas.

Some wars end without ending, and without producing a state of peace or stability, as is the case today in Somalia, in Afghanistan, and—so far—in Iraq. These failures result either from an incomplete eradication of the "enemy," as the US government and its military spokesmen tend to declare, or from the defective and permanent "tribal culture" of peoples not organized on liberal-democratic lines, as pundits and area-studies experts tell us. But one also has to ask whether the manner of carrying out a war, when the war is not quite a war, might somehow undermine the permanence of any settlement.

On May 1 of last year, George W. Bush flew to an aircraft carrier and unfurled his banner: "Mission accomplished." Major combat operations were over. The war against the Iraqi government was done. That government was destroyed.

The paradox is that we began to see the crucial conditions of war return only when war was declared over—in an occupation that the United States had not prepared for, and that we citizens are now slowly coming to recognize and understand. We return to war, in some form, at a moment when war is unacknowledged—when an exchange of deaths, a slow and visible process, undoes the one-sidedness of our glorious, barely visible three-week war last March and April.

In mid-April of 2003, tens of thousands of Iraqis protested against an occupation, but that was lost in the end of what we had declared to be our war, while we were preparing to declare it over. US troops fired on the demonstrators twice in three days, killing at least fifteen and wounding seventy-five. Back in April, the first revenge attack was reported in Fallujah—and this news, too, was lost. The United States and the United Kingdom finally declared themselves "occupying powers" in May, seeking the protection of international law to take temporary control of Iraqi oil supplies. The situation worsened rather than improved. By mid-June 2003, the drip of dead Americans, ambushed or bombed, had begun. Attacks on US soldiers during the fall, Patrick Graham recently reported in *Harper's,* reached "roughly fifty per day" in Al Anbar province alone. By January of this year, 2004, says Rick Atkinson of the *Washington Post,* US forces were suffering an attack, on average, every forty-one minutes. Whatever the frequency of attacks, as of this writing, 810 American soldiers have been killed in Iraq, only 108 of them during the three-week war. Nearly 4,700 have been wounded—some of them grievously, we know, since US medicine can stop death and undo wounds but can't save exploded arms and legs, which have to be replaced with artificial limbs.

"Heroes without war" acquires another meaning, in the Iraq situation—when US troops fight so remarkably, and against such weak states, that a "war" can be held to twenty-one days, too short a time for anyone to understand what is occurring, too quick a sequence of battles to be meaningfully represented by the press. It also made too compressed a victory for either the defeated population or the victor to learn whom they would be living with, in the odd intimate proximity of an occupied nation and a distant foreign power—as we shipped our reserve troops and entrepreneurial citizens over, to speed the transformation.

We begin to learn, however. And so do the Iraqis. By observing the Americans, the Iraqi insurgents could see firsthand how much we watch each of our military lives. The Iraqis could not kill our best fighters in a planned war. But it didn't matter who a dead American was. It didn't matter, in the occupation, if the person killed was a fuel convoy driver, an Army Reservist rotated from weekend training to overseas duty, a National Guardsman who usually protected the USA from natural disasters, or a Marine patrolling the street.

No Iraqi can face off against our frontline fighters. And it doesn't matter if the American is not faced down. He or she can now be blown up by what even the press calls an IED, an "improvised explosive device"—an old artillery shell, invariably, wired with a fuse. A highway full of booby traps, like a barrage of carelessly fired mortar rounds, will eventually hit someone. And the new deaths are added to the balance sheet of American lives, each one mattering more than fifty or a hundred Iraqi fighters in our calculus. So the Americans' higher register of life can be used against us. A steady hemorrhaging of lives, one or two a day, could force our recognition of the opposite side, whom the American fighters still find unintelligible, and whom the American public hear about only as "dead-enders," "foreigners," or "terrorists."

The act of mutilation—performed by boys and townspeople, though the ambush was arranged by fighters—is a way of getting us to see what we Americans value most, as we watch it be undone. We respect "clean" killing; this is filthy mistreatment of the already dead. We care more about one or two or three of our own inviolable and invincible soldiers' bodies (and our military cares, especially) than we do about mass killing. Six civilians and a journalist had been shot dead in Fallujah by US troops the Friday before the mutilations. Very well, the civilian mob would show us what we are like.

Ironically, several weeks before the mutilations, the Marines had been brought in to replace the 82nd Airborne in part because they were more polite, more decent, closer to the ground in their fighting methods than the paratroopers they replaced, more likely to win "hearts and minds." Then the mutilations occurred. The Marines joined a battle more like Mogadishu than anything that had occurred in Iraq during the actual war. Reports have been spotty and contradictory. The Marine tactic seems to have been to enter the city to draw fire, then pulverize the sources of fire. Close air support was used in neighborhoods inside the city, from Cobra helicopters launching Hellfire missiles, to cannon-firing AC-130 gunships, to bombs from F-16s. The director of the Fallujah General Hospital reported six hundred people killed and twelve hundred wounded in one week. He said the majority were civilians; the Marines insisted 95 percent were "military-age males."

April also proved to be the bloodiest month for American forces since the war. One hundred and thirty-five soldiers died and eleven hundred more were wounded. The Fallujah insurgency continued a year-long chronology of Sunni Muslim resistance. Simultaneously, however, the Shiite Muslim forces of Muqtada al-Sadr and his anti-American Mahdi Army were rising against US troops in Najaf, Karbala, and elsewhere. Twelve Marines were killed in a single seven-hour firefight in Ramadi on April 6—nearly two-thirds of the number killed in the long-ago fight in Mogadishu.

We swore the people we are fighting would cheer their liberation. We are living inside our worst-case scenario, in which Sunni and Shia can be united for only one cause, to resist us. This is something for the political scientists and intelligence agencies to explain. But the wider

issue is that the news reports seem to indicate that the many disparate insurgents—who themselves are often destabilizing and extremist
groups—are coming to look like representative forces. I do not mean
that the actual fighters represent the will or ideas of a majority, or even
a significant minority, of the people (or peoples) of Iraq. I simply mean
that these varied groups, fighting a common enemy, are coming to seem
like a force with whom citizens can come to identify or disidentify—
just as Americans identify and disidentify with the actions of the US
military and its civilian leaders, who order our fellow citizens to kill and
die in our name.

This occupation, in reassuming the condition of war, will change the
self-conception of the Iraqis, or our own—if only we have the nerve to
look steadily at it, and think. The United States is making a claim on
what Iraq should be: secular, human-rights-based, economically priva-
tized and open to foreign investment, and as democratic as it can be
while ensuring permanent friendly ties with the United States. When
we make this claim backed by our military, we are also making claims
about our United States—for example, that we have the moral, national,
and humanitarian authority to overthrow tyrannical governments in
favor of democracy and free-market economics.

The insurgents, in turn, are making claims about the way they want
their own country to look: theocratic, Islamist rather than Western,
traditionally repressive rather than egalitarian and rights-based, "Arab"
rather than globalized, independent rather than occupied. They are
also making claims about how they want the United States to be: not
expansionist, not dominant, not spreading Western values, not capable
of imposing rights-based freedoms, equality-based democracy, or free-
market globalization.

And these conflicting conceptions—the "policy" at stake in our
unwanted new war—will be deliberated upon by two populations, and
not the jihadists and ideologues who started it, in that odd and terrible
form of deliberation that is greased with lives, pain, suffering, and loss.

In this sense, "resolve" is a word that has been grossly misused in
recent months, and yet is most relevant. The administration makes it
mean resoluteness, a steadfast quality of refusing to change course, in

war, regardless of events. The siege of Fallujah in April was even called "Operation Vigilant Resolve" or "Iron Resolve." Yet the word has a more honorable place in our democracy. It is the oral formula in which all acts of public deliberation are put forward, from town councils to the Congress: "Be it resolved, that . . ." The significance of a resolution is not its finality, but that deliberation goes on. At this moment, war once again becomes a cause for thinking. The thinking must go on in public. Our administration's certainties are not America's. Our resolve is a public self-discovery that has yet to be made.

[2004]

SEEING THROUGH POLICE

A surprise of being around police is how much they touch you. They touch you without consent and in both seemingly friendly and unfriendly ways. The friendly touch is the first surprise. A policeman allowing protesters to cross the street touches you on the arm or back as you cross. Face-to-face, police will put a hand on your shoulder, from the front, intimate as a dog putting his paw up. It is unnerving. Women say male police know very well how to touch, even in public sight, in ways that are professional and neutral, and also in ways that are humiliating and sexual, with no demonstrable distinction dividing the two. The police know, and you know. Like a reversal of electric polarity from protective to hostile, this conversion of mood does not only follow the policeman's individual initiative. It traces something like an atmospheric charge among police in groups, their silent experience of a phenomenon, their habitual tactics in response.

In confrontations on a curb (when you stay on your sidewalk, because the public street is forbidden except to police), they may press lightly on your collarbone, "holding you back," just measuring out the distance with their arms. You can even be held up in this way, if you relax. Shoving you requires a separate, additional level of their energy. Batons and gloves extend the police field of touch, insulating them from the brutality that their arms and hands will do. A gray-haired professor of history I know put his hand on the top rail of a metal police barrier, at a protest, as one will do when standing still. An officer forbade him to touch it. All macho, the historian refused to move his hand. The policeman smashed it with his baton, splitting the flesh but not breaking the bone. That was a conflict over the reciprocation of touch: the rail and the baton were proxies. The unspoken rule is that the citizen must never return touch.

Singling out an individual for arrest, the next escalation is to grab the citizen body at the neck or shoulders—attacking from the front, black-gloved fingers grip the face, while from behind, the palm shocks the base of the skull—pushing at the fulcrum of the neck to hurl the person down. Sometimes the cop's left hand pulls up or tears at the arrestee's shirt or outermost garment while pushing with the right hand. A poet in his forties I know was thrown to the ground like this because he stepped outside a crosswalk at the beginning of a march. Other officers swarm the downed man or woman and pull at arms and legs, and kneel on the back or the neck or head, or mash the face into the pavement under their palm while cuffs go on. The final escalation is punching, beating, or kicking. Sometimes this is reserved for the arrestee on the ground who is already restrained, as a form of punctuation. Sometimes it is done in the van or on the way to it. Police are more likely to do this only when they believe they cannot easily be recorded with cameras.

The purpose of touching by police is to make persons touchable. Touch readies more touch. It is preparatory. The restraints in civilization on attacking anyone, especially a citizen who portends no harm or threat, are fairly high. For most forms of violence that breach civilized norms, even if it is one's art or profession, steps of habituation are needed. The "sudden" violent arrest at a protest is almost never sudden if you have been watching the officer and the longer sequence. The process of change in an officer who will then bring someone down is not oriented to the target, but seems interior, oriented to the self; by the expressions that pass over his face, usually in an instant of stepping back, withdrawal, and the cessation of interaction or negotiation or "management," you can detect a kind of change of availability that prefaces the attack. It very often seems to surprise, even astonish or trouble, nearby officers, when the attack comes, yet they still know to capture and cuff whichever citizens wind up on the ground (sometimes the wrong ones, as the trailing officers will often also push down and even cuff bystanders who happened to get knocked into indirectly in the attack).

Police are different things to different people. Not because each person has his or her own subjective view on the constabulary, but because the meanings of the functions of police vary with a citizen's identity, as one or another possible target or beneficiary of policing.

"Directing traffic." This function of restricting and encouraging movement through a city may be the very oldest job of police. Police maintain a spatial order. The most manpower and work time are still devoted to it. What is traffic? Certain neighborhoods contain certain types of people and behavior. Others contain others. Various subjects must move through corridors of the city to redistribute themselves over the course of the day and night. But they must not unsettle police's fundamental sense of who belongs where. Today, when police are accused of racial bias in their traffic stops and pedestrian searches and must justify themselves, they speak with *pride* of the fact that they will not just stop and question black people but also stop and question white people caught in black neighborhoods and rich people cruising in poor neighborhoods. This, to their minds, is parity. They don't recognize their role in making up the boundaries of these neighborhoods in the first place, or why not all neighborhoods are functionally the same for the activities of life.

"Catching criminals." This is the activity police truly like to identify with, however little of their time it occupies. Occasionally police stumble on red-handed robbers, or thugs fleeing an assault. The bulk of "catching" people lies in traversing the city, as necessary, to find some people on the word of other people. Police act as go-betweens for antagonists who may even be practically within arm's reach—yelling outside their cars in a fender bender, or giving opposite accounts of a domestic dispute. Real "investigation" and "detection"—the glorious business of tracing an unidentified malefactor after the fact of a crime, without just finding out, from the witnesses closest at hand, who did it—is an activity that exists in police departments, but only among a tiny number of specialized personnel who don't even have to wear uniforms.

Where the police identify a crime against the city, state, or law, rather than an affronted person—the so-called victimless crimes of illicit possession, unlicensed work, or unlicensed sale—we can best speak of another police function as distributing crime. The legislature declares certain objects and unlicensed commerce illegal. The police then go and distribute these violations. Street drugs are made illegal (prescription drugs are fine), hidden and unlicensed weapons are illegal (mostly carried by those on unsafe streets, which is to say the poor), flawed cars are illegal (unlit taillight, noisy muffler, unpaid insurance). Thus police spend a large part of their time distributing crime to the sorts of people who seem likely to be criminals—the poor and marginal—and the prediction is prophetic: these people turn out to *be* criminals, as soon as they are stopped and frisked and forced to turn out the contents of their pockets or glove boxes. (Leave them alone, and most would never be "criminal" at all.) The majority of violations technically listed in the tables of the law are of no interest to uniformed police. Those committed in the course of doing business, in the professions, and in government aren't likely to be actively detected or sought by anyone. They are accidentally or competitively disclosed—leading to the awkwardness of the need of some settlement, which is then dealt with by regulatory agencies, guilds, or accrediting bodies, plus, at the far extreme, civil-court proceedings and court-mandated money exchanges. Very rarely are police or even criminal justice ever brought in.

The most admirable and defensible of the exemplary police activities is "keeping the peace." It is also the least discussed, the least subject to written laws and directives, and the vaguest. In a democracy of equal citizens, people will inevitably conflict, even through no fault or crime of one party or the other. Someone will take advantage, or threaten. The role of the police here is to pacify—and pacification, in a civil democracy, is no bad thing intrinsically. It is a vital, valuable thing.

Enforcing racial terror: this exemplary function, unofficial or officially denied though universally known, owns no familiar phrase. In recent decades, African-Americans have made proverbial the facetious offenses that police seem to be pursuing: "driving while black," "shopping while black," "walking while black." The history of racial terrorism by whites is old. Police have gradually taken up its responsibilities in a process that goes back more than a century. Police departments' role in racial terror has survived even where racism has waned and their forces have integrated nonwhite officers. Racial terrorism is simply a part of the job for local and metropolitan police forces in America—any policing at the level of the city, broadly construed. This may have been replicated in foreign municipalities, as in London policing of Caribbean and South Asian populations, and Paris policing of North Africans in the *banlieues*. Racial terror does create enormous complications for any ordinary theory of what American police do, however—just as it carves a fundamental division between the experience and expectations non-African-American citizens have of police and those held by African-Americans.

I would like to add a different essential function of police: being seen.

If you want sometime to sympathize with police, watch young ones when they don't know they're observed. The young cop stands on a corner, squinting in bright winter sun. Pedestrians approach from every side, with questions, asking directions, or start talking without introduction, boring him, because he is part of the street like a stop sign. Or, as one does with a stop sign, they ignore and veer around him (sometimes deliberately, pointedly, despising him for his uniform).

You can see how hard it must be to ready a face for each of these people that will look authoritative rather than deferential. Between encounters, you could watch the front fall, strained by all these obligations. That is why our comic picture of a moment of rest for the harried policeman requires he take off his patrolman's hat and wipe the perspiration from his face, as if smoothing down the instrument that's put to such exhausting work.

The basic ambition of a policeman is never to cease to project force, stolidity, an unbroken front, seriousness, intimidation. But that's impossible. Policing contains daily humiliation at each inevitable failure of the policeman's front. The uniform itself, the badge in its widest sense, like the luster of all shields meant to dazzle, is meant to maintain this front regardless of the individual inside. But the uniform can never succeed entirely. You would need RoboCop. All police are mortal. There is something in the cladness of police, their preoccupation with holding the uniform together, that makes us aware of all their armor's shortcomings, or inspires imagination of these human beings naked, their uniforms taken away. The traditional English name for the mana with which police uniforms are invested is surely awe. Erving Goffman, in his famous conceptualizations of front, face, and performance, recalled Kurt Riezler's point that the inevitable obverse of awe is shame.

The coupling of awe and shame among police comes out in our awareness of police symmetry and asymmetry. A shield is worn on the peak of the hat, while a second one covers the heart. The gun descends from one side of the utility belt, and, traditionally, the stick hangs from the other. Sometimes a heavy flashlight substitutes. Looking at individual police, they almost always seem lopsided. The belt pulls down on one side. The blouse comes undone. They are constantly hiking up their pants. The regulation shoes are the same as those of nurses, waiters, and mail carriers. Heaviness gathers at the waist, in a sedentary, slow, caloric job. There is something in police that droops.

The symbol of police in this dimension in North America is the donut. The donut is equivocal. It is not loved as apple pie is. It has no national or official standing as apple pie does. It has a local message only. Donuts, like other deep-fried delicacies, do not travel well. Yet donuts have our rueful affection. Really, it is the pursuit of coffee that drives police to donut shops. Donuts confirm what they will not admit with their badge and gun, that they are the ones who must be awake all the time, in public, in the extremely boring job of sitting in a place, either thereby to assure passersby and the public that they *are* sitting there, watching, or to ensure that other people *don't* sit there. This sitting is being added to their nature; the stasis gathers at their waists. They are living traffic cones. Traffic cones, too, would drink coffee and eat donuts to stay awake.

Most surprising, perhaps, is that the more time you spend looking at police, the more you see that the law is not a true resource for them. A rationale, yes, but a thin one. Police lack law. I didn't notice this until I really started watching them, thinking about what I had seen, reading about them and reading research done on them. The original television version of *Law & Order* split each episode into two parts. First, policing; second, courtroom proceedings. It took me years to notice that the title was backward. Police are order. This explains the police perception of, and anathema toward, any symbol of disorder or mess. In their daily practice, police pledge at every level to avoid mess or clean it up. The cliché from Mary Douglas's *Purity and Danger,* her cross-cultural study of the constitution of dirt and taboo, holds up here: What we call dirt is only "matter out of place." Police clean up.

It is always hard to remind or convince police that their stated loyalty is to the Constitution. It's not their fault, really, so much as it is the fault of a municipal organization of authority that keeps legal thinking at a level "above their pay grade." A bad consequence is that it's quite difficult to make police feel responsible for civil-rights violations or unjust laws, since rights and the law of the polity are not theirs to know or decide. The police reformer David Harris describes the experience of a friend in the Oakland Police Department, directing police retraining around racial violations, which crystallizes a general truth.

In 2001, Captain Ron Davis, a twenty-year veteran . . . led an in-service training session on racial profiling. . . . Davis began by asking the assembled officers a simple question: "What is your job?" . . . "What I want to know," he asked, "is, what is your mission, and the mission of your department? To what are you dedicating your time, day after day?"

Most of the answers were variations on "fighting crime": "Catching bad guys"; "Getting criminals off the street"; "Keeping the streets safe from predators"; "Chasing crooks"; "Taking down the guys that need to be taken down"; "Responding to nine-one-one emergencies"; "Helping the department achieve its goals"; "Carrying out the chief's orders." . . . Then he asked, "What does your oath say? When you graduated from the academy and became a cop, you all raised your hand and took an oath. What did you swear to do?" . . . Silence. . . . Eventually, an officer gave Davis the answer he sought: "We swear to uphold the law and the Constitution." Another officer spoke up. "Well, sure, that's the oath," he said, "but everyone knows what this job is really about."

I'm not sure anybody knows. Not us, but also not police themselves, not politicians and government, and not political theorists.

Part of the reason police seem at present unreformable is that they have no intelligible place in the philosophy of democracy. It's possible they never have. When our theories of democracy took shape, police as we know them were a minor tertiary agency and an afterthought. If police don't take stock of the Constitution, I sometimes wonder, might it be because our Constitution can't conceive of them?

"Police" as a word and concept exists in Europe from the fifteenth and sixteenth centuries forward, as a word for the administrative state management of population and territory—*Polizeiwissenschaft,* for the incipient German bureaucracies. Modern Anglo-American police forces date to the urban development of private hired watchmen and guards for merchant or guild-professional spaces. Benjamin Franklin helped reorganize and rationalize one such force, among his many civic projects, in Philadelphia before the American Revolution, as he relates in his *Autobiography.* Their major urban institutionalization occurred in London under Robert Peel in 1829 in the Metropolitan Police Department (yielding officers nicknamed "bobbies," for their founder, and the traditional abbreviation for the department, "the Met").

This metropolitan form of police organization marked a dividing line with the tradition in Europe. On the Continent, crown monarchs had kept even the prosaic functions of policing tied to the sovereign. This meant that the European tradition, emanating from France, wove military power, spying, and control of the poor in with urban regulation and penal justice. First abolished by the Revolution, police surveillance was reconstituted a decade later under Napoleon. In *Discipline and Punish*, Foucault described the position of European police with the 1768 motto of Vattel: "By means of a wise police, the sovereign accustoms the people to order and obedience."

"Police" and *"policy"* are cognate: our liberal political tradition has focused on the second. The most revealing juncture in classical liberalism may come in a rare discussion from Adam Smith, in the 1762 lecture given the title "Of Police." For Smith, what matters to civil government as "police" possesses sufficient dignity only when it speaks to what we would call economic policy. The constabulary is acknowledged as a necessity for its execution of the criminal law but is beneath political notice:

> Police is the second general division of jurisprudence. The name is French, and is originally derived from the Greek πολιτεια [*politeia*], which properly signified the policey of civil government, but now it only means the regulation of the inferiour parts of government, *viz.* cleanliness, security, and cheapness or plenty. The two former, to witt, the proper method of carrying dirt from the streets, and the execution of justice, so far as it regards regulations for preventing crimes or the method of keeping a city guard, tho' usefull, are too mean to be considered in a general discourse of this kind.

"The proper method of carrying dirt from the streets" and "the method of keeping a city guard": twin practicalities.

Liberal and social-contract theories of democracy—those that begin from Hobbes and Locke and that form the official philosophical background to the American Republic that was constituted in 1789—do have a central place for punishment, but not for police. This is perhaps because, on a strong version of contract theory, police ought not to exist. How could democratic agreement fail to be self-enforcing in its daily practice if the agreement is real, sustained by each individual's consent? Social-contract theory does include the discouragement and rectification of error after definite breaches of the contract, as punishment will address the convicted wrongdoer who either gave in to the temptation of interest or was perverted to it by some personal flaw. But the right agency for requital is penal law. Crime and punishment belong to judicial proceedings and courts, where the cause can be unfolded after the fact. There is no location *alongside* or *outside* the citizens and their contract, for a supplementary force or additional locus of authority and violence, for mediation or interruption. There is no place for any intervening agency with *political* force, except as a kind of collector or picker-upper of persons—hence, one very much like a trash picker or one who carries dirt from the streets, as Smith proposed.

With the growth of the role of police in democratic societies, a theory of their presence and place in government has simply not emerged in proportion to their power and variable function. The only really worthwhile thing we have is empirical description, from the late-twentieth-century field of police sociology—and this research has been most useful in dispelling illusions, not creating comprehensive philosophy. An impressive number of practical things have been studied and yielded surprising findings, on such topics as work hours, organization, decision making, dramaturgy, constituencies, professional attitudes, and differential application of the law to people of different identities and situations. The radical theorist Mark Neocleous gives some results:

> Both the "law and order" lobby and its Left critics have failed to take on board the implications of a mass of research on the police. . . . The overwhelming majority of calls for police assistance are "service" rather than crime related: in an average year only 15 to 20 percent of all the calls to the police are about crime, and what is initially reported by the police as a crime is often found to be not a crime by the responding police officer. Studies have shown that less than a third of time spent on duty is on crime-related work; that approximately eight out of ten incidents handled by patrols by a range of different police departments are regarded by the police themselves as non-criminal matters; that the percentage of police effort devoted to traditional criminal law matters probably does not exceed 10 percent; that as little as 6 percent of a patrol officer's time is spent on incidents finally defined as "criminal"; and that only a

very small number of criminal offenses are discovered by the police themselves. Moreover, most of the time the police do not use the criminal law to restore order. In the USA police officers make an average of one arrest every two weeks; one study found that among 156 officers assigned to a high-crime area of New York City, 40 percent did not make a single felony arrest in a year.

The disillusioning thrust of this work on the usual mandate for police—stopping crime—had already been distilled forty years ago by the most famous and influential sociologist of police, Egon Bittner. As he archly put it in 1974: "When one looks at what policemen actually do, one finds that criminal law enforcement is something that most of them do with the frequency located somewhere between virtually never and very rarely." Yet the next step of theorizing from this new knowledge, a task also authoritatively identified with Bittner, pushed this ironic mode into the theory itself. What even the most original sociology of police seems to show, again and again, is that police are paradoxical and their strictures unworkable. They don't fit philosophically. As a stopgap profession poised between other philosophically grounded institutions, police are "impossible." Perhaps police ought not to exist, thinking theoretically, since their behavior is inadequately supported by the democratic social order's explicit justifications. Yet they must exist, practically—despite their errors—precisely because they have proved themselves in democracy as both "first responders" and a "last resort," a mobilization of nondefinition and nonfixity for all sorts of situations: the agency thrown at anything in society that can't be accommodated or that we don't want to see. Bittner's formulation is the one that has lasted, and haunts the field as the only really original and lasting philosophical contribution to what our police are:

> I propose to explain the function of police by drawing attention to what their existence makes available in society that, all things being equal, would not be otherwise available. . . . My thesis is that police are empowered and required to impose or, as the case may be, coerce a provisional solution upon emergent problems without

having to brook or defer to opposition of any kind, and that further, their competence to intervene extends to every kind of emergency, without any exceptions whatsoever.

And that's all they are—that's their essence. "The assessment whether the service the police are uniquely competent to provide is on balance desirable or not, in terms of, let us say, the aspirations of a democratic polity, is beyond the scope of the argument," Bittner apologizes.

In his analysis, the key term from his definition may well emerge to be "impose," or "coerce"—and the sine qua non for Bittner's picture of police becomes availability of force (or even violence). The apparently damning body of Bittner's work has been embraced by police chiefs, perhaps because it furnishes executives with the only plausible apology in the face of continual criticism. One major professional association now gives out its annual Egon Bittner Award to a municipal chief who has survived more than fifteen years of service—not ironically, but in earnest.

Suppose, though, we did want to find the place of police in a democratic polity, in the sense of what version of their role *can* be desirable for democracy.

Their feature of visibility might be a place to start. Police lift accidents, events, and gatherings into vision. They enhance situations but no one mistakes them for the main show. The officers are a blue aniline dye, poured into channels of society, down alleyways and interstates, sketching in blueprint the lines of public space, how we distribute dispersion, how we distribute assembly, how we distribute crime, how we distribute safety. Or in a sense police are the grease or gunk—the fluid or sand—that speeds or obstructs shifts in the constitution of social reality.

Police are piped along the edges and borders of spontaneous or planned gatherings, installing for others, in the moment, the outline of public significance. One knows to walk toward anywhere that police are standing, where they mark the significance of something *else:* a parade, a concert, a demonstration, or an arrest, an abuse, an accident.

One can go to enjoy them, their offer of theater and ritual to daily occurrences, as they establish a space of eventfulness. Or to watchdog them, to make sure that their handling of people can't occur invisibly and unaccounted for.

Secrecy by police in any public place always identifies them as suspect. Yet police departments hold tightly to their capacities for secrecy and claim them to be necessary for their heroic function of detection and investigation. Insofar as detection of crime is what police *wish* their job were about, police are likely always to strain for greater secrecy in a democracy.

Where sight disappears, in the paddy wagon and the police station, abuse becomes possible. (And indeed these are the sorts of places, along with jails, a democratic police might seek to eradicate or open up.) One knows the hush that occurs in a crowd when an arrestee disappears into the closed, windowless wagon; the citizen, even as a criminal, has temporarily disappeared from the democratic public (until arraignment, the space of salvation by *habeas corpus*—then one looks for marks on the face, marks on the wrists and the body, from abuse). This is one of those gaps into which citizens fall where democracy can disappear.

Yet the real rival of sight is not just secrecy but touch, which registers itself only between bodies that know what has actually been done but can't prove it by other means. Police possess touch, citizens should possess sight. A question is why a third element that could stand between sight and touch doesn't come much more to the fore, when we think of police, in some way that we would find democratically recognizable: talk. Talk is the actual basis of a democracy. It is the specifically democratic dimension of human relations. It restores the assurance of neighborliness. Talk is also what police actually mostly do in encountering the public; yet one doesn't think of police as talkers and listeners first, but as bullies. What happens when citizens and police talk in the fateful encounter? *How* do they talk? And if they don't talk, why not?

Suppose we say this: Police are negotiators, but without access to contract, law, or eloquence. Their medium is not law. They do not always use entirely memorable or wholly coherent words. Usually they enter situations of conflict which they did not cause, but which they are required to enter into as third parties. There, they are deliberately distracting, grandstanding observers. Turning the attention of other parties away from each other and instead to themselves.

When you look at them in the right way, focusing on the middle range between space-holding inaction and violent attack, negotiating can be seen to be what the police do unendingly, habitually—but unfamiliarly, because in some way they generally refuse to recognize or care about the original goals of negotiating parties. They bring a separate set of criteria to bear, and not always appealing ones. Is this chargeable? Should this person be removed or transported temporarily? When can I leave, and how do I scare these citizens a bit so as to feel they won't come into conflict again, and police won't need to come back? Police negotiate without an obvious, single, unitary reference or goal—other than to end the necessity for their being there. And they are always asking themselves a separate question of whether to lift a person out of the horizontal conflict and into the vertical mechanism of criminal justice—a process for which the cop won't really be ultimately responsible, and which he won't have to enter himself.

Even a traffic stop, for the most minor infraction at a stop sign or in a twenty-mile-an-hour zone, becomes a negotiation. Here the negotiated outcome may be a "warning," when a warning is ostensibly a name for something official although in fact "the official" has been denied or put away. "Okay, I'm going to let you go with a warning." The "warning" is not known to the statute book. It does not exist as a juridical category. But it is one of the major categories of police thinking, and one that—instead of objecting to its arbitrariness, or uneven application—we might want to preserve. Because it is a key moment when police, without breaking "front," without admitting deficiency, acknowledge that negotiation has been won by the citizen.

Police exist so we can see them on the corner, or on the subway platform, so that we know, when we move in public, that no other person can take us for unseen, to rob us or molest us without defense. They exist sometimes just to mark a lane closure (by standing in it) or road construction (by standing in front of it) or a town fair (by standing at its entrance). They announce eventfulness, and in some way their mere presence stands against danger.

Of course we feel differently if we think the danger they might think they see is us. Or if we resemble their idea of obstruction, or of notable event. When police eye African-Americans, harass African-Americans, obstruct the movements of African-Americans, and wind up drawing their guns and murdering African-Americans—which even in the twenty-first century they do with regularity and impunity, no matter the police department or region of the United States—it's first because America still sees racially. Kidnapping an African labor force to build the country is still the country's unrepented sin. The mad but ingenious mechanism of coding the difference between free and slave by "color," not by an actual spectrum of tans but "white" and "black," as metaphysical as day and night, bright and dark, sight and obstruction, nobility and stain, lingers. Police, as devotees of sight and seeing, sustain this way of looking at every citizen of recognizable African ancestry.

What differentiates a place that seems clean, orderly, and peaceful from the same location with items out of place, mixed up, confusing, noisy, and conflictual isn't just aesthetic norms in the neighborhoods police come from, but what they think that "we" want, by how *we* see. But who are we? The police sociologist Peter K. Manning, one of the best ethnographers of police departments, has strongly made the point that one thing police tacitly depend on most is how they think their client citizens view them as they undertake patrols and arrests—yet many of the formalizations they use to imagine such "law-abiding citizens," "good people," "the public," rigidly enacting an absent standard of order, alienate them from their actual citizenry. The place they possess least guidance and clarity is on what "good people" want and how we want to be treated:

> The police were designed to respond to citizen demands and requirements for service as much because this represented prevention or deterrence of the sources of crime as because the police were intended to act symbolically as one citizen would to another in time of need.

The symbolic centrality of police action as standing for the collective concern of people, one for another, cannot and should not be underestimated. Law has grown up as a means of formalizing the conditions under which the police *must* act and *cannot* act but does not provide the basis on which they do or should act.

Violence, too, is given to police as a technique they alone can use, in the service of the overall nonviolence or pacification of society, such that citizens need never use violence legitimately upon one another—they route it through police, so to speak. But this formal device, too, winds up defining police by their application of violence. They wind up originating violence as a means of resolving any social deadlock. Police add violence to situations. If we can see, and see through, police, we may see that this becomes a way of injecting *testing* violence or domination into the heart of society in a *public* way. Small comfort, perhaps, since there is no guarantee that we will oppose the wicked things that police may show us. Our neighbors may support that wickedness. We may have no idea how to fix it. Still, police violence differs from forms of violence and domination which have no visible presence, or public check. The police measure out in public what the society will tolerate, even to our shame.

Is it ever possible to love police? Certainly at the personal level, momentarily, it's possible, when they save us from direct violence, or return a lost child home. I mean beyond that. Perhaps the other scenario really is when we know they have order or law on their side, and they don't apply it—because, they hint, their adherence is to community, not to the State. "I see you, and I let you go, for the sake of an order you and I share which is yet not the law."

This reaches to a completely different part of theories of democracy—to fraternity, solidarity, sympathy, sociability, trust—the least formalizable part, the part most betrayed in recent years (or maybe always) by moneyed politics and corrupted government. The least articulable part, and a place to start.

[2015]

VIII

THOREAU TRAILER PARK
THE MEANING OF LIFE, PART IV

In Concord, Massachusetts, opposite Walden Pond, during the decades when I was growing up nearby, the maples and oaks that fringed Walden also shaded two lots of concrete, where there rested a congregation of flat-roofed oblong trailer homes, like caskets of ivory. Cinder-block front steps tied the screen doors to the earth. Fabricated to move, these homes had lost their mobility. The state had purchased the land underneath them. Divided from these lots by a state highway not much widened from the old cart road it had paved, the dark woods, the deep pond, the wan beaches, and vast tracts of forest past the railroad tracks constituted Walden Pond State Park, a nature preserve, and also a historical memorial, controlled by the Commonwealth of Massachusetts. Thus there was the state park, and then there was the trailer park. The two must be at odds forever. For if the low, undistinguished dwellings across the road made a "trailer park" in the American parlance, this name marked them off profoundly from the logs and grasses and falling leaves, paths and overlooks, fenced in so that anonymous citizens could enjoy them (for a modest entrance fee) as long as they left no trace. "Trailer park" bespeaks a corral for retirees and the working class, poor enough not to own houses not on wheels, but not deprived enough to be picturesque or pitiable; not poor enough to lack garish collections of cars which nosed up to vinyl siding, and oversized televisions that twinkled in daytime through windows of automotive glass, cutting out silhouettes of plastic flowers on the sills, or glinting through the mazes of chintz curtains. "Trailer trash," referring to human beings, is the rare American phrase of contempt that lacks an organized group to resent it. Throughout my childhood, the state park service prosecuted a war of attrition against the trailers: forbidding transfer of their sites to heirs or newcomers, prohibiting return to anyone who planned to use his wheels and then come back, finally disposing of each carcass as its owners died.

Walden Pond is historical, not just natural, because Henry David Thoreau philosophized there for two years in the 1840s. This source of notoriety is unlike that of the other state parks down Battle Road at the other side of Concord, entering Lexington, where patriots touched off the American Revolution, or War of Independence, by shooting at massed British soldiers in 1775. Thoreau, just two generations of "Americans" later, moved into a small house he erected on borrowed land on Walden's shore, grew beans and potatoes for sale, and noticed as the seasons turned who wandered through his neighborhood, both human and animal. He made his contribution to the tradition in philosophy slightly later than Kierkegaard, slightly earlier than Nietzsche, though both are his spiritual siblings. His book of thoughts and observations, *Walden,* and one essay on his idea of the individual and the state, "Civil Disobedience," are enough to make him one of America's most significant philosophers. Thoreau's questions were quite simple: what, truly, living is; how much more of it could be done if one withdrew from customary obligations, especially the command to "make a living," hold a job, own property, swear to debts and credits. He counseled making one's business only spiritual, or interpersonal. The precise site at Walden where his cabin rested has been forgotten, but visitors have deposited a cairn of rocks behind the pond's northeast cover. It mixes stones worthy of a New England farm wall with smooth balls the size of hands. A rebuilding of Thoreau's dwelling, to the dimensions described in *Walden*'s first chapter, in the main parking lot, wears the refined look of machined and store-bought lumber. It is periodically vacuumed clean. Nearby, a bronze statue of the philosopher meets the weather. The gift shop sells quotations from Thoreau's writings, printed on bumper stick-

ers, coffee mugs, T-shirts, and day calendars—"In wildness is the preservation of the world," "Simplify, simplify," "Beware of all enterprises
that require new clothes"—alongside complicating goods: pieces of new
clothing and walking equipment for navigating the well-trodden paths
in Walden woods. It also sells every one of Thoreau's books.

The state park is a wonderful invention; I don't want to make fun.
It saved my suburban childhood in many ways. It preserves woodlands,
and husbands oaks, pines, and birches; shrubs and weeds; chipmunks
and frogs; owls and chickadees. It makes a swimming pond available to
anyone regardless of town residence, one hardly bettered west of Boston, which provides relief for so many in the summer heat. But that
trailer park, while it lasted, was a beam in everyone's eye. To the park
service, to journalists, to preservationists, to visitors, it couldn't be a
plausible place to live the simple life, or a place for philosophy; it was an
eyesore, an offense. The trailer residents, who are all dead now, bought
their groceries in Acton or other poorer towns than Concord, the fancy
community in which they were called "the gypsies." Their presence,
through my childhood in the 1980s, was an important mystery to me.
As each trailer disappeared, it left behind a gray rectangle of cement
like an old bed. I crossed the chains and Do Not Trespass signs to the
last one standing but I was too short to see in. And as I came to know
Thoreau better, through his writings, in my young adulthood in the
1990s, I thought the trailer park might be one of the few things Thoreau
would defend, against so much that was done, at Walden Pond, for his
name's sake.

It is hard to remember what Thoreau said because it is all so disturbing.
It is easier on us to think of a thin man who erected a cabin with his
own hands on the shores of a lovely pond. Thoreau deliberately didn't
build his cabin from scratch. He hacked a free timber frame from someone else's trees, got friends to help him raise it, and recycled the rest
from a laborer's bivouac, buying cheap, for boards and roof, "the shanty
of James Collins, an Irishman who worked on the Fitchburg Railroad."
This was philosophical, with all its shortcuts and offenses. Thoreau's fire

burned to irradiate a fundamental mutation into "economy." Economy for him followed from his theorem: "The cost of a thing is the amount of what I will call life which is required to be exchanged for it, immediately or in the long run." Knowing "life" in two senses—holding a yardstick to it, putting it on the scales, to measure it and value it, while at the same time experiencing it, submitting to its manifestations—is the chief philosophical, and daily, task. The challenge reminds me of Schiller's metaphor of social reform, in *Letters on the Aesthetic Education of Man,* as repairing a clock without stopping it or failing to let it tell the time.

In Thoreau's Concord, farming seemed the most estimable pursuit. Economic concentration, as at the big farms in his neighborhood, was revealed to him, once he had begun his fateful measurements of life, as an enslavement from which only death would free its beneficiaries: "When the farmer has got his house, he may not be the richer but the poorer for it, and it be the house that has got him." Instead of the farmer gathering his necessities in the least expensive and destructive way, he abstracts magnitudes he doesn't need. "To get his shoestrings he speculates in herds of cattle." It might be better, Thoreau suggested, that we sleep even in coffin-sized toolboxes, of the kind he saw among the railroad tracks; we could dwell in them at less expense to our lives, anyway, than that exacted by the big coffins, called houses and properties, on which we pay a thirty-year mortgage. "Many a man is harassed to death to pay the rent of a larger and more luxurious box who would not have frozen to death in such a box as this."

All of his words can be hard to bear, but no American is spared. "I began to occupy my house on the 4th of July," Thoreau boasts, and he means to rival the pretenders to the Fourth of July—those founding Americans of 1776, who claimed they fought for independence, freeing the new nation, when really they left it in ignorant bondage. Thoreau makes war on jobs; debts; houses; inheritances; governments; states. Only his economy can give the country a new chance in its bankruptcy. Thoreau passionately adores the pond and the woods, to be sure, and wildness, and nature, but not because they are adornment, or refreshment, or comfort to human lives. They are, for human life, brute lessons. Beautiful nature is beautiful for men and women because it strips our life to essentials, reflects us, dismisses us, and smashes our idols and objets d'art. "Before we can adorn our houses with beautiful objects the walls must be stripped, and our lives must be stripped, and beautiful housekeeping and beautiful living be laid for a foundation; now, a taste for the beautiful is most cultivated out of doors, where there is no house and no housekeeper."

The philosopher occupied a cabin, because he wished to live outside all houses. He left Walden, too—apparently Heaven—once he had gotten what his soul needed at that time. "Perhaps it seemed to me that I had several more lives to live, and could not spare any more time for that one."

Occupy Wall Street occupied a park in the financial center of the United States, not because it wanted to sleep out of doors, but because its participants wanted to live in a democracy. Was that connection clear, to all who saw it on TV, to everyone who held an opinion of it? Eight weeks it lasted—eight weeks!—and then it was shoved out with sticks and fists by police, its experiment uncompleted. I was there on the Sunday morning it started, and blocked from the park by police on the weeknight it ended. I had known parks, and tents, and little camps—seriousness and play; the American landscape is littered with them. So what was Zuccotti Park, which the inhabitants insisted on calling by an alternate name (which may have been the old, original name), Liberty Square? Was it a Walden, a project in philosophy? Was it another trailer park, cleared by the state, a disreputable idyll of those who lacked greater means?—despised for that reason, as will be all havens of those too weak to impose their wills upon their betters?

Walden Pond, for all its beauties, is a pond only, not a lake or a seashore—a puddle in the grander scheme of things. Thoreau knew that well. Liberty Square, a tiny rectangle of unlovable paving, hardly ever deserved the name of park; one knew how unwanted it was, how undesirable and unknown. What made it seem a park was just the legal guarantee that it must stay open for the public twenty-four hours a day, though that contract, too, was intermittently abrogated by its "owners." (The park had been promised as a permanent public space, in a deal in the 1960s, in exchange for allowing its owners to build new office space in violation of existing laws. Thus this leftover plot could be "public," yet not owned by the public or managed by the state. This mutual irresponsibility proved essential to Occupy, as the mayor and realtors dithered over who should suffer the bad press of destroying it.) What sort of park Zuccotti was becoming, though, depended on the angle from which you looked at it. To me, in my idealism or naiveté, it seemed a renewal of the basic reference of America, the visible presence of the People, the living unruliness at the core of dead memorials. Six days before the first Occupy gathering, September 17, 2011, officials had opened, a few blocks away, a foolish, meaningless September 11 memorial, on the tenth anniversary, while we could see them continue to build a giant tower of private corporate office space above the hole, the real offering, amidst their crocodile tears, to the mass murder of American citizens. The free speech emerging in Zuccotti Park was the living memorial in the building's shadow.

The occupation's purpose was to address the economy. No one could deny that private Wall Street banks had, in 2008, nearing collapse, made themselves whole with billions from the taxpayers' treasury, and put great sums from the rescue into their own pockets. They took taxpayers' money and foreclosed on taxpayers' homes. They unhoused the middle class while the executives renovated their third and fourth and fifth vacation houses. But principally banks, brought back from the brink of death, cast their weight, and all the power the democracy restored to them, against democracy: spending the citizens' money in election funding and lobbying, to ensuring that good old laws, born in the Great Depression, retired in the 1990s, which had prevented such profitable (and self-destructive) speculation, could not be restored. Banks spent the citizens' money to guarantee they were heard before any citizen. So the Wall Street occupation was meant as a reminder that the country could still demand its democracy, and put banks under the rule of law, and take something from them in recompense for our foolish generosity. Many cynics who pretended sympathy said: "You should be protesting in Washington, not on Wall Street." But if arsonists burn down houses (and collect the insurance), and the fire department won't rouse itself (or is bribed not to), you should go and stand where the fires originate, and the rags are being soaked and lit—until your neighbors, the whole city, will turn and look.

Still, I underestimated the degree to which Liberty Square had the character of a trailer park, too, not just an experiment in philosophy. Because I am bourgeois. I had an apartment to go to; at night I slept in my own bed. I believed I was at ease with Thoreau in my wish not to make politics take over the rest of my life, remembering the daily individual matters as more important, except when interrupted by injustice. "If I devote myself to other pursuits and contemplations, I must first see, at least, that I do not pursue them sitting upon another man's shoulders." Quite right; and then I went home. In the encampment, however, it became clear that others, much of the core of the occupation, really did want to live together. They wanted to create a democracy not of symbols, but of fact. A bit of the miscellaneous old New York port city or the self-governing Yankee town, a village. A home. People wanted to live democracy together—no matter how bad this looked to those of us, and our less committed fellows, from the home-dwelling petty bourgeoisie. The homeless began to join Occupy. When the vast metropolis of Bloomberg's New York sees them as human trash, littering the parks and squares that business committees primp into window displays, this park alone meant not just a hiding place, but safety, sleep, conversation, amusement, and food, without condescension and conditions.

That a democracy could become a community in actuality, exposing its conflicts and sufferings, with none of the paper stuffing of symbols to cushion it—that a park could furnish people a place to live, under such outside scrutiny—this spelled terrible danger for the protests. As many times as crowds chanted, "This is what democracy looks like" when the police threatened us, I cringed to hear how the words advertised our weakness. Few enough people want to see what democracy looks like, unless it has been cast and burnished in bright symbols. Too much seeing "the Democracy," as the citizenry used to be called, will make it easier for many people to wish that it be gone.

The Democracy does not wear new clothes. Its kindness and manners, transpiring between individuals, will not be visible from boardroom windows high above. From up above, in air-conditioned rooms, one cannot smell that the Democracy is clean, sweet; so it is called smelly, dirty, unwashed. The distant citizenry, cut off from it, treats the Democracy with disgust. And parts of the Democracy will be poor and weak; this, many can't bear to see, especially those closest to the middle or to poverty. It reminds us what we are, where we can fall. So, after eight weeks, without great resistance from other parts of the city, the police were able to hoist their klieg lights, barricade or arrest the press, and beat the Democracy: chase and push the Democracy, arrest it for running into the fists of the police—all in the name, as the mayor's orders came down, of "public health." Garbagemen threw the occupation's five-thousand-book library into the trash to "keep it safe." Those books were ruined, as certainly as if they had been burned. In the empty square, with America's children bruised and bleeding in paddy wagons or on the sidelines, the City of New York brought out the power washers, to make a park glisten, into which no human was allowed. They ended the protests in the name of cleanliness.

I discovered myself, the little bourgeois, pushed by the police, insulted, mocked. So I turned out to be in the trailer park after all. Or, as the thought has gradually grown on me, in one place no one had thought existed with the protesters there, at all: a jail. The liberty of Liberty Square, for those two months, had in fact meant the creation of a jail. On every side, the police lined up facing us—day after day; and I had thought of them as benign. I thought their presence was a gross expenditure and waste of my tax money, certainly; a stimulus to fear, undoubtedly; a sort of marketing gift from the city to the banks, unfairly, as if free assembly, but more specifically *these* opinions, were dangerous. I saw our police line up at the perimeter of Bank of America like employees, fence posts, servants of the bank; but, of course, we pay them. The blue-uniformed guardians stood along the margin with Broadway, facing off with us. They lined Liberty Street, closed it up with police cars and equipment and men. Well, hadn't these silent barriers in the end produced a jail, containing us? Or had the existence of this tiny pathetic space, the one place in the city for the supposed American virtues, of the Constitution's free assembly, and free speech, the Founders' contest of opinions, brought out the jail from the city around it? Each bank building was a bar of our cell, or a stone block of the wall. Now the hideous "Freedom Tower" erected itself, to bar the window of the open sky.

Jail is the other notable site with which Thoreau, the American philosopher, is associated, after the cabin, and the pond. His town of Concord put him there once, when he refused to pay his poll tax, with-holding support from the United States which upheld slavery and jailed the man who wouldn't send an escaped slave back to his owner, which invaded Mexico with its army to kill and terrorize its neighbors for its own territorial ambitions. Thoreau refused to let his neighbors in Con-cord escape the obligation to justify why they did pay, why they obeyed, even to the tax collector—why they went along with injustice, only saying that it was wrong, when they could act together. From "Civil Disobedience":

> Under a government which imprisons any unjustly, the true place for a just man is also a prison. The proper place to-day, the only place which Massachusetts has provided for her freer and less desponding spirits, is in her prisons, to be put out and locked out of the State by her own act, as they have already put themselves out by their principles. . . . If any think that their influence would be lost there, and their voices no longer afflict the ear of the State, that they would not be as an enemy within its walls, they do not know by how much truth is stronger than error, nor how much more eloquently and effectively he can combat injustice who has experi-enced a little in his own person. Cast your whole vote, not a strip of paper merely, but your whole influence.

The theory behind the practice of occupation, the theory behind all "direct action," in which one goes to a place of injustice or its conduits and symbols and stands there until one is noticed and joined—or carted away unjustly to jail—is, in part, an inheritance from Walden Pond's eccentric, Thoreau. Other reformers accomplished more in action. But Thoreau communicated a clarity to nonviolent direct action in words that found their way to Gandhi in India and Martin Luther King in Alabama. While government can be maintained by voting, the perversion of government cannot be fixed by voting—nor need it be. If your government gives up on justice, the many men and women with consciences must go to the junctures where the government has leagued with injustice and clog them, with their whole selves, body and soul: to force a decision. Won't your countrymen, government servants included, gradually withdraw support for the wrongdoing? Like so many of the edicts in *Walden*, here, too, in "Civil Disobedience," it is only by irritating people, by interrupting their ease and convenience, that their consciences can be awakened to their capacity for choice.

> The government itself, which is only the mode which the people have chosen to execute their will, is equally liable to be abused and perverted before the people can act through it. . . . A minority is powerless while it conforms to the majority; it is not even a minority then; but it is irresistible when it clogs by its whole weight. If the alternative is to keep all just men in prison, or give up war or slavery, the State will not hesitate which to choose. . . . If the tax-gatherer, or any other public officer, asks me, as one has done, "But what shall I do?" my answer is, "If you really wish to do anything, resign your office." When the subject has refused allegiance, and the officer has resigned his office, then the revolution is accomplished.

A couple of months ago, I went to the courthouse to see the trials of the last defenders who were arrested when the police came and emptied Zuccotti Park. They sat down and locked arms in the little kitchen where the community had prepared free meals for hundreds each day. Taken and arraigned in November, they finally were promised a day to speak their case in the public air of court, in June. The State's prosecutor, in court, announced himself unprepared, and, without a word from the defendants, the judge happily adjourned the trials until autumn. A year after the 2011 eviction of Zuccotti Park, there is still no opportunity to learn if the arrests were legal, or against the Constitution, or to let the case be made, within the system of the State, against the unjust State.

But the discovery that shocked my bourgeois sensibilities had to do with the young men and women entering the courthouse for their trial. I was amazed to see they had not dressed for court. They did not wear suits, or proper dresses, or ties. But to win, I reflected, you have to behave in the way that people like this, the lawyers, the judges, will recognize. And with that thought, of course, I had gone off Thoreau's path. From life, back to the rules of the dead in mind and soul. One young man, not more than twenty-one years old, wore a T-shirt that read, "I WILL NOT—BE SILENT." A woman defendant in eyeglasses, a graduate student, had pinned a hand-lettered cloth advocating her student-debt campaign to the back of her denim jacket. I thought, thoughtlessly: "That won't look to a judge like remorse." And I was ashamed again. The voice that spoke inside me had the clamor of the wrong. It was the beat of feet on grooves of dirt worn bald by decades of obedience, not the light footfalls of the daimon on a path unique to me. I had to accept that these men and women would not change before the law. Their character was that of protesters, even here. They were refusing, in their being, an unjust order.

"Beware of all enterprises that require new clothes, and not rather a new wearer of clothes." Thoreau's beloved quotation goes on: "If there is not a new man, how can the new clothes be made to fit?" The instant for philosophy is always now, and every day, because some of us need a lifetime for it. We are slow learners.

[2012]

ACKNOWLEDGMENTS

"Against Exercise" was published in *n+1* 1, Fall 2004, and excerpted in *Harper's,* September 2004 (as "The Fit and the Dead"). It was republished in *The Best American Essays 2005,* edited by Susan Orlean and Robert Atwan (Houghton Mifflin, 2005).

"Afternoon of the Sex Children" was published in *n+1* 4, Spring 2006, and excerpted in *Harper's,* November 2006 (as "Children of the Revolution"). It was republished in *The Best American Essays 2007,* edited by David Foster Wallace and Robert Atwan (Houghton Mifflin, 2007).

"On Food" was published in *n+1* 7, Fall 2008.

"Octomom and the Market in Babies" was published in slightly different form in *n+1* 9, Spring 2010, as "Octomom, One Year Later."

"The Concept of Experience" was published in *n+1* 2, Spring 2005.

"Radiohead, or the Philosophy of Pop" was published in *n+1* 3, Fall 2005.

"Punk: The Right Kind of Pain" integrates elements of "The Right Kind of Pain," *London Review of Books,* March 22, 2007, a review of the book *The Velvet Underground* by Richard Witts, and of "What You've Done to My World," published in *Heavy Rotation: Twenty Writers on the Albums That Changed Their Lives,* edited by Peter Terzian (HarperCollins, 2009).

"Learning to Rap" was previously unpublished in English. It was published in slightly different forms in Germany in the book *Bluescreen* (Suhrkamp, 2011), as a chapbook, *Rappen Lernen* (Suhrkamp, 2012), and as a radio essay for Bayern 2's "Nachtstudio" (broadcast January 2012).

"Gut-Level Legislation, or, Redistribution" was published in *n+1* 4, Spring 2006.

"The Reality of Reality Television" was published in *n+1* 3, Fall 2005.

"WeTube" was published in *Paper Monument* 2, Fall 2008.

"What Was the Hipster?" was published in *New York,* November 1, 2010, as an excerpt and condensation of the essays "Positions" and "Epitaph for the White Hipster" in *What Was the Hipster?: A Sociological Investigation,* edited by Mark Greif, Kathleen Ross, and Dayna Tortorici (n+1 Foundation, 2010).

"Anaesthetic Ideology" was published in *n+1* 5, Fall 2006.

"Mogadishu, Baghdad, Troy, or Heroes Without War," was published in *n+1* 1, Fall 2004.

"Seeing Through Police" was published in *n+1* 22, Spring 2015.

"Thoreau Trailer Park" was previously unpublished in English. It was published in Germany as a chapbook, *Die Edition 4: Berliner Festspiele* (2012).

The author expresses his gratitude to the original publications and their editors.

ABOUT THE AUTHOR

Mark Greif received a BA summa cum laude from Harvard in history and literature and an MPhil from Oxford in English as a British Marshall Scholar. He earned a PhD in American studies from Yale in 2007. In 2004, in New York, he co-founded the literary and intellectual journal *n+1*, and has been a principal at the magazine since then. Since 2008, he has been on the faculty of the New School in New York, where he is now an associate professor. His book *The Age of the Crisis of Man: Thought and Fiction in America, 1933–1973* was published in 2015 by Princeton University Press. In 2013–14, he was a member of the Institute for Advanced Study in Princeton, New Jersey. For 2016–17, he is a fellow at the Center for Advanced Study in the Behavioral Sciences at Stanford.